Can These Bones Live?

CAN
THESE
BONES
LIVE?

The Art of the American Folk Preacher

REVISED EDITION

Bruce A. Rosenberg

University of Illinois Press
Urbana and Chicago

© 1970 by Oxford University Press, Inc.
New material and revisions
© 1988 by the Board of Trustees of the University of Illinois
Manufactured in the United States of America
5 4 3 2 1 C P 5 4 3 2 1

This book is printed on acid-free paper.

Library of Congress Cataloging-in-Publication Data

Rosenberg, Bruce A.
Can these bones live?

  Rev. ed. of: The art of the American folk preacher. 1970.
  Includes index.
  1. Preaching—United States—History.
2. Oral-formulaic analysis. I. Rosenberg, Bruce A.
Art of the American folk preacher. II. Title.
BV4208.U6R67 1988   251'.00973   87-5895
ISBN 0-252-01415-4 (cloth : alk. paper)
ISBN 0-252-01416-2 (paper : alk. paper)

For Ann and Sarah

Contents

Acknowledgments

No research, whether in the sciences or the humanities, takes place in isolation. It is realized within a context, a tradition; it depends on the research and the contemplation of others. The most novel and imaginative idea is thus the product of a collaborative effort. The 1970 edition of this book, *The Art of the American Folk Preacher*, depends upon the ideas and the fieldwork of Milman Parry and Albert Lord for its conceptual grounding. As I mentioned in the first edition, my own fieldwork was greatly aided by the advice and specific contacts given me by several UCLA graduate students, especially David Evans, and by Alan Jabbour, Robert Murray Davis, Mary Lou Abram, and Chuck Perdue. I remain particularly indebted to the practical advice and theoretical wisdom of UCLA's D. K. Wilgus, a gratitude undiminished after fifteen years. As I benefited then from conversations with Donald K. Fry, Robert Kellogg, David Young, Clayton Wilson, Francis Lee Utley, and others, in the past decade the list of my creditors has lengthened to include Father Walter Ong, Roger Abrahams, John M. Foley, Jeff Titon, and Edson Richmond.

This revised edition includes material that appeared in three articles, "The Aesthetics of the Folk Sermon" in the *Georgia Review* 25:424–38, "The Genre of the Folk Sermon" in *Genre*

4:189–211, and "The Message of the Oral Sermon" in the new journal *Oral Tradition* (forthcoming). My thanks to their editors for permission to reprint sections of those essays.

While this edition was in preparation, another book on the same subject (black folk preaching) appeared: *I Got the Word in Me and I Can Sing It, You Know*. The further recognition and credit that Gerald David's book affords spiritual preachers is greatly deserved by them. More than fifteen years have passed since *The Art of the American Folk Preacher* first studied these men and their churches, and a fresh approach to the subject may enlighten us all.

Linguist Ann H. Stewart has educated me in the scholarship of her discipline, teaching me about the linguistic psychology of oral composition, from which has come a greater appreciation of the art of American folk preachers. She has given me the decisive encouragement to rewrite this book and has even suggested the title. The content is mine, but it has been written in her spirit.

It is said that once, in London, England, there were a group of artists and entertainers—in the city—and by some scheme some enterprising person was able to get most of them together in one place, so as to demonstrate their gifts. And when all of them had gone through their routines, they came down to an orator and a minister. And both of them were requested to recite the Twenty-third Psalm. The orator employed all of his innate gifts of speech, called upon all of his skill, and gifts of oratory. And when he had finished his recitation of this psalm, the house went up in thunderous applause. And then the minister arose rather solemnly, and proceeded to recite the same passage. When he had finished it is said that nobody applauded, but there was hardly a dry eye left in the house. The M.C. upon commenting on the two who had recited this passage, said the orator recited this passage like a man who knew it and was gifted to recite it; but the minister recited like a man who knew the shepherd of which it speaks.

—C. L. Franklin
From a sermon on the Twenty-third Psalm.

PART I

1

The American Folk Sermon

The 1970 edition of this book had intended, in part, to challenge many of the components of the Milman Parry–Albert Lord theory of oral composition. Nearly all of their fieldwork had been done in Yugoslavia, though some recording had been undertaken in neighboring Balkan states. Their resulting research and the conclusions drawn from it were based on a language that few interested scholars could read, much less analyze. *The Art of the American Folk Preacher* was going to correct that problem by using and analyzing materials that were immediately available to English speakers. The reasoning proceeded thus: if, as Parry and Lord argued, the *guslars* used compositional techniques like those of Homer—thus making him accessible in ways that had not been possible before—then the preachers, whose techniques of creation were also analogous, could be analyzed so as to more richly understand both. In the event, most folklorists found that the academic "discovery" of the folk preacher (of a certain kind) only reinforced the Parry-Lord thesis, and that American folk preaching was an analogous instance of the Yugoslavian experience.

As the Serbo-Croatian epic tradition waned in the past half century, scholars interested in oral composition had to resort to the internal evidence of the texts themselves (or else learn some exotic language such as that of the Kirghiz nomads of central Asia, and then travel there to record their sung narratives). Hence the impetus and potential usefulness of studying the American folk preacher: not only to learn something more about the composition of oral epic verse specifically, if that was still possible, but to find an extant, vital, oral tradition that might further endow our conceptions about the nature of the composition and transmission of such "illiteratures."

The original intention of the first edition of *Folk Preacher* had been to address oral formulaic theory, indirectly, through a detailed examination of American folk sermons spontaneously composed and performed aloud; but during the course of the initial recording and interviewing—1966 to 1970—the compelling expressive power of American folk preachers commanded attention in its own right. In the final measure, my research and that of others concentrated as much upon the preachers themselves and their talents as upon the principles of composition in Homer and a sprinkling of medieval narrators. Rev. Rubin Lacy, Rev. Elihue Brown, and Rev. D. J. McDowell quickly crowded off the pages of this research the more august names of Homer, Turoldus, and the *Beowulf* poet. After the diachronic and cross-cultural comparisons have been made, the American folk preachers have proven to be of interest not only for what they can reveal about the oral compositional process (as in the making of such poems as *Beowulf*), but for themselves and an American oral tradition.

This book would not be possible without the previous scholarship of Parry and Lord. Milman Parry created and subsequently developed the idea that the Yugoslavian epic singers composed their oral poems (as had Homer—Parry was a classicist) by the skillful manipulation of metrically consistent phrases, some memorized and some spontaneously composed (based on lexico-syntactic models known by the singers), which skill enabled them to spin out narratives at great length.[1] Their memorization of the narratives in their repertoires was such that they could also perform basically the same story months or even years later, the "same story" meaning another narrative employing the same string of what Barthes has called "distributional elements."[2] Verbatim repetition, as in all oral traditions, is never achieved.

Parry called these metrically consistent phrases "oral formulas," which he had defined as "a group of words regularly employed under the same metrical conditions to express a given essential idea."[3] This definition has been the subject of controversy almost since its appearance. Advocates of the oral-formulaic theory found, in applying Parry's notion to other narrative traditions, that formulas sometimes consisted of a single word, that "regularly employed" has meant "repeated," that "the same metrical conditions" had to be interpreted quite loosely if it was to describe the formula at all, and that "a given essential idea" was not as precise as, say, psycholinguists would want.[4] Nevertheless, after all the quibbling, the modifications, the adjustments and alterations, the extensions and hesitations, Parry's definition is still the one most commonly used and remains the most useful one yet devised. Michael Nagler has modified it, to the satisfaction of most, but it remains Parry's creation.[5]

Fieldwork for this project began in Bakersfield, California, and ended there (temporarily) as well. Between my two stays in that San Joaquin Valley town, I traveled to Oklahoma, Kentucky, North Carolina, and Virginia, as well as to other areas in south and central California. There I found a tradition of oral composition that is vigorous, widespread, and available to researchers. Many preachers (most of whom happen to be black), originally from the South, compose their sermons spontaneously by using techniques that have been made familiar to us in the writing of Parry and Lord. During the past sixty years many of these preachers and their families (and congregations) have migrated to the East, the West Coast, and many of the major cities of the Midwest; and they have carried their culture with them. The preachers rarely objected to having their sermons recorded, once I could convince them that my intentions were not deprecatory, and so it has been possible to conduct fieldwork in the "living laboratory" of practicing churches and to study an oral tradition here in the United States. The biggest difference between the Yugoslavian oral epic and the American oral sermon is the undisputed narrative quality of the *guslar*'s songs and the peculiar generic blend of the American pulpit stories. Stylistically, the uttered lines of the sermons are less metrically regular. But as for most other aspects of composition and product (the transcribed text), the two forms have much in common.

Almost of secondary interest to this research—but perhaps of primary interest to some folklorists—are the collection and study for its own sake of the spontaneous chanted sermon. Few other such examinations have been undertaken. Jeff Titon has worked extensively with the Reverend C. L. Franklin in Detroit and Brother John Sherfey in Virginia's northern Blue Ridge, while Sammie Ann Wicks has looked closely at Old Regular Baptist traditions in eastern Kentucky.[6] Newman I. White, Alan Lomax, J. Mason Brewer, and a few others have published oral sermons or fragments of sermons, but almost never with analytical comment.[7] White's sermon looks suspiciously literary; but literary or not, it is one of the few such recorded sermons even pretending to an authentic oral tradition. James Weldon Johnson was heavily influenced by preachers he had heard in his childhood when he wrote seven sermons for a book he called *God's Trombones*. But they are literary poems, not oral folk sermons, and moving though they may be they are not of a kind with the authentic items.

However, in one way the starting point for this introduction to the sermon is Johnson's observation that the oral chanted sermons are the materials of folk art.[8] The sermons rarely end-rhyme, they seldom alliterate, the imagery is meager; yet they are poetic. The lines are metrical, the language is ordered, and the effect is often pleasing. Harry Caplan has called preaching a "sacred art";[9] the oral sermon is certainly artistic. Its oral style echoes *Beowulf* and the Homeric epics, but it is usually not a sophisticated poetry. It often mediates between oratory and oral narrative and frequently mediates ineptly, but it is folk art for all of that. Johnson remembered hearing sermons that he thought were passed along from preacher to preacher and from region to region with only minor variations.[10] During this study it was not possible to trace a sermon so thoroughly, but there is no doubt whatsoever that an active oral tradition of the chanted sermon is still alive and influences many aspects of American life.

The idea first occurred to me when as a graduate student in Ohio I would occasionally pick up evangelists' sermons on local radio stations; after a while—after I heard parts of several sermons—I realized that I was hearing the same phrases repeated, much as are formulas in Homer. At the Santa Barbara campus of the University of California, Professor David Young of the Classics Department one day happened to remark that he thought that J. Charles Jessup's sermons—performances he also admired—were heavily formulaic. Jessup, based in Gulfport, Louisiana, was carried to the southern California area over radio station XERB, Los Angeles. Young was interested in formulaic approaches to literature through his studies of Homer. But what was crucial to my research was his independent corroboration of my hypothesis; after that, my work began in earnest.

Professor D. K. Wilgus of the University of California at Los Angeles supported this project from its conception, and it was he who provided my first contact. Several of his graduate students had been recording in the California interior, especially in Bakersfield and Ridgecrest, and they had first met the Reverend Rubin Lacy there. Their purpose was the collection of folk ballads; Lacy was a blues singer in the late twenties and early thirties, and he and friends of his had proven helpful to the UCLA folklorists. One of them, David Evans, had recorded parts of sermons, and from his description of them I felt certain that a visit to Lacy would be profitable. It was. Lacy was friendly and cooperative from the beginning and introduced me to several of his colleagues.

The nature of these sermons made the positioning of the microphone important. With the microphone placed on the rostrum much greater fidelity was obtained; however, with a preacher who moved back and forth continually there was little to do except continually adjust the recording level. That generally worked out well so far as clarity was concerned, though sometimes at the expense of the effect of the sermon. Even with the microphone on the pulpit, at least part of the audience was clearly audible. I mention this fact specifically because audience response is vital in an antiphonal service. Later, the effect the congregation has on the preacher's performance will be discussed: sometimes it is "filled with the Spirit" and at other times it is merely listless, bored, and unresponsive. The state of the audience is important, and one cannot understand any sermon of this type adequately without knowing the responses of the congregation during its performance.

My presence did not appear to alter significantly the progress of the service, and most important for my immediate purposes, the performance of the sermon. The very young children gave me coy and quizzical glances, but for the most part I was ignored by the adults. They shouted, clapped, and sang, paying no particular attention to me, but this was not always the case with the preachers. The first few visits to each church made a difference in the sermon, however slight. Lacy, for instance, saved his favorite numbers for me, which turned out to my advantage. Other preachers may have felt that because they were being recorded they should perform better; one man actually told me so, though jokingly. It is difficult for me to evaluate what difference these factors made in the "texts" I recorded and later analyzed, but I do not believe it was linguistically significant. Primarily this appears to be so because radio sermons that were monitored manifested the same formulaic characteristics as those that I personally attended. Then, after a short time, the preachers did not pay special attention to me. Finally, having heard several successful sermons at the outset, I had a concrete basis for comparison with later performances.

The only difficulty I did encounter was in the interviews, and that was the result of the nature of the subject: it is sacred matter and not always translatable into lay terms. I was told very early in my relationship with Lacy and the Reverend Elihue H. Brown that there was no use talking about the preacher's language because it all came from God. That was the end of it. When I recorded a traditional folktale during one sermon the preacher was reluctant to discuss its source except in terms of the Holy Ghost. I later recorded a preacher in Virginia, the Reverend Theodore Roosevelt Hanner, using a striking metaphor during a sermon: "Out of His mouth/ Come a two-edge sword/ Cuttin' sin/ Both right and left." Lacy had used the identical metaphor months before in California; and while Revelation does have the two-edged sword, it does not use it in this way. Hanner was insistent that "the Lord" gave it to him, even in response to my suggestion that the specific diction might be humanly derived.

My basic plan of study was to cover four geographic areas in the United States, and to fill in some of the spaces by monitoring radio broadcasts. Of the areas chosen, one was to reflect a society in transition or dislocation (southern California); one, a stable portion of the South (Virginia and Georgia); one, a border area, preferably in the hills (Kentucky and Tennessee); and one, the middle Southwest, an area between the stable East and the demographically fluctuating Far West (Oklahoma City and Tulsa).

Radio broadcasts from Mississippi and Texas were plentiful, and were frequently monitored. Within each area the procedure was to get a sampling of about twenty preachers, but also to concentrate on two or three and to know their styles thoroughly.[11] In southern California the sermons of over twenty preachers were recorded, concentrating on Lacy and Brown, who were both available and cooperative. Ultimately, the difficulty was in deciding when a sample was sufficient. Since one can never be certain, I continued recording as a matter of routine, but so far as this study is concerned I have heeded the maxim of Vladimir Propp: when you stop finding new material, the collecting may be terminated. For the specific aspect of the sermon that was studied, I have not recently discovered new qualitative data.

NOTES

1. Milman Parry, "Studies in the Epic Technique of Oral Verse-Making. I: Homer and Homeric Style," *Harvard Studies in Classical Philology* 41 (1930).

2. Roland Barthes, *A Barthes Reader*, ed. Susan Sontag (New York, 1965), pp. 263–64.

3. Parry, "Epic Technique," p. 80.

4. H. L. Rogers, "The Crypto-Psychological Character of the Oral Formula," *English Studies* 47 (1966), 89–102. Also see the more recent strictures of anthropologist Ruth Finnegan, *Oral Poetry* (Cambridge, 1977).

5. Michael M. Nagler, *Spontaneity and Tradition: A Study in the Oral Art of Homer* (Berkeley, 1974), p. xxiii.

6. Titon's work with Brother Sherfey appeared as *Powerhouse for God: Sacred Speech, Chant, and Song in an Appalachian Baptist Church*, two 12″ LPs and booklet (Chapel Hill, 1972); his presentation of the Reverend C. L. Franklin's life story and sermons, *Give Me This Mountain*, will be published in two volumes by the University of Illinois Press. See also Sammie Ann Wicks, "Life and Meaning: Singing, Praying, and the Word among the Old Regular Baptists of Eastern Kentucky" (Ph.D. diss., University of Texas, 1983).

7. See Newman I. White, *American Negro Folk-Songs* (Hatboro, Pa., 1965), pp. 126–28: the artistic and sometimes elaborate "stage directions" suggest an editor's hand; Edward C. L. Adams, *Congaree Sketches* (Chapel Hill, 1927), pp. 41–47; Edward C. L. Adams, *Nigger to Nigger* (New York, 1928), pp. 211–13: suspiciously fluent; Orlando Kay Arm-

strong, *Old Massa's People* (Indianapolis, 1931), pp. 226–27: short fragments and patronizing tone; Alan Lomax, *The Rainbow Sign* (New York, 1959), pp. 185–209: the sermon is given completely, but the editor's comments are overly dramatic; Marcellus S. Whalley, *The Old Types Pass Away* (Boston, 1925), pp. 84–97: the sermon is fragmentary and the editor's tone condescending; and J. Mason Brewer, *American Negro Folklore* (Chicago, 1968), pp. 119–38: one of the most authentic collections of sermons so far.

8. James Weldon Johnson, *God's Trombones* (New York, 1948), p. 1.

9. Harry Caplan, "Classical Rhetoric and the Medieval Theory of Preaching," *Classical Philology* 28 (1933), 96.

10. Johnson, *God's Trombones*, p. 1.

11. More than two hundred sermons of about fifty preachers from about a dozen states were examined for this study. Some preachers, such as the ones cited most frequently in this book, were studied intensively, while others were sampled. Fieldwork was conducted in the four geographic areas mentioned in the text; radio sermons from relatively inaccessible areas were also monitored.

2

The Church

Most Americans have now heard some of the chanted/sung sermons that this book examines. Relatively very few have heard
them in their churches, but several of the sermons of the Reverend Martin Luther King, Jr., and the Reverend Jesse Jackson
have been so influential and widely broadcast and telecast that
few have escaped this experience. Other public performances—
especially King's "I Have a Dream" speech—were not perceived
as sermons, but as political orations; the millions who heard it,
originally and since, have thus been witness to this most effective
style of public oratory, but not with an understanding that they
had heard a sermon. Styles blend and intermingle. The sermon
is a hortatory oration on sacred matters, and King's "Dream" was
founded in Christian faith. The so-called oral style emerged from
a reading of a prepared text that day in front of the Washington
monument. In this age of nearly universal literacy, when the
influence of print culture has seeped into every molecule of
Western life, a few fundamental distinctions between styles and
modes of performance will be useful.

According to those who preach spontaneously—that is, without
the aid of a manuscript—a minister is either a manuscript preacher
or a "spiritual" preacher. This is a basic distinction, made by the
preachers themselves (and thus native), and is useful to the analyst from outside the culture. In the event, there is often some
bleeding between categories, some transitional performances: a
few sermons were begun with the aid of printed matter and

evolved into extemporaneous recitation; and a few preachers use note cards to guide their memories during performance. Usually, the difference between those portions that are read and those created at the moment is easily recognizable. And for the scholar looking for the interstices between these two performative modes, such texts are more interesting than specimens of the "pure" style. Absolute taxonomic classification is not possible in many such instances, nor is it desirable to try to force such categorization. It is more interesting to live with the impure performances, for they can tell us the most.

Stylistic blending occurs when prepared, written texts are (partially or wholly) abandoned by the preachers, who consequently break away from the prose of the printed source and into the rhythm with which they are more comfortable; the resulting demonstration is of the spontaneous creation of metrical utterances. When the preacher departs from a prose text for the sake of metrical consistency, the sermon becomes "spiritual" (as the preachers themselves call it), or "oral" or "spontaneous." An acoustic recording of the performance, and not merely the written/printed transcription of it, is necessary to realize the difference. Folklore, to cite an old aphorism, is everything that gets left out when the performance is transcribed.

Spiritual sermons also are of two types—chanted and non-chanted—although the distinction here is not nearly so marked. The chanted spiritual sermon is the one with which this book is chiefly concerned: if the sermon is not chanted and the length and metrical consistency of each uttered line is not regularized, the formulas of which Parry and Lord spoke will not occur. The music of the performance creates the formula in that the preachers attempt to fit their language into metrically consistent patterns. In the chanted sermon, the verses are preponderantly formulaic (in the Parry-Lord sense), there are extended passages with parallel syntax, and the constructions are direct with almost no periodicity.

Of the spiritual preachers in America, themselves a minority, only a few chant their sermons. These preachers are found largely in the South where they were born and where they learned to preach, though some now live in every major city in America. Although most are black, there are whites in the eastern Kentucky hills and in parts of Ohio and Pennsylvania who still preach this way. Where the sermon first was chanted is very difficult to determine, owing to the scarcity of documents on this specific aspect of American religion, but certainly blacks have developed it most fully. In Kentucky, white "old-time country preachers," as their neighbors call them, were surprised to learn that the chanted sermon was not exclusively theirs.

The orally presented prose (nonchanted) sermon, on the other hand, has more of the characteristics of conventional oratory and even of conversational speech. In such performances logical development from sentence to sentence occurs more frequently than in chanted sermons, with fewer parallel developments and almost no memorized formulas. The language will have a rhythm of its own but it is regular, so formulas do not develop. The syntax is quite free in this kind of sermon, as flexible as conversation, which, aside from the conventions of oratory and preaching, it resembles when transcribed. Most spiritual preachers are of this sort, especially those whose congregations are middle class. One such preacher, the evangelist Maxie Boren of Austin, Texas, found the chanting strange yet interesting, though neither he nor any of his colleagues preached that way; among other things, he lacked the musical ability.

We shall have to confront, finally, the matter of nomenclature, since it is simply too cumbersome to refer continually to a sermon as spontaneously composed, orally presented, and metrically ordered. Actually no one name is ideal. Neither "oral" nor "spontaneous" distinguishes the chanted sermon from the spoken, although occasionally in the forthcoming pages both are used when the contexts make their meanings clear. To label a performance "metrical" ignores its oral spontaneity. Francis Lee Utley suggested "Pentecostal," probably because of the word's association with that phenomenon of verbal ecstasy, speaking in tongues; but many spiritual preachers do not belong to the Pentecostal church. We do think of a denomination when we hear the word, and such a name might well be confusing. I opt for "chanted," for despite its obvious shortcomings it does describe the one feature of these sermons that is most important in this study.

We are fortunate in having eyewitness accounts of these services in the early nineteenth century, undoubtedly because their abandon so disturbed the sense of decorum of visitors, particularly European visitors, to the United States. The following description is that of Henry Fearon, published in 1818:

> Having heard that American Methodists were distinguished for an extreme degree of fanatical violence in their religious exercises, I visited the African church, (all houses of religious assembly being denominated churches), in which were none but blacks; and in the evening, "Ebenezer Church," in which were only whites. I went at 8 o'clock in the evening. The door was locked; but the windows being open, I placed myself at one of them, and saw that the church within was crowded almost to suffocation. The preacher indulged in long pauses, and occasional loud elevations of voice, which were always answered by the audience with deep groans. When the prayer which followed the sermon had ended, the minister descended from the pulpit, the doors were thrown open, and a considerable number of the audience departed. Understanding however that something was yet to follow, with considerable difficulty I obtained admission. The minister had departed, the doors were again closed, but about four hundred persons remained. One (apparently) of the leading members gave out a hymn, then a brother was called upon to pray: he roared and ranted like a maniac; the male part of the audience groaned, the female shrieked; a man sitting next to me shouted; a youth standing before me continued for half an hour bawling, "Oh, Jesus! come down, come down, Jesus! my dear Jesus, I see you! bless me, Jesus! Oh! oh! oh! Come down, Jesus!" A small space farther on, a girl about 11 years of age was in convulsions: an old woman, who I concluded was her mother, stood on the seat, holding her up in her arms, that her ecstasies might be visible to the whole assembly. In another place there was a convocation of holy sisters, sending forth most awful yells. A brother now stood forward, stating, that "although numbers had gone, he trusted the Lord would that night work some signal favours among his dear lambs." Two sisters advanced towards him, refusing to be comforted, "for the Lord was with them": another brother prayed—and another. "Brother Macfaddin" was now called upon, and he addressed them with a voice which might almost rival a peal of thunder, the whole congregation occasionally joining responsive to his notes. The madness now became threefold

increased, and such a scene presented itself as I could never have pictured to my imagination, and as I trust, for the honour of true religion and of human nature, I shall never see again. Had the inhabitants of Bedlam been let loose, they could not have exceeded it. From forty to fifty were praying aloud and extemporaneously at the same moment of time: some were kicking, many jumping, all clapping their hands and crying out in chorus, "Glory! glory! glory! Jesus Christ is a very good friend! Jesus Christ is a very good friend! Oh God! oh Jesus! come down! Glory! glory! glory! Mere exhaustion of bodily strength produced a cessation of madness for a few minutes. A hymn was given out and sung; praying then recommenced; the scene of madness was again acted, with, if possible, increased efforts on the part of the performers. One of the brothers prayed to be kept from enthusiasm! A girl of six years of age became the next object of attention. A reverend brother proclaimed that she "had just received a visit from the Lord, and was in awful convulsions—so hard was the working of the spirit!" This scene continued for some time; but the audience gradually lessened, so that by ten o'clock the field of active operations was considerably contracted. The women, however, forming a compact column at the most distant corner of the church, continued their shriekings with but little abatement.[1]

Descriptions of black church services at about this time are far more plentiful, with the focus of the writer almost invariably upon the passionate vehemence of the preacher and his congregation. William Eleasar Barton wrote the following vignette of a black service he witnessed in Mississippi:

The company has long been swaying back and forth in the rhythm of the preacher's chant, and now and then there has come a shout of assent to the oft-repeated text. Each time the preacher's almost incoherent talk becomes articulate in a shout, "I have trod de winepress;" there are cries of "Yes!" "Praise de Lawd!" and "Glory!" from the Amen corner, where sit the "praying brethern," and the Hallelujah corner, where sit the "agonizing sistering." In the earlier demonstrations the men rather lead, but from the time when Aunt Melinda cries out, "Nebbah mind de wite folks! My soul's happy! Hallelujah!" and leaps into the air, the men are left behind. Women go off into trances, roll under benches, or go spinning down the aisle with eyes closed and with arms outstretched. Each shout of the preacher is the signal for some one else to start; and, strange to say, though there are two posts in the aisle, and the women go spinning like tops, I never saw one strike a post. I have seen the pastor on a day when the house would not contain the multitude cause the seats to be turned and take his position in the door with a third of the audience inside and the rest without, and have heard him provoke the most ecstatic response to a reference to his wife such as this, "O, I love dat yaller woman out dar in dat buffy, but I love my Jesus bettah!" I have seen the minister in grave danger of being dragged out of the pulpit by some of the shouters, who in their ecstasy laid hands on him. I have seen an old man stand in the aisle and jump eighty-nine times without moving a muscle of his thin, parchment-like face, and without disturbing the meeting.[2]

Unfortunately, no mention was ever made of the preacher's chanting or singing during the sermon, or of any rhythmical recitation that would break up his utterances into metrically consistent units. The closest one comes to a description of rhythm is in a service witnessed by Clarence Deming: "All through the sermon the preacher is stimulated by the chants of the sisters, the shouts of the brethern, and a swaying, rhythmical movement which swings the whole congregation in unison."[3] Not even the "Baptist whine" appears to be exactly what we are here seeking, though the chanted sermon may well have derived from it: contemporaries described (and derided) the rising and falling of the preacher's voice, and its resultant play upon the congregation's emotions, though the style is said to have developed as a means of relieving the strain of preaching in the outdoors.[4]

A contemporary description of the chanted sermon was sent to me in 1969 by Alan Jabbour, then at Duke University, now head of the American Folklife Center. Jabbour knew little about the kind of preacher I was seeking, but was helpfully seeking information for me in Durham, North Carolina. After attending the church services of the Reverend W. T. Ratliff, he sent me the following letter:

Rev. Ratliff begins his sermon in normal, though stately and carefully measured, prose. As he gets into his subject, he gradually raises the intensity of his delivery (though with well-timed ups and downs). About one third of the way into his sermon the prose has verged into a very rhythmical delivery, punctuated into periods (more or less regular) by a sharp utterance which I suppose might be called a vehement grunt. I haven't timed these periods, but I would guess that they fall about every three seconds, sometimes less. Within the rhythmical framework, the rises and falls eventually build to a climax when he lapses into a sort of chant, still with the same punctuation, but with a recognizable tonic [tonal center]. Some of the congregation (who respond *ad libitum* throughout) here lapse into humming along with him. After this climax he breaks off dramatically into normal prose, then builds back again, and finally tapers off into a subdued normal delivery at the end.

Jabbour's letter was so accurate in its description of the kind of sermon I had been recording (it might well have been the description of over 90 percent of them) that I recognized it at once, and asked him to arrange an interview for me. What was true of the South had been true of California, for the people I met in the San Joaquin were southerners practicing (in their terms) old-time, not newfangled, religion. This study began in the black churches of California and was extended back to the preachers' former land, where the faith originated. And the church service itself in California was much as Jabbour and I found it in the South.

It is unlikely that all of the churches are hot all of the time, but it always feels that way. The buildings, often fibre or plywood siding nailed on wooden uprights that barely support the low ceiling, are in effect dutch ovens. Everyone is sweating all the time. All during the services cardboard hand fans with mortuary advertisements on them are swished back and forth, giving the singing and the sermon an undertone of humming. If the congregation is prosperous the church will have a large swamp fan built into the wall, as noisy as an old Ford, which blows warm air around; but when it is 108 degrees even warm air pushed in one's face feels good. I think that everyone expects the service to be hot, for regardless of the weather, regardless of the swamp fan, nearly all flick the mortuary fans in front of their faces.

The services are as informal as though the congregation felt that God was an old friend (a friend to whose house a jacket and tie are worn, however). No real effort is made to stop children from signaling to and giggling at one another, or to stop the infants from crying. The women usually sit together on their side of the aisle toward the front with their children. The men, who are relaxed and jovial as they joke outside, come in at the last minute and sit near the back. At many services one or two of them sleep through the sermon. Preachers sweat more than anyone because they are as active as actors strutting on a stage. They gesticulate, twist their faces into theatrical masks, and wave their arms. Regularly they lift their handerchiefs to their mouths to clear their throats and to wipe the perspiration from their lips. If the sermon is especially effective the audience may dance in the aisles, fall on the floor, or speak in tongues, but most of the time their response is limited to relatively more sedate cries of "Yes, Jesus" or "That's right," to clapping, and to controlled toe tapping.

These contemporary services are conservative in that they attempt to conserve what the preacher and congregation consider to be the best of the past. On a national scale we now realize that the "past"—the relation of the black to American Protestantism—is a shameful one, but it will be useful to review a segment of it here. This sketch must be brief and will only touch upon the highlights of what we know about preachers in colonial and pre–Civil War frontier days; my purpose will be to explore the possible origins of the chanted sermon.

New England must first be considered: although the settlers in this region paid scant attention to the religious needs of either slaves or the freed, some black churches were eventually formed. The vast majority of slaves were never given Christian training by the Puritans,[5] and it is estimated that only a small proportion of the blacks in the colonies were even nominal Christians.[6] Nevertheless, some blacks were exposed to the faith of the whites—usually to foster docility and obedience—and we should not discount the possibility that, in part, the contemporary chanted sermon derives ultimately from such exposure.

In Philadelphia during the last quarter of the eighteenth century the remarkable Richard Allen bought his freedom from a sympathetic master in the same year of his conversion, and later established the Free African Society and the African Methodist

Episcopal church. Membership in this church initially was small,[7] though in the second decade of the nineteenth century branches of the AME church had been formed in Baltimore, Wilmington, and several Pennsylvania and New Jersey towns. In 1820 there were 4,000 black Methodists in Philadelphia, half that number in Baltimore. Despite this impressive growth, however, Allen's influence in the South was checked by the hostility of southern planters who, after the Denmark Vesey insurrection of 1822, repressed the appearances of Allen's followers below the Mason-Dixon Line.[8]

We are thus tempted to discount Richard Allen's influence on the spontaneous chanted sermon, despite his undoubted importance in the early black church. There is no evidence, moreover, that his preaching or his services were characterized by the outpouring of the sort of emotion we have described. Nothing in contemporary descriptions of his style suggests the kind of performance witnessed, for example, by Alan Jabbour. Rather, he has been described by those who knew him as "a plain-spoken, matter-of-fact, young Negro. . . . His words were simple and instructive and sincere."[9]

The influence of New England religion may have been felt in the South in two ways, though as we have seen, it is difficult to measure the intensity of that feeling. The first is in the structure of the Puritan sermon—what some modern ministers glibly call the "text and context" form. The preacher began with a quotation from Scripture (the text), proceeded to explain it (context), raised a doctrine from the passage, and then, in the section that most interested the preacher, applied that doctrine to everyday affairs. The structure of the sermon was simple and ordered by a straightforward setting forth of argument after argument, an arrangement that Perry Miller has likened to a lawyer's brief.[10] This pattern was followed with little variation for over a century following the settlement of New England, and we find that this pattern informs many chanted sermons.

The second important element to spring from New England is that of freely expressed passion in divine worship; one thinks immediately of the "Baptist whine" and of such men as John Davenport and George Whitefield (whom David Garrick once said could bring an audience to tears merely by intoning the word

"Mesopotamia").[11] The Anglicans attacked their more passionate colleagues for their vehement pathos, their histrionics, the "tuned voice" (of Whitefield); and there is ample evidence of this early theological quarrel.[12] Nowhere do we find the statement that the sermons of these men of the "New Lights" were chanted, as are those of the men who interest us here; however, the emotionalism, the free expression, and the "musical tone" of the preachers suggest that this aspect of the chanted oral sermon may have begun in this context.

It was only during that wave of religious fervor in 1800 and 1801 called the Second Great Awakening that large numbers of blacks were proselytized and converted.[13] The Baptists and Methodists especially, out of favor in New England because of their "barking" and "jerking" and other "primitive traits,"[14] were prominent in this new wave of enthusiasm on the frontier. The camp meeting enlarged the physical scope (at least) of divine service; for example, at Cane Ridge in 1801 over 20,000 worshipers gathered to pray, while during the sermons men and women danced and shouted aloud.[15]

The Methodists and Baptists succeeded with the whites as well as blacks in the South (while the Anglicans and Presbyterians failed in comparison) because of several sociological reasons. The Baptist preachers, for the most part lacking the education of their Anglican peers, appealed to those whom E. Franklin Frazier has termed "the poor and the ignorant and the outcast."[16] The Baptists and Methodists emphasized feeling as a sign of conversion, and this doctrine was readily accepted by the socially repressed. The Protestant middle-class communions were already concerned with national and political issues; the "unrestrained emotionalism" of preaching the gospel continued among adherents of the Second Great Awakening and is, as we have seen, continuing today. The clergy of this movement, often circuit riders and farmer-preachers, were given easy access to the slaves since they usually taught a religion of consolation rather than of revolt against white masters; several Episcopal planters are known to have requested Methodist preachers to come and console (i.e., quiet) their slaves.[17]

The Reverend Dr. Joseph Washington, Jr., has shown us how the slaves thus received a substandard Christianity.[18] The white preachers taught Christian morals—especially patience and endurance—to be sure, but not the tenets of faith or ethical concerns such as the immorality of slavery. But the hypnotizing effect of the Baptists was compelling, and very quickly many slaves took up preaching on their own. It is possible, therefore, that the chanted sermon as we know it today was also influenced by these first black "exhorters." On the issue of worship for blacks the southern planters were of two minds. We have seen how they encouraged Methodists to preach to their slaves, yet it was often thought necessary to repress the blacks' preaching for fear of sedition and rebellion. Between 1830 and 1835 the fear of insurrection was so great that services without white supervision were prohibited; five or more slaves could not assemble in the absence of a white.[19] The historical evidence, therefore, indicates quite strongly that although many blacks may have first witnessed Christianity from other blacks, by far the majority in the South learned about it from whites.

The reasons for locating those areas that were most heavily proselytized during the Second Great Awakening as the birthplace of the chanted sermon are compelling. New Lights preaching in New England appears not to have reached many blacks there, but was tremendously effective among the slaves after 1801. We find many descriptions of blacks responding to the emotional fervor of the Baptist and Methodist preachers in the South, but seldom in the North; and the type of sermon with which this book is concerned appears to be primarily a southern phenomenon. Finally, if the border states were the locale where white preachers passed the chanted sermon along to their black brethren, one would expect to find whites reciting in this style. My field trips to eastern Kentucky showed this to be the case.[20] Chanted sermons are well established in the area among whites who say that neither they nor their grandparents ever preached differently.

If there is any validity to the theory just presented—that the chanted sermon as we today know it either began or was widely popularized during the Second Great Awakening—then its history is roughly parallel to that of the spiritual. Beginning, as Don Yoder has traced it,[21] in eighteenth-century New England, the spiritual migrated south where it was widely adopted (and adapted) by blacks. By using popular tunes as the vehicle for evangelical hymns, the spiritual also developed the chorus that has come to characterize the camp-meeting spiritual. The practice of "lining out" hymns was common, probably because many of the congregation could not read, but just as plausibly—as whites in Kentucky claim today—because hymnals were scarce: the leader sang out a line and the congregation responded by re-singing the same line, often in their own melody. If worshipers wished to sing harmony, or sing either their own words or melodies, or if they wanted to shout, they were free to do so. This kind of antiphonal performance was already in the black work-song tradition and was readily adapted into their services.[22]

One is inclined to approach the origin of the chanted sermon by the circuitous route of the spiritual for several reasons. The sermons are repetitious in the same ways the spirituals are. And an extraordinary number of sermon lines come directly from spirituals; for instance, the following ten lines, taken verbatim from a sermon by the Reverend D. J. McDowell of Bakersfield (a former gospel singer) have several lines from spirituals:

> God is our refuge
> And strength
> A well-proved helpmate in trouble
> I'm in trouble this evenin'
> 5 Yes I am
> I said I'm in trouble this evenin'
> I need someone to go all night long
> If you never hear me no more
> Keep your hand, in God's hand
> 10 He'll make a way for you

No doubt this borrowing will occur as long as spontaneous folk sermons are preached.

There are other similarities; as we shall later see, the sermons are most often chanted in the pentatonic, a popular scale of Baptist hymnals. The rhythms are the same in spirituals and sermons, and the informal, concrete tone appropriate to a personal relation with one's God is present in both. Satan and God and all the saints are treated as real and living people, not as abstractions.

So it is in the spiritual sermon, where one often hears the preacher say, "Jesus said to me last night."[23]

Functionally, the chanted sermon is an ideal conflation of the prose sermon and the spiritual. Both of the component genres are approved expressions of worship, and the conflated form has proved equally acceptable. We can never know for certain why the chanted sermon initially came to be wedded to music, but perhaps our common sense can provide a reasonable answer. Sermons can be dull, especially long sermons and particularly when they are solemnly intoned. The first black preachers in America, like their white counterparts on the frontier, had little formal education and even less training in formal rhetoric or public speaking. We may speculate that chanting or singing was first used both to liven a potentially dull sermon and to establish a rhythm so as to make the performance as emotionally stimulating as the obviously successful spirituals. Singing is difficult to sustain in an extended form such as the sermons; so chanting is clearly a more practical expedient, though some talented preachers occasionally break into song for short periods. Whites in Kentucky today hum after each line of their spiritual sermons so as to establish rhythm. The congregation is moved to religious ecstasy by this style, which embodies the emotional power of music and the (ostensibly) rational power of the spoken word. Musical instruments are not needed; the preacher's voice is the full orchestra.

If the chanted sermon is in fact a conflation of forms, one would expect to find transitional "texts" showing an intermediary form of the conflation more clearly; and such performances have been recorded. For the following "song" I am indebted to Charles Perdue, who recorded it in Rappahannock County, Virginia, in 1968. The singer is Newton Jackson who was an experienced deacon in his church. He was active in church affairs, and though it was not known whether he was preaching extensively or not, Perdue thought that he was. The first three verses as well as the last were sung; the twenty-six lines between were chanted in the style of the spiritual preacher:

> How I got over,
> How I got over,

My soul looked back and wondered,
How I got over.

How I got over,
How I got over,
You know, my soul looked back and wondered,
How I got over.

You know just as soon as I can see my Jesus
That, that made me free.
I'm glad that He suffered
And He died for you and me.

I want to thank Him 'cause He brought me,
I want to thank Him 'cause He taught me,
I want to thank Him because He kept me,
I want to thank Him 'cause He never left me,
I want to thank Him for the Holy Bible,
I want to thank Him for good old revival,
I want to thank Him for heavenly visions,
I want to thank Him for old-time religion,
Don't you know, I'm gonna sing, "Hallelujah,"
Yeah, I'm gonna shout, "Glory,"
Oh, I'm gonna thank Him for what He's done for me,
Don't you know I'm gonna wear a diadem,
In the New Jerusalem.
Gonna walk the streets of gold,
Goin' to the homeland of the soul,
Gonna view the hosts in white,
You know they travel both day and night,
Comin' up from every nation,
On the way to the great combination,
Comin' from the North, South, East, and West,
Yes, on the way to the land of rest,
You know I'm goin' to join the heavenly choir,
Well, gonna sing on and never get tired,
Hallelujah, you know I'm gonna sing, sing "Hallelujah,"
Yeah, I'm gonna shout, "Glory,"
Oh I'm gonna thank Him for what He's done for me.

Well, it's how I got over,
How I got over,

Lord, my soul looked back and wondered,
How I got over.

This performance is part spiritual and part sermon, though the influence of the latter is not as strong as its chanting in sermon style makes it appear. Although heavily repetitive, it appears to be largely memorized rather than entirely improvised. Most of the lines rhyme, indicating that Newton knew most, if not all, of the couplets by heart. Probably he knew additional rhymes that might have been added to or substituted in this passage when it occurred in other performances, as his memory and other factors permitted. To the extent that he was relatively free to add and to delete these rhymes, none of which are necessary to this sequence, the performance is spontaneous. The rhymes themselves were almost assuredly memorized as units, making the section in effect a short sermon. A conventional sermon would be less highly memorized, more improvisation would occur, and (in authentic sermons) rhyme would rarely be used.

We should not think, however, that music necessarily came to the sermon historically through such transitional forms, though the idea seems plausible. Rather, what Newton's performance does illustrate is that among those whose religion has always been communicated by the chanted sermon, the singing of spirituals is intimately related to preaching and is religiously acceptable within the context of so serious a form as the sermon. Even if Newton's performance does not recapitulate the historical blending of prose sermon and spiritual, it is illustrative of the attitude of the preachers interviewed toward the symbiotic roles of singing and preaching in their religion. As we shall later see, one preacher volunteered his belief that blues were suitable for church as they often were as "truthful" as hymns. And it is no coincidence that every man interviewed for this project was either a former professional singer, choirmaster, or singer of some talent, though perhaps only with amateur status. As the first sermon to be chanted was the product of a man with musical as well as oratorical genius, so the same talents are obvious in the tradition today.

The principal informants in Bakersfield for this study were the Reverend Elihue H. Brown, pastor of the Union Baptist Church, and the Reverend Rubin Lacy, who had just given up his own church in Ridgecrest, California, and was then in Brown's congregation. Later Lacy pastored in Corcoran. Brown was born near Helena, Arkansas, in 1916; Lacy's first home was in Pelahatchie, Mississippi, where he was born in 1901. When I first met Lacy in California he was preaching about once a week, either at the Union Baptist or at one of the other churches in the area. Lacy was otherwise unemployed and supplemented his welfare money with the "offerings" he got for preaching. Sometimes he was paid a flat five or six dollars for each service; at other times he got half of the congregation's offering, the other half going to the host pastor.

Most of the preachers in Bakersfield (like those with small congregations around the country) could not support themselves on their church earnings, and held other jobs. A few could: a handful in Bakersfield, and some of the more popular with larger followings in big cities. In the main preachers depend upon their skills as orators to draw members to their congregations. The Reverend Edmund Blair of the Omega Baptist Church in Chicago was reported to have built up his congregation in a few years from eight to 3,800. The Reverend D. J. McDowell (who did live on his preaching and pastoral duties alone) believed that one must be careful about what the congregation is told: "People don't like to be told that they are bad." Part-time or free-lance preachers do not have to worry as much about offending their audience, but neither will they disregard its feelings. Even if they don't depend upon the congregation for a living, their pride is involved in their popularity (i.e., they are ineffective as God's ministers if no one wants to hear them), and some money, however little, is involved.

Every one of the preachers recorded during the course of this study was born in the South, though many of them either lived or spent much of their time elsewhere. Lacy attributed this movement to the eastern seaboard, Chicago and Detroit, and southern California simply to "civil rights." The situation was, I believe, far more complex than that, but for our immediate purposes the important fact is that the effect has been to spread a portion of southern culture across the nation. Those who migrated to the North, East, and West wanted to worship in the old way, and brought their religion with them. The migration created a demand and encouraged other ministers to follow their flocks. The pastors went with their congregations or else formed new ones in the new land; the healers and evangelists found new areas for conversion and reform, and strengthened their positions on both coasts and in the Midwest.

Functionally, the clergy in this study divided themselves into four groups: the pastors, the preachers, the healers, and the evangelists. Their authority is Ephesians 4:11: "And He gave some apostles; and some prophets; and some evangelists; and some pastors and teachers." The pastors run the local churches and tend to all the organizational and administrative matters concerned with keeping the congregation together. Preachers, on the other hand, are not necessarily the heads of their churches and might have nothing to do with local administration; they have been given the gift of preaching and may do so anywhere. Some preachers are members of an organized church, as Lacy was a member of the Reverend Elihue Brown's Union Baptist Church of Bakersfield. But Lacy often gave guest sermons at Brown's church and at others in the area. The preachers believe that Paul was the first of their number. Healers can be, though often they are not, limited to specific churches: A. A. Allen, for instance, was not only interdenominational but interracial and international. Relatively little of Allen's time was spent at his home base in Miracle Valley, Arizona. The evangelists almost never have churches of their own; their role is to bring converts to the churches of the pastors. However, most churches have "evangelistic services" on Sunday evenings, and more often than not they are led by the local pastor.

In practice it is nearly impossible to distinguish functions except for specific times and individuals. Lacy called Brown a pastor, yet Brown preached often and skillfully at his own church, the Union Baptist, and at others as well. He spent many summers doing evangelistic work in his home state of Arkansas that was unrelated to the immediate welfare of his congregation. I would personally classify A. A. Allen as a healer. His monthly magazine, *Miracle Magazine*, was devoted largely to his healing miracles, but Lacy called him an evangelist. And no doubt the same ambiguity of roles could be found in the evangelist Kathryn Kuhlman and the healer Oral Roberts.

Possibly because roles are not clearly defined and functions overlap, tensions are often strong among the various types of clergy, much as it was in the Middle Ages. Chaucer records the reputed licentiousness of pardoners and friars and some parish priests, and the ease of getting absolution from some of them in exchange for certain favors. And we know that after the thirteenth century tension existed between parish priests and the Franciscans and other preaching orders. Lacy at first denied, for the record, any conflict between pastors and evangelists. He was keeping his own house in order. But at another interview he said that his wife used to send money to A. A. Allen, money that might have gone to his own church. Lacy had forgotten his earlier statement, no doubt, but such conflicts are not hard to detect. Allen himself frequently attacked the established church clergy not only for their "false theology" but for their "greed." And I heard, though not with such great frequency, similar attacks made by J. Charles Jessup of Gulfport, Mississippi, and Neil Glasse and Brother Bob MacElroy, both of the Claremont-Ontario area in California.

Lacy defined pastors as "feeders"; they "feeds Christians," specifically their flock, with spiritual food. As Lacy explained to me, a "pastor" is a place where one feeds (folk definition: a "pasture"). When a "pastor" is dry, Lacy told me, there is no food for the flock.[24]

According to the clergymen I interviewed, the calling to the church comes from God. There is no other way. In nearly all instances, as was also the case with Lacy, Brown, and McDowell, the calling came against the will of the preacher. On one occasion Lacy said that he did not want to preach when he first felt the Spirit of God come to him, and he resisted for many years. He was a marginally successful blues singer and had various odd jobs until 1932 when he was in a railroad accident. He says a voice came to him then and said, "The next time it will be death." Thereupon Lacy gave away his guitar and went into the Missionary Baptist Church to do the Lord's work. Yet he recalled that when he was very young he was considered "peculiar" and given to religious thought; his grandfather, by whom he was raised, was an African Methodist preacher.

A person may be called to do the Lord's work, but to preach requires "spiritual power." This feeling that one is divinely summoned is important in understanding sermon techniques. Only spiritual power allows one to preach well; that can come only from God and "it don't take nothing but faith." (Yet at another interview Lacy said that a man could either be born to be a preacher, or else he could be called, but Lacy could not clearly distinguish between roles.) Lacy may well have been born to be a preacher; others, like J. Charles Jessup, appear to have been called. The story is told (not only by Jessup) that one day, while he lay upon "the bed of affliction," Jessup insisted on being locked in his room for forty days and forty nights, and that when he emerged he was a new man and one of God's ministers. Lacy tells another story about a friend who was deathly ill and who called out, "God, if you spare me I'll do what you want, and become a preacher." God did; and the man kept his promise.

The spiritual preacher finds ample scriptural support for his style of sermonizing. The preacher need not be learned, and in fact should not be educated, except in the ways of the Bible:

> And, behold, I send the promise of my Father upon you: but tarry ye in the city of Jerusalem, until ye be endued with power from on high. (Luke 24:49)

The important point here is that the apostles are not instructed to school themselves or to attend a seminary, but are merely to "tarry" until the Spirit comes to them. The spiritual preacher's understanding of the Bible, the truth, will come only and directly from God:

> Then opened He their understanding, that they might understand the Scriptures. (Luke 24:45)

For the holy preacher there is only one fit subject, the kingdom of God:

> The law and the prophets were until John: since that time the kingdom of God is preached, and every man presseth into it. (Luke 16:16)

God is with the preacher at every moment, inspiring and informing his/her words:

> Go ye therefore, and teach all nations, baptizing them in the name of the Father, and of the Son, and of the Holy Ghost, teaching them to observe all things whatsoever I have commanded you: and, lo, I am with you always, even unto the end of the world. Amen. (Matt. 28:19-20)

And the Holy Spirit shall forever be his comfort:

> Then had the churches rest throughout all Judea and Galilee and Samaria, and were edified; and walking in the fear of the Lord, and in the comfort of the Holy Ghost, were multipled. (Acts 9:31)

The matter of being born to be a preacher and being called is no different from what the laity think of as the preacher's education. Lacy was raised by his preacher grandfather and as a child was thought to be destined to be a clergyman. He said that at the age of seven he used to "practice preach" and would give sermons to the birds and the trees (like St. Francis?) in Pelahatchie. At that time, he said, he used to imitate preachers he heard in the area. In other words, he grew up in a clerical tradition where preaching, like gospel singing, was a vital part of his life. He got religion at home; like most black Baptist children he went to church more than once a week, and he also went to revivals and other camp meetings. When the Spirit of God finally moved him to take the cloth in 1932, he could draw upon a very rich and very vigorous tradition.

The tradition is still vital,[25] though its vigor may be waning. Lacy, like many of his colleagues, listened to radio sermons and watched revivals on television. He heard a few sermons that were recorded (on the Battle and Chess labels). He went to church three or four times a week and heard not only his own pastor but guest preachers from neighboring towns—Pixley, Delano, Taft, and Arvin. What he got was a cross section of styles from many places in the South and from many transplanted southerners. That cross section of styles was within a definable tradition. None of the preachers whom Lacy heard "live" prepared written sermons: they chanted (and sometimes sang), using stock phrases, stories, and ideas. Lacy not only learned and assimilated the language of his colleagues, but contributed his own innovations to the tradition.

In another culture, Albert B. Lord has identified three stages in the development of the singing career of the Yugoslav *guslars*. At first the *guslar* is a nonparticipating listener, learning the stories, songs, and language of the performing singers. The second stage begins when the apprentice first begins to sing. The final stage, according to Lord, is when the singer has become accomplished enough to move freely in the tradition.[26] Roughly the same paradigm describes the preachers. At first, as young children, they sit in church and learn the stories of the Bible, the popular sermon topics, the melody and rhythm of gospel songs (and, more important, the melody and rhythm of the pastor's chanted sermons), and, however unconsciously, many of the phrases that will later become formulas. The incipient preachers will also hear sermons and gospel singing at home on the radio, on records, and on television. All these aspects of style and lessons of theology they absorb as children, whether they have it in mind ever to become preachers or not.

A second stage often comes when the apprentice becomes involved with church work and attends services more frequently. Rev. Elihue Brown sang in a choir for several years before stepping forward to the pulpit, and during that time the music of songs and sermons became firmly ingrained in him. Many preachers are former deacons of the church who began their new roles gradually by reciting short prayers before the sermon proper;[27] when the prayer has been mastered a short sermon may be attempted, perhaps in front of the children's Bible class. Gradually the assistant pastor can work into the church's schedule until ready to take a church on his or her own. The sermon of such an apprentice, William Robinson of the First Baptist of Santa Barbara, is included in this book. Lacy skipped this second stage, learning his music as a blues singer; but his childhood was saturated with the music and rhythms of the church, and he attended services regularly while singing for his living.

The final stage begins when the preachers take their own churches; at this point they must feel that their repertoires are sufficient to sustain a congregation week after week, and that their skills are sufficient to master the intricacies of individual sermons. They then become an active part of the tradition: they have mastered certain aspects of language and certain rhythms that are sure to elicit a predictable response. The ratio of the interplay of free-floating materials (shaped by the preacher's imagination) to necessary elements makes a comparison with improvised jazz helpful. Rarely do jazz musicians completely improvise with no relation to the work they are currently playing; almost always they know their scores perfectly, have played them many times, and have thought about them even more frequently. When, during a performance, they break free of the limits of the standard's notes, they have a good idea of what they are going to do, at least in general terms. But the important point of comparison is that the improvisation is possible only when the basic score has been mastered, however simple or difficult. Thus, in the same way, preachers do not move away from what they know well, even if the standards are their own texts, until they have mastered the technique.

One could predict with certitude how a taped sermon by Detroit's C. L. Franklin or one by the Reverend Mr. Gatewood would be received; such sermons are in, are part of, the idiom.[28] And one could with equal certainty predict how flat a sermon by a white, northern Presbyterian would sound to a southern Baptist congregation. C. L. Franklin, filled with the Spirit of God, would impart that Spirit to any black congregation (whose own pastor was a spiritual preacher) even though they had never heard him before.[29]

NOTES

1. Henry Bradshaw Fearon, *Sketches of America* (London, 1818), pp. 162–67.

2. William Eleasar Barton, *Old Plantation Hymns* (Boston, 1899), p. 41.

3. Clarence Deming, *By-Ways of Nature and Life* (New York, 1884), p. 361.

4. William Warren Sweet, *Revivalism in America* (New York, 1944), p. 95.

5. Joseph R. Washington, Jr., *Black Religion* (Boston, 1966), p. 173.

6. E. Franklin Frazier, *The Negro Church in America* (New York, 1964), p. 7.

7. Frazier, *Negro Church in America*, p. 28.

8. John Hope Franklin, *From Slavery to Freedom* (New York, 1967), pp. 162–63.

9. Marcia M. Mathews, *Richard Allen* (Baltimore, 1963), p. 18.

10. Perry Miller, *The New England Mind: The Seventeenth Century* (Cambridge, Mass., 1963), p. 352; see also Robert Henson, "Form and Content of the Puritan Funeral Elegy," *American Literature*, 32 (Mar. 1960), 12.

11. Sweet, *Revivalism in America*, p. 108.

12. Alan Heimert, *Religion and the American Mind* (Cambridge, Mass., 1966), pp. 228–31 and passim.

13. Washington, *Black Religion*, p. 190.

14. Heimert, *Religion and the American Mind*, p. 230.

15. George Pullen Jackson, *White and Negro Spirituals* (New York, 1943), pp. 80–83. Mrs. Franklin Trollope describes a camp meeting she attended in 1829 in which blacks were numbered among the 2,000 or so faithful. Her account is contemptuous of the sobbing, shrieking, groaning, and screaming all around her, so that her picture of American life must be accepted with reservations: *Domestic Manners of the Americans* (New York, 1901), pp. 237–41.

16. Frazier, *Negro Church in America*, p. 8.

17. Washington, *Black Religion*, pp. 194–95.

18. Ibid., pp. 196 ff.

19. Frazier, *Negro Church in America*, p. 3.

20. Compare the observations of Sammie Ann Wicks, "Life and Meaning: Singing, Praying, and the Word among the Old Regular Baptists of Eastern Kentucky" (Ph.D. diss., University of Texas, 1983).

21. Don Yoder, *Pennsylvania Spirituals* (Lancaster, Pa., 1961), pp. 1–32.

22. The history of this phenomenon has been efficiently summarized by Bruce Jackson, "The Glory Songs of the Lord," in *Our Living Traditions*, ed. Tristram P. Coffin (New York, 1968), pp. 108–19. For an early description of an antiphonal service of lining out and response, see Bruce Jackson, *The Negro and His Folklore in Nineteenth-Century Periodicals* (Austin, Tex., 1967), pp. 122–23.

23. See Jackson, "Glory Songs," pp. 115 ff.

24. Lacy's etymology is not particularly creative in this instance: on another occasion he told his congregation that "Sunday" was named for the "Son" of God, which was why we all went to church on that day.

25. The tradition I speak of in this book is that of oral preaching in which the sermons are metrical and are spontaneously composed. Al-

most all such preachers either come from the South or learned this style from a southerner. Often the preacher is black, although some whites, in Kentucky, Ohio, and Pennsylvania, also preach this way.

26. Albert B. Lord, *The Singer of Tales* (New York, 1965), pp. 21–26.

27. After several weeks of attending services, I was myself able to make a rather specious leap into the second stage by reciting a formulaic "testimony" I had devised. In most Baptist churches guests are asked to "say a few words" before the congregation is dismissed: I found that the testimonies were heavily formulaic, and after listening to several such performances I was able to give my own. What I lacked in years of experience in making such statements I overcame because I knew the linguistic principles on which such short speeches were made. Professor Donald R. Howard thinks that Chaucer would have had a place for people like me among the Canterbury pilgrims, but I hope that my "testimony" will be understood as a verbal exercise rather than as religious hypocrisy:

> Thanking the Lord above all things
> It's good to be in His house this mornin'
> And it's good to hear the words of the preacher
> We thank him for his message
> I thank the Lord for giving me another night's rest
> I thank Him for letting me rise this morning
> And I thank Him for letting me have another day
> God bless this congregation
> God bless the pastor
> God bless the deacons
> And bless this house

28. Lacy once insisted that his favorite preacher was John Allen Chalk, whose Sunday morning sermons originated in Abilene, Texas, and who was heard in Bakersfield over KUZZ. It was obvious, however, that Chalk was a manuscript preacher and not the kind Lacy usually admired. Curiously, on the several mornings when I asked Lacy questions about Chalk's sermon, he said that he had not listened. Certainly Lacy did not admire Chalk's style of delivery; one can only speculate about his admiration for his colleague.

29. Charles Keil, *Urban Blues* (Chicago, 1966), pp. 7–8, notes that speaking in tongues, healing, "possession," frenzied dancing, hand clapping, tambourine playing, singing and screaming, and constant participation by the audience are alien to the "prevailing conception of

Protestantism." The ineffectiveness of a white minister in a black church was noticed over a century ago: see Jackson, *Negro and His Folklore*, p. 66.

3

Singing the Word

All oral preachers insist that their sermon material comes from
God. There is no question in their minds about that, and it is a
touchy matter to try to discuss more secular sources. Lacy could
sit at home for a week and think on and off about his sermon for
the following Sunday, but he knew that God drove him to deliver
that particular sermon on that particular day, even to choosing
the passages from Scripture that he would use or quote; and most
important, at the moment of performance God, and God alone,
would inspire him to say the words that he would actually use.
The most articulate expression I have heard of that belief—the
relation of inspiration to the spiritual sermon—came not from
Bakersfield, however, but from the Reverend Rufus Hays of
Louisa, Virginia, in a personal interview in 1969. Hays's opinion
would be heartily endorsed by all spiritual preachers:

> As you concentrate and meditate open-hearted and mind, God can
> relate to you the interpretation properly, and He can bring out
> the message that He has in the particular points to the people that
> He has to speak of. As you know the Scriptures tells a story; they
> relates commands; they relates demands; you might be reading a
> particular experience of Israel. In that particular statement or con-
> versation there is a point of verse; and the Spirit of the Lord dawns
> on you out of that particular point of passage of Scripture. The
> Lord utters deeper inspiration, maybe not relating to the same
> subject or thought that was spoken to Israel at that time, but that's
> the way God's word is.

The preacher's words come from the Holy Ghost, but the preacher must be familiar with Scripture, for instance, in order to know how to interpret the Holy Ghost's message. Only after I came to know them better did Lacy and Brown discuss their sources. The most fertile field for religious ideas is the sermons of other preachers, especially ones the preacher has heard in childhood. Then, scores of books are available that anthologize sermons either in their entirety or in outlines, and occasionally list suggestions for sermon themes.[1] And radio, phonograph records, and television church services are other valuable sources.

Exposure to the sermons of fellow preachers is extensive, even without the intensifying of that exposure through radio and television. For instance, Lacy and Brown went to Arkansas nearly every year to participate in the revivals there; and of course they listened to the sermons of their colleagues who had made the same pilgrimage from other parts of the country. A man like Lacy was able to pick up ideas for sermon topics from preachers all over the South without doing extensive traveling himself. The annual Baptist conventions also brought the faithful together for several days of prayer and preaching. One of Lacy's favorite sermons, for instance, was an elaboration and application of the Old Testament parable "The Eagle Stirreth Up Its Nest." Lacy said that he had heard it often. It also happens to be an extremely popular sermon topic among southern Baptists, having been recorded on disc by C. L. Franklin, J. M. Gates, and Calvin P. Dixon. Lacy had heard records made by Franklin, although he didn't remember which ones, and he might have heard the others.

Especially popular is "Dry Bones in the Valley" (from Ezekiel 37): Lacy and Brown could recite their own versions of it, and the story has also been recorded by Gates, Joe McCoy (as "Hallelujah Joe"), Elder Charles Beck, and the Reverend Leora Ross. A further indication of the popularity of this story may be seen in its version as a spiritual ("Ezekiel Saw the Wheel") and the popular tour de force of years ago ("Dem Bones, Dem Bones, Dem Dry Bones"). Both traditions were united by Lacy in a sermon recorded in 1967. The repeated use of a specific passage from Scripture along with the similarity of development of many of the sermons suggest at least an indirect influence within a tradition.

Other popular sermon topics are worthy of mention here: "The Four Horsemen," "The Twenty-third Psalm," "Moses at the Red Sea," "Dead [or Live] Cat on the Line," "The Horse Paweth in the Valley," "Jesus Will Make It All Right," "Jesus Will Lead You," "The Prodigal Son," and "The New Jerusalem."[2] Certain preachers favor certain stories and will use them more often, but most preachers with several years' experience will be able to preach on all these topics.

Now most preachers are not willing to admit that their ideas come from other preachers. Lacy, for instance, preached a sermon in June 1967 on "The Deck of Cards," which he at first claimed was his own invention; people in Bakersfield had never heard such an idea, he said. The sermon's basic theme was that the standard deck of cards has religious significance: the ace is the One God, the two suggests both parts of the Bible, the three stands for the Trinity, the four-spot corresponds to the four gospel writers, and so forth. When pressed by another member of the congregation, Lacy recalled that he got the idea from a spoken country-and-western record made by T. Texas Tyler sometime after World War II. The same story has since been recorded by Tex Williams, Tex Ritter, Ernest Tubb, Pee Wee King, Wink Martindale, and even by Phil Harris. It has been satirized by Ferlin Husky (as "Simon Crum") in a version called "The Hillbilly Sucker and the Deck of Cards." Lacy recognized a good thing when he heard it and used Tyler's idea[3] in his sermon (the "Deck of Cards" sermon is printed in this book). The Reverend J. J. Freeman of Pixley, California, used a particularly inventive theme for one of his favorite sermons, "The Postage Stamp," which compares a person, and especially the church's pastor, to a postage stamp: each person has a place in life, just as the stamp has its place on the envelope. The five-cent stamp (before the rise in postal rates) does the best job it can within its capability, just as we are bidden to do the best we can with the talents God has given us.[4] I was not able to track down the source for Freeman's sermon, if one existed, but I would guess that if it was original it soon entered the tradition as other preachers adopted it.

A second major source of topics is written sermon material, of which there is a thriving literature. Jabez D. Burns wrote several books of sermons and sermon outlines that were very popular among the clergy I interviewed. Lacy often preached on "God's Plowboy," comparing the minister to the farm laborer who fertilizes the spiritual soil, but who toils in the field in hopes of an ultimate reward. The theme came from Burns's *Master Sermon Outlines* (Atlanta, n.d.); Lacy merely used the bare outline and several of the major points as a rough guide, as is usually the method when written sources are used. ("God's Plowboy" and its source have been printed below.) Many southern black preachers are so accustomed to reciting orally and composing spontaneously that when they read from a text the result is usually poor; in the performance of "God's Plowboy" recorded in 1967, Lacy read three or four passages from Scripture contained in his source book, but extemporized the rest, while adhering—as was mentioned earlier—generally to the book's outline.

One should also include with this kind of sermon those that are read directly from the Bible. The Reverend Mr. Goins, from the Bakersfield area, once preached on Genesis, reading directly from Scripture (though one may be certain that he did not have to), gradually breaking into a chant and away from a literal reading.

If we try to find out from the preachers themselves how they compose their sermons, we again run into differing interpretations. Manuscript preachers compose by the inspiration and perspiration method: about 90 percent hard work to exploit 10 percent good idea. But spiritual preachers of the type under consideration are far harder to pin down. Rev. Mr. Brown often said that his inspiration came only from God; Lacy corroborated this, insisting that no preparation was necessary because the sermon was inspired: he simply had to step up to the pulpit and he was "fed" directly from God. These explanations were typical; I have since found the same idea invariably expressed throughout the South.

Yet at times Lacy could announce a week in advance what he was going to talk about on the following Sunday morning and one time let slip that he had been "thinking" and "working up" a particular sermon for several days. On Sunday mornings it was common for the men I interviewed to use many of the words, phrases, and even ideas that they were going to use while preaching. One Sunday morning, Brown welcomed me with the remark that he was thankful that "God's hand" had guided me to Bakersfield, and he excused himself several minutes later, leaving me in "the good hands" of the deacon. His sermon an hour later was on "Being in the Hands of God."

Spiritual preachers "work up" their sermons for several days or, if time is short, for several hours before delivery by reviewing in their minds the basic outlines, much as Parry and Lord found that their Yugoslav informants "memorized" their epics by remembering the basic outlines and filling in the stories with formulas. Spiritual preachers have a stock of themes for use in sermons as well as a stock of sermons that they can use at will. Like the jazz musicians of our earlier example, preachers do not experiment with their sermons until they have learned them well. New sermons are added to the repertoire gradually, and then filled in with stock phrases and even stock passages of ten lines or more. This generalization will almost always hold despite Lacy's claim that the best way to preach is without warning of any kind: "If you got notice you mess up," but when you preach at the last minute you have got to depend upon God. However, preliminary study time was used by some, such as the Reverend Rufus Hays, who gave a fifteen-minute sermonette over WELK, Charlottesville, Virginia, and who studied the Bible in preparation for the day's message just before broadcast time.

Lacy has already been quoted as insisting that the preacher is fed by God, and he used this faith to justify his mild contempt for those who use a manuscript. Yet in his sermon on "God's Plowboy" Lacy used *Master Sermon Outlines* and read the appropriate passages from Scripture. Brown did the same thing when he wanted to be sure to repeat the quotation accurately. McDowell often used a note card, reducing a twenty-minute sermon to one five-by-five-inch card. Goins and others who have recited from the Bible begin with the book in front of them, and though the first several words may be quoted verbatim they soon break into their own idiomatic chants. For instance, Brown once began a sermon with: "In the beginning was the Word. And the Word was with God. And the Word sure was God." In this case the idiomatic "sure was God" was added to regularize the meter of the line.

For the spiritual preacher, then, God works through an extensive tradition of sermon topics derived from other preachers heard live, on radio, records, or television. Some of the topics are explications and comparisons of normally secular subjects, such as the deck of cards or the postage stamp. Others are explications of passages in the Bible. The preacher relies upon stock phrases and passages to fill out the skeleton of the sermon, and develops the message through repetition. T. Texas Tyler's "Deck of Cards" record takes less than four minutes in performance. Lacy stretched it out to about eight minutes, but even that was still only one-third of the piece he called his "Deck of Cards" sermon. He once said that he could use the cards portion of the sermon with almost any message preceding it, though preferably with commentary on "heart." He used the cards portion so often that he could recite it nearly by heart, with only minor lexical variations. The rest of the sermon may not have been so tightly organized or composed, but could be put together by techniques similar to those described by Parry, as we shall later see.

There is a famous literary precedent for Lacy's technique. Chaucer's Pardoner could also preach on any topic spontaneously: "For I kan al by rote that I telle."[5] The Pardoner's technique is not oral formulaic, yet the suggestion is strong that he composes by the manipulation of traditional themes. But the Pardoner's story is a confession of cynicism; he preaches against certain vices in the tale, specifically gluttony and swearing, in order to increase the sinner's offering. His preaching is flexible; he can preach against any sin spontaneously because he has "by rote" learned what to say on every occasion. This historical comparison is important for several reasons. Primarily, it places Lacy and his colleagues in a human and Christian context that is relevant to their lives. This context, which gives us many analogues to Lacy's situation, raises his problems and his skills out of the immediate milieu of his Bakersfield existence and enables us to see how he shared them with memorable characters of the past. And finally, these comparisons remind us that though the immediate focus is the American spiritual preacher, our ultimate concern is with a less chronologically and spatially limited human phenomenon.

We have seen how the Puritan sermon is based on a text-context-application pattern; if we are to judge from Middle English sermons collected in the Early English Text Society series (London, 1940), such was the basic pattern for the later Middle Ages. Once again we may see Lacy, with all his individual genius, still as part of a tradition that has been the common heritage of all of us for several centuries. For this pattern is exactly what many southern preachers, especially those under study, strive for in their own sermon organization.

The text and context organization, the exegetical sermon, has survived through the Renaissance and into our century where, as the Reverend Mr. Robert Howland of the Goleta, California, Presbyterian Church has pointed out, it has been largely ignored by white middle-class churches. The pastors of those churches prefer topical sermons dealing with more secular matters such as civil rights, disarmament, our military involvement in Central America, the "New Morality," and such quasi-secular topics (for Protestants) as birth control. This secularized sermon is another aspect of our heritage from the eighteenth century. The topical sermon occasionally uses scriptural evidence to support the main argument, but it is not at all thematically like the gospel preaching of many southern Fundamentalist clergy. The northern middle-class churches are changing their sermon content; the southern churches, especially the Baptist and Methodist, are in this respect keeping alive a Christian tradition of considerably antiquity.

One can see the structural patterns of which we have been speaking in several of the sermons collected in this volume. They are even more obvious in the sermons of the great, nationally known preachers such as the late Reverend Mr. C. L. Franklin. Many of his sermons have been recorded by Battle and Chess Records in Detroit. Franklin was a master of organization, just as he was of drama. His sermon "Moses at the Red Sea," in particular, with its applicability to those in his congregation who were facing or had faced seemingly insurmountable difficulties by drawing upon the strength within themselves, was created carefully by a man of great sensitivity and reason. J. Charles Jessup, though not black and not Baptist, strove for the text-context-application-resolution formula and usually achieved it.

Lacy and Brown were far less tidy in their sermon organization, especially Lacy: witness his statement that he could begin his "Deck of Cards" sermon on almost any topic, though he tried to think of something that had to do with "heart." His opening quotation was: "The fool has said in his heart, 'There is no God.'" Both Lacy and Brown digressed quite a bit, as did several other preachers in the area, occasionally getting completely off the subject. A sermon of thirty to forty minutes is, after all, difficult to keep on a single subject within a given framework. There is no continuing narrative thread to force the speaker to stay on the track. And it is in the nature of sermons to use examples, proverbs, and parables; understandably, then, preachers who compose spontaneously by welding together such illustrative materials with set passages and phrases can be very easily led astray. In some of Brown's sermons one could hear him struggling to get back to the point after an ambiguous scriptural passage had led him to pursue some irrelevant theme.

When one first hears sermons of the type under consideration, little coherence is found in them. Even in transcribing them I could find little in the way of any principle of organization. Narratives are easier to organize; certain characters have to be introduced at certain points in the story and certain events have to take place. We learn something about Beowulf before he fights his first combat; he sets sail, is encountered by the coast-warden, is introduced to Hrothgar, and is twitted by Unferth before he engages Grendel in combat. The singer of such a tale will have little trouble remembering what is to happen because of the nature of the story: the singer is not likely to forget and place the Unferth episode after Beowulf has beaten the troll—it would not make sense.

But sermons need not have any such consistency. Standardized narrative scenes whose language is memorized—Lord's "themes"—may be ornamental or essential. The former may be used in any given narrative depending upon the whim of the singer; essential themes are necessary for the advancement of the narrative. The sermon singer can be far more flexible: the sermon itself is usually based on a single line of Scripture, and not on an elaborate narrative. That single line may be expanded in many ways, and though the preacher may use passages that are similar in principle to Lord's themes, they are seldom necessary in the way that narrative themes are necessary.

A good illustration of this point is Lacy's sermon on "Dry Bones in the Valley" (printed below). The story from Ezekiel concerns the role of the prophet and preacher, and the fact that Ezekiel was in the desert reminded Lacy of himself in the San Joaquin "desert." But Lacy was also an old man and one of his favorite stories was about St. John as an old man. So he talked about John first in the sermon on "Dry Bones." Then he talked about "Old Moses", gave a sermonized version of "Dem Bones," and finally got around to Ezekiel. Now little enough logic holds in this sermon, yet all these stories are related if we use the associational leaps in Lacy's mind as a guide. St. John's old age is not related to Ezekiel logically, but we have seen how the connection would be made by the preacher. The story of Moses follows: the connection? Moses as an old man led his people to salvation across the desert. The final passage Lacy knows he will have to reach has to do with bones, and that reminds him of the popular song about "Dem Bones." Finally he comes to Ezekiel. As narrative it is near chaos, though there are narrative passages in the separate stories of the sermon. As logic it is something of a disaster; and yet, in a subtle way, all the tales hold together.

But if they cohere in this sermon at least, they, or their order, are not essential to the sermon. No discussion of Ezekiel in the valley of dry bones needs a story of Moses in the desert. All that is necessary to such a sermon is the story of Ezekiel in the valley. The other stories—sometimes they are also themes—are ornamental (like the digressions in *Beowulf*?). Very few themes are essential in this art, so that the preacher has a greater thematic flexibility than the *guslar*. There is this difference: many of the *guslar*'s themes are structured necessarily while nearly all of the preacher's are arbitrary and occur associationally.

A generic description is impossible beyond the few observations that folk sermons are spontaneously composed and orally recited by the preacher for the edification of peer group members. Often preachers have had no seminary training, but exceptions are many; usually no manuscripts are used, though occasionally preachers will refer to notes, particularly if they must use many biblical references and are concerned lest they forget some of them. When manuscripts are used interesting "transi-tional" texts result; usually "folk preachers"—by this definition—will quickly break away from the prepared text toward their personal rhythms and styles. Prepared sermons that are read in their entirety by ministers are almost invariably the mark of sem-inary-trained preachers, who often find employment in com-munities outside of the culturally homogeneous area in which they were raised, if in fact their backgrounds have been so stable.

Neither can one speak of the "genre" of the "oral epic," and for the same reasons. Whether *guslars* in Bosnia or the *akyn* among the Kirghiz, the people who compose such pieces and their audiences have no concept of genre, let alone epic. Many of the Yugoslavian compositions are versified traditional folktales, and some are merely single motifs. The length varies from a few hundred to several thousand lines. The greatest impediment to arriving at a generic description is the flexibility of the singers, who can lengthen or abridge a piece according to their whim or the desire of the audience, or forget an episode or even stitch two or more together if at the moment of composition the fancy strikes. When composition is in this mode, generic definition, which usually relies upon structure, is difficult.

For nearly all of these reasons we cannot precisely define the orally delivered, spontaneously composed folk sermon, because we have found that narrative segments in the Bosnian stories have their counterparts in hortatory sermon components. The preacher can also lengthen or shorten a performance according to the conditions of the moment. Some preachers strive for the tradi-tional text-context-application format of sermons, and most achieve it, but that form is by no means universal, and many depart from it so substantially that the structure is unrecogniz-able. Yet we would not want to say that a sermon is not a sermon if the preacher fails to adhere to this structure. Like the *guslars*, the preachers have little regard for formal structures. Their pur-pose is to convey the Word of God in whatever way they can. The *guslars* entertain with folktales; the preachers edify with exempla.

We should, finally, say a word about artistic merit. Faulkner realized and utilized the emotional power of the sermon in one of the most crucial passages of *The Sound and the Fury*; the the-

matic climax of that novel could well have been expressed in
other modes had Faulkner's aim been solely ideological. Reverend Shegog's ideas offer no challenge, certainly; but for dramatic impact, for the power of its message—as Frederick Hoffman
puts it[6]—Faulkner could not have chosen a more suitable form.
Such sermons can be moving experiences: as Charles Keil has
observed, one need not be black to be moved by a sermon of
Rev. C. L. Franklin.[7] But the final proof can come only during
the live performance.

The chanted folk sermon is never far from the spiritual. The
most striking similarity between song and sermon, the most readily identifiable, is that of diction. A surprising number of sermon
lines are taken from traditional spirituals, probably even more
than from the Bible. As an example, the following ten lines, used
earlier, were extracted from a sermon by the Reverend D. J.
McDowell, delivered in Delano, California, on July 30, 1967:

> God is our refuge
> And strength
> A well-proved helpmate in trouble
> I'm in trouble this evenin'
> 5 Yes I am
> I said I'm in trouble this evenin'
> I need someone to go all night long
> If you never hear me no more
> Keep your hand in God's hand
> 10 He'll make a way for you

Several lines in this excerpt are from spirituals; not only could
McDowell's sermons be examined at length with the same result,
but those of nearly all black folk preachers contain a similarly
high proportion of lines from the spirituals. The same has not
been true of whites, however. Music and the influence of the
diction of the spirituals seem to be more characteristic of blacks.

In addition, we should also consider that much of the sermon
diction that is ultimately biblical in origin eventually finds its way
to church by way of the spirituals. When the Reverend Rubin
Lacy, preaching a sermon on "Dry Bones" on July 16, 1967,
said, "The Word of God/Come to the dry bones/Rise and live,"
he had in mind more the song "Dem Bones, Dem Bones, Dem

Dry Bones" than he did Ezekiel 37:5. The song has "Now hear the *Word* of the Lord"; Ezekiel reads: "Thus *saith* the Lord God unto these bones." Lacy was also thinking of the well-known spiritual line, "Dese bones gwine *rise* again," rather than the Bible passage, where *rise* does not appear. A brief list of sermon diction from the Bible by way of spirituals should suffice to illustrate the point:

'Zekiel saw a wheel (from Ezekiel 1:15)
Daniel saw the stone (Daniel 2:34)
We'll sing a new song (Isaiah 42:10)
He's the Rock of Ages (Isaiah, 2:10)
Dressed in raiment/White as driven as the snow (Revelation 1:14–16)
Rainbow round his shoulder (Revelation 10:1 reads in part: "and a rainbow was upon his head." In this instance the preacher's inspiration was a popular song—"There's a rainbow round his shoulder, and a sky of blue above," etc.—and not a spiritual.)

Another quality of both black sermons and spirituals—not exclusively theirs but certainly characteristic—is the repetition of lines. It would be pointless to cite examples here from the songs, their repetitiveness being so obvious a fact. The demonstration may be limited to extracts from a sermon of Jerry H. Lockett, "This Same Jesus," delivered in Charlottesville, Virginia, March 17, 1968:

> I'm talkin' about Jesus
> I'm talkin' about Jesus
> Talkin' about the one
> Who brought us a mighty long ways
> ⁵ We seen a child way up in Jerusalem
> Seen Him up there settin' down amongst the doctors
> Seen Him up there among the lawyers
> Settin' up there among highly educated people
> . . .
> This same Jesus
> ¹⁰ Told the woman one day
> Same Jesus
> That give sight to the blind one day
> This same Jesus

> Spoke to the dumb one day
> [15] Caused them to speak
> The deaf to hear one day
> That same Jesus

The function of repetitiveness as an aid to oral composition has been discussed in detail elsewhere in this book; here we need only accept the fact that the language is repetitive.

The reasons for this striking repetition may vary for the two genres. In the spontaneous composition of sermons the pace of delivery is such that preachers need as much time as they can afford not only to think of the imminent idea but to formulate its diction and structure. Ballad recitation imposes different demands upon the performer, yet as Gordon Hall Gerould has observed, performers are remarkable in the fluidity with which they can improvise ballad lines: it is often easier for them to compose new verses spontaneously than to remember the old ones.[8] Still, one would be hard-pressed to argue that the psycholinguistic process of song composition was very close to that of sermon making; the point to be argued here is only that the element of improvisation brings the song somewhat closer to the sermon than we would at first expect. (During the summer of 1967, Lacy once inserted most of the "Dem Bones" song into his sermon on Ezekiel, converting the meter of the former to his sermon style.)

It follows, then, that the rhythm of many of the sermon lines is also that of the songs. For instance, Lacy's conversational speech was basically iambic but his recitation from the pulpit, at least those portions that were chanted, were often anapestic, as in the following excerpt from a sermon delivered on July 9, 1967:

> In the mornin'
> When the horses
> Begin to come out
> And the riders on the horses
> [5] Want 'em to come out
> God from Zion
> Riding a red horse
> There's somebody gonna say
> Is that the general
> [10] That I was fighting for

> And I heard another cry
> Saying no-ooo

But then, we should expect Lacy's rhythm here to vary from that of his conversation, since he was chanting, and his first allegiance was to rhythmic fluency and not to the meaning of the language. He was not quite singing (though chanting and singing are often hard to distinguish), and the resultant meter is not precisely that of song, either, nor is it as consistent; but it is songlike nevertheless, borrowing more from the spirituals than from conventional oratorical style.

Neither are we surprised to find that many of the preacher's lines can be notated as though they were songs, and that they have identifiable melodies. Part of the reason lies in the minister's divine joy, which expresses itself melodically; part lies in the traditional role the spirituals have had for most blacks and some whites; and part is concerned with the preacher's retention techniques. After extended observation it was discovered that each preacher chanted certain phrases to a particular melody, probably automatically, and probably to enable him better to recall the phrase without having to think about it. We have seen that preachers compose their sermons much as the *guslar* composes epics and lyrics; automatic phrases are valuable in the composition process in that they enable performers to concentrate on the lines to come, lines that they are subjectively formulating even while they are objectively—and automatically—uttering the phrase of the moment.

The striking imagery that reduces the metaphysical to the immediately physical, a characteristic of spirituals, especially black, is also found in the sermons. Again, this is to be expected, since the same culture (or subculture) produced both, and the song is held nearly as sacred as the sermon. In the spirituals Satan and Jesus have a horse race:

> Win de race agin de course . . .
> Satan tell me to my face . . .
> He will break my kingdom down . . .
> Jesus whisper in my heart . . .
> He will build 'em up again . . .

The preacher is likely to say: "Jesus said to me the other day. . . ."
Or it will be St. Paul; or the preacher will advise St. Peter not
to worry about his children; or the leader of the Jews will be
referred to familiarly as "old man Moses." God and his saints are
real, living, and near at hand; there is nothing distant or aloof
about them. The preacher—and the spiritual singer—addresses
that God and those saints directly and intimately. It is a face-to-
face confrontation in a meaningful world.

We have no trouble guessing why chanting would be added
to the prose sermon. W. W. Sweet claimed that the "holy whine"
of the Baptists, the characteristic rising and falling of voice during

their sermons, was to relieve the strain imposed by preaching
outdoors.[9] But we shall have to go beyond this. Chanting, as well
as other histrionic uses of the voice, reduce the potential monotony of performance by infusing it with a kind of drama. Most
important, chanting builds tension in the performance of the sermon through intensified tone as well as through increasing rhythm.
And it is largely for these reasons that the chanted sermon is
more interesting to hear. It is more exciting than prose sermons,
generally, and has an aesthetic of its own—about which more
later.

Excitement may well be in the minds of the congregation, and
thus may be subjective, but its manifestation is decidedly present,
and no doubt foreign, as Charles Keil has observed, to the "prevailing conceptions of Protestantism."[10] Preachers preach that
way not only because their congregations demand it, but because
they find prose deliveries from a manuscript deadening.[11] They
view themselves in sharp contrast with the dull, lifeless services
of the manuscript preachers whose lack of emotion they may
take as a sign of the absence of God, a feeling they share with
passionate pulpit orators of early America.[12]

Emotionalism is desired, as it was in parts of New England and
throughout the border states during and after the Second Great
Awakening. No doubt such services provide a tremendous outlet
for people of humble social attainment, then as now: E. Franklin
Frazier remarks that the camp meeting provided a sense of sol-
idarity for broken blacks,[13] but this can be generalized to include
the culturally disinherited of both races. In churches where emotionalism is desired, then, we can see how the chanted sermon

is an ideal expression, allowing an exciting aesthetic form to act as the vehicle of transmission for the Word of God, a subject already heavily charged with emotion. The chanted sermon is perpetuated for the same reasons that it was created: it is an ideal medium for its particular message, for in few other art forms is the message so nearly the medium. No other form allows the preacher to communicate the Word of God while singing, clapping, and even dancing, or allows the congregation to participate by yelling, tambourine playing, speaking in tongues, and toe tapping, as well as this one does.

Mainstream Christianity is the inheritor of the Thomistic tradition that God is attainable through reason. For us Revelation may be suspect; passion is downright unacceptable. The sermon should lead us to God by providing an intellectual path that the mind can follow, however narrow and winding the way; such a rationale equates emotionalism with hysteria and hysteria with the negation of reason. If one believes that God is knowable primarily through the intellect, despite Paul's assertion that he had to become a fool to know Christ, then the ideal sermon mode is exposition, not rhythm.

This polarity also has social implications. In the nineteenth century the fervor of the revivals and camp meetings was appealing to many who could be saved by feeling that they were saved.[14] The ministry of the Baptists and Methodists were often poorly educated, especially compared with their Anglican colleagues, and this also made them more appealing to the slaves and dirt farmers who were often their congregations. Poor education usually implies a lower economic standing; the holy services that the poor attend are thus suspect in the eyes of the intellectually superior, whether it be the Presbyterian planter of the antebellum South or the middle-class white today.

A colleague, after hearing several recordings of chanted sermons, suggested that such preachers might be found largely in rural areas (as it happens they have been successful in major urban centers as well) because audiences there are less sophisticated, but that as churchgoers acquired sophistication—by moving to a large city, presumably—they would drift away from the churches of spiritual preachers toward the more conventional. For this man sophistication is the crux.

But the issue is more complex than that. It seems not to be a matter of sophistication—an idea implying that all right-thinking, intelligent, emotionally mature people will think one way while their social, intellectual, and emotional inferiors will necessarily worship another way—as much as a sense of middle-class decorum that one acquires. The middle class cherishes a sense of the appropriateness of things—this is one of the clichés of sociological thought—as they emulate the outward forms, pomp, and ritual of the upper class. We do not clap and shout in church because it is not appropriate or decorous to do so; what is at issue is not our sophistication so much as our concepts of our own dignity.

One of the elements of style is appropriateness to subject. One does not write a eulogy on the death of a queen in limerick form; and when the subject of a poem is bed-wetting one does not employ Homeric similes. This is well understood. The choice of form, of genre, is a conscious one on the part of the poet, investing his product with meaning just as does his language. In the latter case the audience is likely to smile; in the former (depending upon one's politics), one may respond in anger or in contempt.

The confusion that results when form or style is not appropriate to content is unpredictable. Matthew Arnold thought that Chaucer lacked a necessary high seriousness. More to our subject, years ago two great public outbursts of ire and indignation occurred when one of our quasi-sacred songs, the "Star-Spangled Banner," was performed in the colloquial style of the jazz musician. The greatest uproar followed Jose Feliciano's jazz version at the opening of the 1968 baseball World Series in Detroit. Singing the national anthem as he would a Caribbean love ballad, Feliciano was decried for his irreverence, his impertinence, and for degrading the flag. Feliciano was shocked at the reaction his song elicited, but it was futile to protest that he loved this country deeply, and that he sang the "Star-Spangled Banner" that way because it was the way he knew best to show his love.

Feliciano's style was popular, hence profane; but the subject was nearly religious, and the middle class demanded an appropriate style for the subject. Kate Smith would have been ideal. The same reaction that engulfed Feliciano overwhelmed Aretha Franklin after her performance of the anthem at the opening of the 1968 Democratic National Convention. Billed by her press agents as "The Queen of Soul," Franklin—daughter of the Reverend C. L. Franklin—gave what she felt was an honest and heartfelt performance; unfortunately for her audience, she had chosen one of the few songs one must not sing as though it were from the Soul Music songbook. Artistic integrity was not as important as decorum.

The popular style is acceptable in spirituals, of course; but then the middle class does not take the spirituals very seriously, preferring Bach cantatas not only for aesthetic but allegedly for religious reasons as well. However, the popular style is appropriate for many black (and a few white) preachers when referring to or directly addressing their God. In the spirituals we have seen that the imagery is immediate, that abstractions are rare, and that God, Satan, and all the saints and devils appear as real people in this world.[15] And this is just the tone one finds in the sermons. The prevailing attitude of these preachers reveals itself in their diction; for that attitude and that diction the chanted sermon is again an ideal medium.

Functionally, the chanted oral sermon serves well the religious and aesthetic demands of the preacher and his congregation. In holy services where enthusiasm for the Lord is desirable and where an emotional outlet is sought, the chanted sermon performs admirably. Its increasing rhythms induce passionate responses; at the same time its repetitive language—which we have seen is an aid to the audience's grasp of what is being said—also acts to accumulate tension. The informality of such sermons allows active participation on the part of the congregation and in yet another way heightens the emotional impact of the service. One could hardly imagine such active audience responses in a speech by Richard Nixon or in a sermon by Lancelot Andrews. The quality of the service is thus charged for the congregation member, for the sermon allows him to respond ad libitum throughout, and he becomes an active participant in the communion rather than a passive receptacle of the preacher's rhetoric.

The chanted sermon uses the language of popular culture, and thus further relates to the congregation. The spirituals are a serious matter to Baptists and Methodists in the South, and the use of spiritual diction in the sermons is felicitous; it is language with which the congregation is intimately familiar, and more important, it is language that is heavily weighted. Since the preacher often breaks into song, since some songs are known to have come from sermons, and since others have preaching styles of delivery with sermonizing and singing interspersed,[16] the preacher (many, as we have already noted, were former singers) exploits the happy connections between sermon and spiritual.

The sermon is an art form; the chanted sermon is a more expressive art, borrowing from the aesthetics of music as well. The performance, as we have seen, provides an outlet for the congregation. It follows that at the sermon's climax there is a purgation of aggression (or of whatever emotions), and this has in fact been my observation. Interestingly, some preachers are aware of aesthetics, though never by that term. Rev. Otis McAllister, of Bakersfield, acknowledged the artistic element in his performance, but could not (or did not want to) articulate further. James Weldon Johnson thought that the old-time black preacher "was above all an orator, and in good measure an actor."[17] But like most of his colleagues, the Reverend Rubin Lacy did not think in aesthetic terms: when asked about his break at the moment of emotional climax and his resumption of normal prose, he merely said, "When you've said enough, you ought to sit down."

NOTES

1. This literature is surprisingly widespread. The Gospel House of Atlanta publishes several by John C. Jernigan: *My Text Books, Sermons in Nutshells, The Preacher's Gold Mine, Homiletic Treasure, Advice to Ministers*, and several more. Other volumes are available by other authors. For a different appeal a minister may refer to the sermons of Paul Tillich, *The Eternal Man* (New York, 1963), Harry Emerson Fosdick's *Riverside Sermons* (New York, 1958), Elton Trueblood's *The Yoke of Christ* (New York, 1958), and countless others.

2. Harold Courlander, *Negro Folk Music, U.S.A.* (New York, 1963), p. 42: songs about Moses, Joshua, and the visions of St. John were most appealing to slaves.

3. A-T Type 1613 has been traced to the eighteenth century, and very close analogues of Tyler's version have been found in England, for instance in the Frank Kidson Collection, Mitchell Library, Glasgow

(folio collection of Broadsides, vol. 1, p. 125). Ed Cray found an identical version in the United States around 1915: "The Soldier's Deck of Cards Again," *Midwest Folklore* 11 (1961), 225–34. Nevertheless most recordings give Tyler credit for authorship. A year after Lacy first credited "The Deck of Cards" to Tyler, he recalled that it was popular in Mississippi years before Tyler recorded it, having been preached by C. H. Jackson, Chris Gallion and "Rapfoot" Gayden.

4. Matt. 25. As with all sermons (and all preachers), Freeman claimed that his was original.

5. Fred N. Robinson, ed., *The Works of Geoffrey Chaucer* (Boston, 1957). All citations of Chaucer's work are from this edition.

6. Frederick J. Hoffman, *William Faulkner* (New York, 1966), p. 59.

7. Charles Keil, *Urban Blues* (Chicago, 1966), p. 16.

8. Gordon Hall Gerould, *The Ballad of Tradition* (New York, 1957), pp. 268–69. See also D. K. Wilgus and Eleanor R. Long, "The *Blues Ballad* and the Genesis of Style in Traditional Narrative Song," in *Narrative Folksong, New Directions: Essays in Appreciation of W. Edson Richmond*, ed. Carol L. Edwards and Kathleen E. B. Manley (Boulder, Colo., 1985), pp. 435–82.

9. William Warren Sweet, *Revivalism in America* (New York, 1944), p. 95.

10. Keil, *Urban Blues*, pp. 7–8.

11. For an early assertion of this see Bruce Jackson, *The Negro and His Folklore in Nineteenth-Century Periodicals* (Austin, Tex., 1967), p. 66.

12. Sweet, *Revivalism in America*, p. 137.

13. E. Franklin Frazier, *The Negro Church in America* (New York, 1964), pp. 8–9.

14. Ibid., p. 8.

15. Bruce Jackson, "The Glory Songs of the Lord," in *Our Living Traditions*, ed. Tristam P. Coffin (New York, 1968), pp. 115 ff.

16. Courlander, *Negro Folk Music*, p. 64.

17. James Weldon Johnson, *God's Trombones* (New York, 1948), p. 5.

4

The Charms of Music

What strangers to chanted sermons find most striking is that during most of the performance, and especially during the chanted portions, the congregation is actively involved in the service. They hum, sing aloud, yell, and join in the sermon as they choose, and almost always their participation is rhythmic. The quality of the congregation appears to have a great effect upon sermons, influencing the preachers' timing, their involvement in the delivery, and sometimes even the length of performances. Such have been my observations despite Lacy's claim that it did not matter whether his audience numbered three or three hundred. He said that he could preach alone in his own house with no audience, or to me alone; but he never tried, because only the church evoked the Spirit of the Lord. Some preachers who do a lot of radio work where there is no congregation present have become less dependent on audience response, but with those who do both face-to-face and electronic preaching there is a difference in styles. In Lacy's case, after one sermon to a particularly deadening congregation he complained to Brown that he had to "carry it" by himself. For instance, his pacing and timing were nearly perfect in the 1967 "Deck of Cards" sermon, and the audience's response was so vigorous that many of Lacy's words were obscured by spontaneous shouts and singing. But in a later sermon on "Revelation" his timing broke down, he stumbled over his words like a drunk over footstools, and emotionally never got out of bed. His occasional efforts to rouse up the spirit of the congregation—by shouting, by singing some of the lines, and by calling "Amen!"—fell flat, and he himself was punctured and drifting.

Lacy's chanting failed because his congregation was not with him—had no empathy with him—that time. But Lacy was correct in theory: as he explained it, chanting seems to "attract people's attention," though that is a great understatement. Clearly, chanting builds up the emotions of the congregation as can no other means, and it is at such moments of emotional intensity that the Spirit of God is most noticeable. The sermons begin in prose and (should) end in song, passing through and pausing at various stages of chanting.[1] To illustrate this difference of style within the same sermon, I quote the following lines from the beginnings and endings of two performances. The first selection is from a sermon delivered by Lacy on July 9, 1967:

> For the Lord's portion is His people
> Jacob is the lot of his inheritance
> He found them—watch this—in a desert land
> In the waste howling land
> 5 He led him about and He instructed him
> And kept him as an apple of His eye

I have set up Lacy's "sentences" in this transcription as though they were metrically consistent in order to compare them with the following chanted lines from the same sermon:

> Eagle has got an eye
> Look at the sun
> The beams of the sun
> All day long
> 5 Don't have to bat his eyes
> He don't turn his body around
> Jus' set there in one place
> Turn his neck around

The most obvious difference between these two passages is that the chanted lines are shorter, and usually have five or six syllables. But when one heard Lacy the difference was far more noticeable than the printed comparison indicates. The first passage was recited calmly, as though from a book: the cadence was casual, almost relaxed. But when the second passage was chanted or sung, the short lines, such as line 4, were drawn out; metrically, "all" and "long" were given a time value of two or three syllables. Musically, the words were rendered glissando so that the time interval was made consistent with lines 3 and 5. And those lines with more than six syllables, such as line 6, were compressed by garbling and by shortening the notes to bring them nearer the standard.

Perhaps because of his experience as a professional singer, Lacy's chanting was more metrical (and more rhythmical) than some. Here is the beginning of a sermon on "Revelation":

I want you to understand this, it don't be mornin' all over the world
    at the same time
It don't be mornin' in the world—all over the world—at the same
    time
Sometime it's evenin' here when it's mornin' there
But I believe He's comin' in the mornin'
⁵ I don't know what time He be here
But I believe He's comin in the mornin'
And I know He's on His way
I know He's on His way because I seen too many signs
The average person don't care nothin' about God

The following lines are from the same sermon after Lacy had begun to chant:

    And God told John—break a twig Amen!
    And hold up a twig
    As proof to you that I'm on the island
    And John broke a twig—God from Zion
   ⁵ And held the twig up on the island
    And the four winds began to shake a twig
    In old man John's hand
    The Spirit kep' on callin' to John
    God from Zion
  ¹⁰ And told old man John
    Umm-hmm

In the second passage Lacy was alternating between a nine- or ten-syllable line (such as lines 1, 3, 4, 5, 6, and 8) and the shorter half line (or its metrical approximation) as in lines 2, 7, 9, 10, and 11. Line 4 has been transcribed as a nine-syllable line, but might just as easily have been valued at two lines of five and four syllables.

Making a line-by-line transcription of the passages from the first part of any oral sermon is slightly harder than marking the limits of the chanted line. At first the "reading" is performed as though from a conventional manuscript with appropriate pauses at the end of each "sentence." Usually the sermons begin with a reading of Scripture and the preacher follows the Bible's punctuation. But these sermons are antiphonal in nature, and soon the audience's response—so active and cogently felt—actually delineates each line, each formula. Metrics govern. To punctuate the beat the congregation shouts "Amen!" "Oh yes," "Oh Lord," "That's all right," etc. Most of the time there is no doubt about the end of the phrase: the congregation clearly makes it known. Or else the preacher punctuates the lines with a gasp for breath that is usually so consistent it can be timed metrically.

These chanted passages are, as Lacy said, the times when God's Spirit has taken over completely. At such times the preacher is being "fed" by God directly, is almost overcome by a "spiritual feeling," and tries to convey the Spirit to the congregation. At such moments, the preachers say, the words come so fast that they have to pause to straighten them out in their minds. Hence, said Lacy and Brown, the frequent use of such phrases as "Am I right this evenin'," "God from Zion," and "I want you to know." But more of that later.

The better to describe this chant in musical terms for those readers who have never heard a sermon sung—and who will never hear the field tapes—Professor Clayton Wilson of the Music Department at the University of California, Santa Barbara, offered to notate the chants of Lacy and Brown musically. The phrases were selected for their musical quality and because they were also representative. The first two are from a sermon of Brown's.

Although these lines are used to illustrate their music, the first one is a stock phrase that Brown probably used a dozen times a sermon. If read, one would give it six syllables, but the way Brown chanted it the line has a value of seven and, depending upon how "know" is noted, possibly eight. The second line was eleven syllables when spoken, but when chanted—as noted by the triplets—the words are elided and compressed so that it has the value of about a seven count. Brown was happiest with a tetrameter line, but when a phrase was too short, as in the first example below, he lengthened it, and when the line was too long, he squeezed it musically to fit, or nearly fit, his meter.

Lacy's professional training had given him an advantage so far as concerned metrics. The following lines were taken from his sermon, "The Eagle Stirreth Up Its Nest":

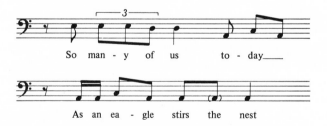

Lacy usually prefered a pentameter line or variations of it, especially two half lines of six and four, or single half lines of five syllables.

Wilson also noted that both men chanted in a pentatonic scale, as did most of the men recorded in this study, even when their chanting was barely distinguishable from the spoken part of the sermon. The scale is a common one in the Baptist hymnal—one would expect the preachers to be at home with it—and we found that the congregation also hummed or sang along in the same scale. On one occasion, before Brown chanted, "Oh I want you to know," one member of the congregation sang the same notes, anticipating his pastor by a second or two. This came to our attention because the singer's voice was interfering with Wilson's notation of Brown's music, and the same line had to be replayed quite often before it could be notated properly. But the same phenomenon happens often, so often that it strongly suggests that not only do the listeners know what ideas and phrases are to come next, they can also anticipate the preacher's music. In an antiphonal art such as this, music provides yet another means of mutual communication. Music may also provide a bridge between lines as an aid in composition: repeated phrases are often chanted to the same musical notes and may aid the preacher in the selection of the notes of the next line. Participation by the congregation in the performance brings additional rapport with the preacher on a level other than linguistic. The musical element of the sermon, then, not only aids the preacher with the metrics and arouses the emotions of the congregation, but helps them to anticipate the message. "Message" is carefully used, for in few other arts is the message so clearly the medium as in this kind of preaching.

Each preacher has a particular message, and that will vary from preacher to preacher even though the text for the day be the same. The music encourages verbal, semantic, and emotional variation. Lacy's short line and intense emotion (once he got going) gave his message a dramatic compulsion; Brown's longer line and even pacing gave his sermons a lyrical quality appropriate to his lamenting tone; and the Reverend Mr. McDowell was capable of both drama and lyric and could use both within a single sermon. Each preacher has a style, a melody, timing, and tonal quality that help determine the quality of the message. A few, like McDowell, can vary that tone within a sermon, but too many variations seem to be distracting to the preacher's concentration. The meter or rhythm of oral sermons begins in prose and works toward metrical verse. The flow is not always smooth, the metrics may be poor (and may vary during the sermon), and the preacher may alternate between prose and metrical sections. It is sometimes difficult to know exactly when the preacher is chanting (rather than talking) or singing (rather than chanting). It is, of course, a matter of degree. This is one of the reasons why visual scanning of transcribed sermons is often not helpful as a descriptive technique. The most superficial look at any of the sermons shows that more lines are hyper- and hypometric than are "standard." This happens for reasons other than the preachers' unconcern about whether they are talking, chanting, or singing at any given moment.[2]

Most preachers do not seem to have a particularly strong desire to maintain the same meter throughout their sermons, and one often hears syncopated lines that although not peculiar to blacks are characteristic of their music. This has been observed countless times in black ballads and it has apparently carried over to the religious literature. A syncopated beat, especially when used in a hyper- or hypometric line, will appear even more irregular when printed, though its time value may be the same as a regular line in performance. And further confounding any attempts to scan this literature as one would text poetry is the element of improvisation. Gerould has commented on this in ballad studies[3] and it, too, is characteristic of the oral preaching style.

When Lacy said that he thought chanting "caught the attention" of the congregation, I asked him about the appropriateness of the blues in church services.[4] His answer was simple. The blues he defined as "a worrying mind." Hence only a Christian could really sing the blues, he thought, because only the Christian was concerned about sin and its punishment. The sinner is carefree— he doesn't worry, and so could not sing the blues the right way. Therefore, Lacy thought, the blues are all right in church. In fact, he thought that often the blues are "more truthful" than conventional church hymns. He used as an example some lines from a song he used to sing:

You never miss your water till your well runs dry,
Never miss your good gal till she said goodbye.

For Lacy, who had known days in Mississippi when the wells did run dry, that song had truth. But some church songs "tell lies" such as "When I take my vacation in heaven." A vacation, said

Lacy, is something that you come back from, and you do not come back from heaven. (Obviously, however, many people have felt that heaven is analogous to a vacation: there is a record cut by the Reverend D. C. Rice about the "Vacation in Heaven" on Vocalion 1502.) At least as far as Lacy was concerned, then, the church has something to learn from the secular world of blues. I do not want to generalize from this one opinion, but I have found it typical. No one who has heard the soul music of Aretha Franklin, Dinah Washington, Sara Vaughn, Nancy Wilson, or Stevie Wonder can doubt the easy exchange between gospel singing and that type of rock; some soul music lyrics are even taken from the church: "I Want to Testify." To the laity more familiar with psychological than with ecclesiastical terms, there seems to be little difference, quantitatively, between the joyous hand clapping of rock enthusiasts and ardent congregationalists.

Preachers are considered skillful when they have mastered several aspects of their craft, including singing. Most of the better preachers have good voices that enable them to sing many of the lines. The effect is aesthetically pleasing as well as spiritually moving. Lacy was a blues singer; McDowell also sang professionally with small groups; and Brown sang in his church choir for many years. Others, like Freeman, were not accomplished singers but could do the next best thing, that is, chant on key. In Freeman's case it was good enough. C. L. Franklin hardly sang at all, but he had greater control over the tone, inflection, and timbre of his voice than most professional actors.

Timing is at least as important. Lacy knew intuitively when to sit down. He knew when he had reached that point in his sermon when to go on further would lose the high pitch to which he had brought the congregation. Skillful preachers develop their sermons with care and with the emotions of the audience in mind. This is a test of a preacher's aesthetic sense; timing—the development of ideas and sentiments—is part of the sermon's structure and it too must please in order to move.

Rhythm is perhaps the most important aspect of the preacher's musical art. Timing, in this immediate context, is concerned with the architecture of the entire sermon; rhythm is the property of the delivery of single lines. Rhythm is an ongoing skill: it must be sustained and properly paced throughout the sermon to be truly effective. A few—but only a very few—of the most skillful preachers can sustain the rhythm of their lines regardless of the reaction of the congregation and regardless of whether they have a live audience before them or not. Jessup preached more over radio than he did to a tent full of worshipers, and thus had to develop his timing and rhythm without the response of an audience. It should be pointed out, however, that Jessup did not sing his sermon, and his lines are not easily divided into formulas. But a man like McDowell had enough presence of mind to maintain his rhythm and to bring the congregation to his level rather than fall to theirs. In an art where the language is so intimately tied to rhythm—where the language itself is determined by the meter of the line—a faulty rhythm causes various problems. When a preacher's rhythm is off, nearly everything will fail; in the 1968 sermon on "The Twenty-third Psalm," Lacy reached out some distance to use a theme on the four horsemen of whose rhythm he was sure. When that portion revived so did the rest of his performance.

The verbal skills of preachers can be judged by their ability to compose formulas, and the craft with which they manipulate formulas and themes both for sense and for the emotional power they exert on listeners. The manipulation of formulas is at least a twofold process; many are fitted spontaneously into the metrical pattern prevailing in the sermon of the moment whether the language so manipulated is being read, is known by heart, or is being used for the first time. And many "memorized" formulas used behind the pulpit are no doubt conceived in the privacy and peace of the pastor's home. Regardless of how the formulas are created, at the moment of performance they must be fitted into the proper semantic and metrical mold. (The psycholinguistic process involved will be discussed later.) And the right lines must be used in the right places within the sermon, in relation both to other formulas and to themes. Formulas often occur in a set order within the themes, and the themes have to be employed in proper relation to each other and to the sermon as a whole. In all this manipulation and usage, flexibility rather than rigidity must govern; there is no one proper or effective way to preach any given sermon. Everything is in flux: the congregation and its moods, the rhythms, diction, syntax, and the emotions of the preacher, and the message for the day. A skillful preacher will take all, or nearly all, of these considerations into account, however unconsciously, and will mold the sermon accordingly. The end result should be the movement of the Spirit of God in the church.

When an audience is responsive the preacher catches its enthusiasm. The singing before a sermon begins is a sure indication of the congregation's emotional level. If the people are "high," the songs will be sung energetically and many of the verses will be repeated, with various improvisations by the piano player and lead soprano. (Brown's congregation was blessed with two fine gospel singers, his own wife and Mrs. Lucille Mukes.) When the congregation is "down," the preacher is likely to recite the sermon woodenly; only the most patient exploitation will bring them around. When they are "up" the preacher gestures, struts, acts out the narrative, and makes asides to various members of the congregation, the choir, or the visiting pastors.[5] A congregation must itself feel the urgency and truth of the sermon before it becomes involved in it. An "up" congregation punctuates the preacher's phrases, as already noted, with shouts, chants, and singing. At such moments they are filled with the "Spirit of God," as are Lacy and Brown and the others, yet it is the preacher's avowed purpose to tell the "truth of God," not merely to arouse the crowd. As William Butler Yeats once wrote about his own verse: "The purpose of rhythm, it has always seemed to me, is to prolong the moment of contemplation, the moment when we are both asleep and awake, which is the one moment of creation, by hushing us with an alluring monotony, while it holds us waking by variety, to keep us in that state of perhaps real trance, in which the mind liberated from the pressure of the will is unfolded in symbols."[6]

Rubin Lacy said on the one hand that the idea is the most important part of the sermon, yet his diction was such, and the congregation's response was often such, that much of what he was saying was unintelligible. What was intelligible was his driving rhythm, his musical chanting, and the great passion he exuded through emphasis, expression, and gesture. As he said, "The people should be glad twice; glad when you get up and glad when you sit down." On the matter of making the audience glad when he sat down, Lacy intentionally made his sermons short, about twenty minutes or less. He wanted to get the people "home on time." And his build-up to an emotional climax was excellent—when his audience had empathy with him. He built gradually and steadily from prose to chanting and then to singing, gradually getting louder and more dramatic, and then so as "not to go too far," he broke off sharply. He caught himself, he said, so that he and the congregation could "come down" to "talking normal." Lacy could feel when he had gone too far and should stop, and his consciousness of it suggested more than a passing interest in his congregation's emotions and in the aesthetics of his own performance.

When Brown or Freeman or the Reverend Bennie C. Blair began singing or chanting movingly, Lacy himself, from his position behind the pulpit with his fellow clergymen, responded much as did the rest of the audience. On one such occasion Lacy kept calling out to Brown, "That's preaching," and "You say it, preacher." Such moments are not common; they occur only when the tempo has increased, audience response is high, and the preacher is chanting, but they indicate that many preachers themselves understand the role of emotion in divine worship, by whatever terms they may happen to use to describe it.[7]

Emotion in church is a controversial matter. To the visitor who went to Brown's church for the first time, the most important aspect of the service may have seemed to be the congregation's emotional expressiveness. The pastor and any visiting ministers at the same service would have considered such emotion a manifestation of the Spirit of God. To them the difference would not be semantic; it is one thing to be emotional, quite another to be filled with the Spirit. Yet at least one clergyman who liked to stimulate his audience to a frenzy was not ashamed of it. A. A. Allen attacked some Pentecostal churches for playing down the roles of passion and glossolalia.[8] Referring to the Reverend Harry Faught's attempts to reduce the level of emotional reactions during services, Allen asserted that "the fact that there is no emotion in his [Faught's] church is a sure sign there is no revival!" Allen was long disdainful of what he termed "dead, formal church organizations" that were "trying to get a little action back into their dead churches" through means Allen didn't approve of.[9] We should not enter this controversy here, however; the point is that overt passionate expression is not shameful in certain circles, and has not been in the past. We have already cited George Whitefield, who could wring tears from his listeners by enunciating "Mesopotamia"; the records of religious services, both black and white, following the Second Great Awakening are extensive and eloquent. Foreign visitors were especially intrigued by this unusual form of worship.

Contemporary white middle-class churches do not indulge themselves in emotion and seem embarrassed by the passion displayed in other more Fundamentalist churches. The Reverend Mr. Robert Howland, Presbyterian, who shares this view, felt certain that his congregation would at first look on such a man as the Reverend Mr. Brown as a talented performer, but would soon tire of him. American middle-class society, for the most part, is ashamed of public emotion: we do not weep in public, and we do not shout in church. Howland's opinion is no doubt true, yet passionate sermons and weeping, howling congregations are well established in Western traditions. Again, we can return to the Middle Ages and the preaching of the Dominicans and Franciscans: contemporaries describe the weeping, work coming to a standstill, and a steady flow of malefactors throwing themselves at the preacher's feet.[10]

I do not suggest that the preachers of the Missionary Baptist church are counterparts of the medieval friars or that there is necessarily any similarity between their preaching styles, but that there are parallels and precedents that should not be ignored.

NOTES

1. James Weldon Johnson, *God's Trombones* (New York, 1948), p. 5.

2. Mainly, I think that the art of oral preachers who chant their sermons is not as precise as that of other allegedly oral poets: Homer and the author of *Beowulf*. When a poem such as the Anglo-Saxon epic

gets written down, whether by a scribe or by the poet, care can be taken to regularize the lines. This assumes that the performance is less regular than the text that has survived (in the case of *Beowulf*, Cotton Vitellius A XV). Lord found that the *guslars* were fairly regular metrically even during performance, but in such poetry there is apparently a tradition to be so. And, the *guslar* maintains pretty much the same meter from the beginning. However that may be true of Lord's experience, when I visited Yugoslavia during the summer of 1969 I found the performances of the *guslars* even less songlike than those of most of the preachers I had recorded; also more hypometric and hypermetric lines occurred than in the chanted portions of many sermons.

3. Gordon Hall Gerould, *The Ballad of Tradition* (New York, 1957), p. 269: "Better than any other singers, who have been carefully observed, they [blacks] show the power of instantaneous response to a stimulus of any kind and a very general habit of composition under stress of excitement."

4. The matter needs closer study. Harold Courlander mentions some spirituals that may have originally been sermons: *Negro Folk Music, U.S.A.* (New York, 1963), pp. 52–56; he also describes some songs as having a "preaching style of delivery, with sermonizing and singing interspersed" (p. 64).

5. Johnson, *God's Trombones*, p. 6, mentions similar histrionics of preachers; Alan Lomax, *The Rainbow Sign* (New York, 1959), p. 190, calls the preacher "a trained actor."

6. W. B. Yeats, *Ideas of Good and Evil* (London, 1903), pp. 247–48.

7. A former colleague at the Santa Barbara campus of the University of California spent a good part of his youth in Texas at Baptist revivals and Sunday services; he recently admitted to me that the selection of hymns was crucial to the amount of the offering on any given day. His father was a Baptist minister. The service would begin with a slow song, followed by a fast-paced number. It would slow down again during the third; then subsequent songs would rapidly escalate in tempo and consequently in emotion, which would hit a peak just before the offering. This informant, who has asked that he not be named, claims that stimulating a congregation is a commonly practiced art, though not usually for personal profit.

8. The scriptural authority for glossolalia is in Acts, 2:2–4: "And suddenly there came a sound from heaven as of a rushing mighty wind, and it filled all the house where they were sitting. And there appeared unto them cloven tongues like as of fire, and it sat upon each of them.

And they were all filled with the Holy Ghost, and began to speak with other tongues, as the Spirit gave them utterance" (King James version).

9. *Miracle Magazine* 12 (July 1967), 3, 22.

10. Johan Huizinga, *The Waning of the Middle Ages*, trans. F. Hopman (New York, 1956), pp. 12–13.

5

The Sermon's Formulas

When we try to learn in some detail how the preachers compose their sermons, we get little help from them in language that is meaningful to the secularly oriented laity. Whatever is to be learned must be from observation and by translating the preachers' remarks into secular terms. I have described the delivery of sermons without any manuscript and usually without notes of any kind except, perhaps, a Bible. However, most preachers do prefer to have some time to think about their sermons, though sometimes sermons are given (and hence composed) extemporaneously without any immediate preparation. Occasionally preachers are asked to say a prayer or a few words of one sort or another without prior warning, and in effect a short sermon is delivered. Once a guest preacher delivered a sermon on a topic selected without the knowledge of the host pastor; but the subject pleased the pastor so much that as soon as the guest had finished, the host began preaching yet another sermon on the same topic, the Twenty-third Psalm. The second sermon was obviously composed spontaneously; yet because it contained, naturally, language that the minister had been assimilating and arranging for many years (with his first words he said that he liked preaching the Twenty-third Psalm because it was the topic of the first sermon he ever gave), the man was able to preach spontaneously for about fifteen minutes in the metrical style that characterizes the genre.

As with Yugoslav epic singers whom Parry and Lord investigated during the thirties and fifties, these compositions are put together with formulaic systems,[1] which are handled quite flexibly throughout the sermon, and of nearly memorized themes,[2] which if anything, are even more flexible than the themes of narrative epic poetry. It does not matter that the Parry-Lord singers composed narrative epics while the American preachers compose sermons: the modes of creation are similar and comparisons may still be made. The sermons are hortatory, certainly, but even a superficial glance at the sermons collected in this volume will show that they are also largely narrative. Narrative and dramatic exempla are used throughout, as are narrative stories from the Bible. Yet what is most important is that the language of the preachers is heavily formulaic in the sense that Parry meant,[3] and that their sermons are composed by using language that is largely formulaic.

For the spiritual preacher the moment of composition is the performance. Two sermons on the same subject or from the same text are never identical, though the structural skeleton may be the same. What is memorized is the sermon's outline and perhaps several themes, but the language that fleshes out the skeleton fluctuates substantially, even if two sermons are delivered by the same man on the same subject. The preacher of sermons is the composer of sermons.

We know how preachers learn: from their own pastors as children, from hearing others in neighborhood churches, from radio and television, and from reading religious matter. In the beginning they will sit passively and absorb the phrases of their informal masters, and just as important, they will develop the senses of rhythm that will determine their own styles later on. Eventually they may "preach to the trees and the birds" as Lacy did, recite the benediction in church while deacons, give an occasional sermon as assistant pastors, and then command pulpits of their own.

All along, the basic problem is to fit the ideas of the sermon to the basic rhythmic pattern. As James Weldon Johnson observed long ago, the black preacher knows that the secret of oratory is a progression of rhythmic words.[4] The rhythm is the message; congregations have been moved to ecstasy by the rhythmic chanting of incoherencies. During many sermons it is physically impossible to hear what the preacher is saying—so loud

is the singing, shouting, chanting, and humming of the audience—
even if what is said is of some great import. Yet the congregation
feels that it is receiving the truth of God. Often the tapes, recorded with the microphone on the pulpit, are for many seconds
blurred and indistinct. Evoking the Spirit of God is the aim of
these sermons, and rhythm best rouses that spirit.

The kind of meter spiritual preachers use is quantitative: the
"line" depends upon the length of time required to pronounce
the syllables, and is not usually determined by stress or accent.
The rhythm—not only within but between lines—proceeds with
the regularity and inexorability of a metronome. If the words or
syllables within a given line are too few, they are drawn out to
the required time value by singing, *recitativo*; if they are too
many, they are compressed so as to fit into the allotted space.[5]
Not all preachers are consistent and not all have a fine ear for
timing. Rhythms vary, not only from preacher to preacher, but
from sermon to sermon and even within a single sermon. It may
be occasionally necessary to fit the rhythm to the subject. And
in an effective sermon it is always necessary to gradually increase
the rhythm so as to inspire the congregation, and to build toward
an emotional and spiritual peak through rhythm, whether that
peak be at the end of the sermon or near its middle.[6]

To fit a group of words expressing a given idea to metrical
conditions, a special mode of communication had to be developed, identical to the mode that Lord called formulaic. The formula must be identified, in this stage at least, as repetition, despite the inadequacy of the idea. For instance, in one of the
sermons collected below (D. J. McDowell's "The Christ of the
Bible") one finds a striking repetition of certain phrases:

The Christ of the Bible	24 times
Am I right about it?	15 times
I know that's right	11 times
Amen [used as metrical line]	11 times
Keep your hand in God's hand	5 times

One would expect to find the phrase "The Christ of the Bible"
in a sermon with that title and one whose subject matter is an
attempted adumbration of the Christ of the Bible. But twenty-
four times is far more than accidental, and a bit more than rhetorical. Furthermore, McDowell used the same phrase (though

not as frequently) in other sermons, just as many of the phrases—
and entire sections or themes—are used elsewhere and in different contexts.

As a demonstration of the extent of composition by formula of
a spiritual sermon I cite a passage from the same source. Most
of McDowell's work was heavily formulaic, and to that extent
the use of his material does load the argument; however, many
more heavily formulaic passages, by McDowell or others, might
have been used. The most obvious examples have not been selected: the following passage is fairly typical of McDowell, and
illustrative of oral preachers generally. The convention of des-
ignating verbatim formulas (solid underlining) and formulas from
systems found in other performances (broken underlining) used
by Parry, Lord, and other scholars, has been followed here for
the sake of clarity.

> Keep your hand in God's hand
> And your eyes, on the starposts in glory
> Lord said He would fight your battles
> If you'd only be still
> 5 You may not be a florist
> Am I right about it?
> But you must tell them, that He's the Rose of Sharon
> I know that's right
> You may not be a geologist
> 10 But you must tell them, that He's the Rock of Ages
> I know that's right
> You may not be a physician
> But you must tell them, that He's the great physician
> You may not be a baker
> 15 But you must tell them, that He's the bread of life
> Am I right about it?
> You must tell them
> That He's a friend
> That stick close t' his brother
> 20 He said, I'll not cast y' out
> In the sixth hour, and in the seventh hour
> I didn't know I was turnin' you out
> If y' keep your hand in God's hand

Of the twenty-three lines, nine (including 2 and 23) are repetitions of others within the same sermon. Eight lines are nearly identical: the syntax is consistent, with the verb in the same relative position, though the nouns are varied (florist, geologist, physician, baker). Four lines are syntactically analogous to phrases found outside this sermon, either communally or personally. At least twenty-one of the lines, then, are in effect repetitions—or 91 percent. The remaining lines (19 and 22) may also have been repeated elsewhere in sermons not recorded or heard.

These figures are illustrative and not representative; a sampling of several other preachers showed that the percentage of those lines that we would underline on a formulaic chart, with a solid line or a broken one, is somewhat lower. All the samples were taken from the chanted portions of the sermons, when the prose of the introductions had given way to metrics. When one hundred lines of his sermon were sampled, McDowell was found to use repeated lines 19 percent of the time and systemic formulas 67 percent: total, 86 percent; the Reverend Rubin Lacy of Bakersfield had 32 percent repeated formulas, 41 percent systemic: total, 73 percent; Brown used repeated formulas 13 percent of the time, systemic formulas 55 percent: total, 68 percent; and J. J. Freeman of Pixley had a relatively low 20 percent and 38 percent: total, 58 percent. For comparison, I also sampled a professionally recorded sermon by Detroit's C. L. Franklin: 17.5 percent were repeats, 62.5 percent were systemic. The total was, I think, an atypically high 80 percent.

The following passage is from a sermon by Lacy, "Dry Bones":

> Ezekiel come on the scene
> That great prophet of God
> Told him Ezekiel
> Go out yonder
> 5 Go an' pastor that land
> Save everybody
> Way they die out there
> By the millions
> Out yonder in the valley
> 10 Prophesy
> To the dry bones

The Word
The valley is white
Bleached with dry bones
15 Go out yon
And prophesy to 'em
Tell 'em
To wake up
And hear the Word of God
20 Ain't God all right?
God from Zion
Ezekiel went out there
Begin to prophesy
Dry bones
25 Ezekiel said
I heard
A mighty rattlin'
The rattlin' of bones
Shakin' through the valley
30 Hark Hallelujah

Allowing for only the strictest interpretation of "repetition," there is still a high concentration of repeated material. Six of the thirty utterances are repeated within the same sermon; one other was used in other sermons; and twelve lines are close approximations of utterances used here or elsewhere by Lacy. Close approximations are those lines in which only one word has been changed (in lines of two or more words), though two words may have been substituted for the deleted (or changed) word. For instance, this sermon has the lines, "Said prophesy" and "Prophesied again," close approximations to lines 10 ("Prophesy"), 16 ("And prophesy to 'em), and 23 ("Begin to prophesy"). Seven of the thirty lines are repetitions, or 23 percent; nineteen of the lines are either exact replications or close approximations—63 percent.[7]

Again, as with McDowell, passages could have been chosen from Lacy's sermons that would come quite close to being 100 percent repetitious. If an exhaustive study of Lacy's style were ever to be made, the percentage would rise beyond the 63 percent in the above passage. But we are probably never going to find a sermon in which all the lines are traditional or memorized, if for no other reason than that the sermons begin in prose and the prose of the preachers is too varied and too flexible to be formulaic.

After several texts are examined closely we should return to Parry's original definition of the formula, for only then can we see that its utility is as a broad guideline; it will not stand close application to lines actually uttered during performance. Objections are many; for instance, if mere repetition characterizes the formula, then any utterance I might make today that repeats one uttered several years ago, however coincidentally, would be a formula. Such utterances would be formulaic, but are not helpful in understanding oral composition. Donald K. Fry has shown that the definition of formula depends entirely upon how broadly one wishes to interpret "a group of words which is regularly employed under the same metrical conditions to express a given essential idea,"[8] Parry's original conception.[9] Since Parry's initial pronouncement, the idea of the group of words that is "regularly employed" has been expanded to mean "approximately repeated." And the original qualification "under the same metrical conditions" has been loosened in practice to become "under no metrical conditions."[10] As far as our immediate problems are concerned, in the American sermon, should we distinguish (formulaically) between McDowell's "Pray with me church" and "Are you prayin' with me now?"; or between "Help me Lord Jesus tell your story" and "Help me tell God's story"?

As Fry has argued, the basis for understanding the composition of oral poetry (or oral narrative) is not the formula but the formulaic system, the verbal mold into which a variety of words are poured, but which remains relatively consistent through similarities of diction, syntax, accent, or alliteration. Lord defined the system as "patterns that make adjustment of phrase and creation of phrases by analogy possible." The Anglo-Saxon poet and the American spiritual preacher create formulas by analogies with others: the system generates nearly all formulas.

Fry was working with Anglo-Saxon poetry, and his definition of the formulaic system is applicable only to that language and that poetry: the Old English system is "a group of half-lines, usually loosely related metrically and semantically, which are related in form by the identical relative placement of two elements, one a variable word or element of a compound usually supplying the alliteration, and the other a constant word or element of a compound, with approximately the same distribution of non-stressed elements."[12] Each poetry that employs oral formulas must have its different kind of formulas and systems to meet the specific demands of the poetry. While Fry accurately describes Old English verse, it will not do for us: spiritual sermons seldom alliterate; they almost never employ rhyme; but they are metrical. We might then modify his definition by saying that sermon systems are "lexico-semantic sets, related in form by the repetition and identical relative placement of at least half the words in the group." Thus, "You may not be a geologist, but you must tell them, that He's the Rock of Ages," is of the same formulaic system as, "You may not be a florist, but you must tell them, that He's the Rose of Sharon." These groups of words, when recited, are metrically consistent, though when they are written and scanned they are not. But, "Help me, Lord Jesus, tell your story," is not of the same formulaic system as, "Help me tell God's story," though they are close enough for us to guess that one came from the other.

All of these scholarly concerns with the applicability and true and universal meaning of Parry's definition have become a kind of academic game. The definition is a powerful one in describing his idea, though it is moot whether he intended it to be a standard against which all the narrative utterances of the world were to be judged, and upon which scholarly opinions would stand or fall. It is better to understand Parry's idea as a perception of the repetitiveness of orally generated language, and a suggestion about its genesis. Since we know that when speakers make an utterance they are aware both of what they have just uttered as well as (however sketchily) the utterances to come, repetitions are likely to occur in ordinary speech. One has to train oneself, or be trained, not to be repetitive; witness the experience of newcomers in the formal act of dictating prose, particularly for eventual rendering by a typist. Whether, therefore, two closely related groups of words are formulas by the strictest application of the Parry definition is secondary to the way in which the work of Parry and many psycholinguists has enabled us to understand the relationship of such word groups—originally in the mind of the speaker/singer/preacher. Formula or not, "Help me, Lord Jesus, tell your story," and "Help me tell God's story" were related in the preacher's mind when he preached both of them. And knowing that present and future utterances were in his mind simultaneously, we understand how one was psychologically related to the other, how one would quite unaffectedly be spoken after the other had been just shortly before uttered.

Every preacher I interviewed rejected the idea of the formulaic theory of composition, no matter how the idea was put to him. In an interview with Lacy I asked him if he ever repeated himself; he said that he definitely did not: once he said something, "it's gone." He didn't have time to repeat what he had said, and if the congregation didn't get it the first time it would never come again. When the preacher is giving a sermon the words come directly from God. Sometimes, Lacy said, he received words so fast that he would hum, but that was only to catch his breath. As the Reverend Rufus Hays of Virginia explained it to me, at such moments the preacher is merely the instrument for the Holy Ghost, who is really doing the speaking: the preacher is only lending Him a mouth and tongue and lips.

One time with Lacy when I played back a tape of his own recent performance and pointed out that he used phrases like "Hark Halleluja" and "God from Zion" several times each, he admitted that perhaps he did repeat himself, but that was because God was feeding him so fast at such moments that he needed time to correctly sort out his thoughts. He even had special terms for such repeated phrases: "bywords" or "habitual words." But when I played a taped sermon by his friend the Reverend Mr. Brown and pointed out the repetitive language, Lacy said: "Oh, he's just stalling for time." According to Lacy, Brown couldn't think of what to say next and so needed the stall to work out the next line. Lacy knew that other preachers repeated themselves, but he thought that he seldom did himself. When I questioned Brown on the matter he had a different response. Such language was a rest "on the highway, where you could pull off and regain your strength to drive on." The fact that he described the phenomenon metaphorically suggests that he had long been thinking about it. He used certain formulas, in other words, to give him time to compose the next line; and all of his colleagues did the same. The formula was strictly for his own benefit, and even though he looked straight at the congregation at such moments he was actually "seeing" ahead "on the pages of the book" to what was to come next: he saw nothing of the faces before him, only the next line.

I have been able to identify five different kinds of memorized formulas, which have been classified according to their function within a particular sermon. The most popular, the most widely used, and the most stable are those that in some way resemble a ballad refrain, yet do not function in exactly the same way: refrain formulas do not advance the narrative or develop an idea, and they do not appear as regularly as ballad refrains. (To illustrate their positioning within a sermon the reader should read the works themselves, as it is impractical to reprint an entire sermon or even a large portion of one here for this purpose alone.) Lacy's refrains, to repeat, included "Hark Halleluja" and "God from Zion." Brown preferred "Am I right this evening" (or "morning") and "I want you to know." McDowell liked "I know that's right." Other common refrain formulas are listed here:

> Do you know what I'm talkin' about (Brown and C. L. Franklin)
> God from Glory (B. J. Blair)
> I want to tell you (J. Charles Jessup)
> Don't you know this evenin' (Brown)
> I say unto you tonight (Neil Glasse)
> I'm gonna tell you (Jessup)
> I'm tryin' to tell you (Lacy)
> I want you to know this evening (Brown)

Although I have attributed the above formulas to the men from whom I first heard them, none are unique to one preacher: the same phrases have been found in Virginia and North Carolina and I would be surprised not to find them throughout the South. Given the limited subject matrix from which they come and the common dependence on spirituals and Scripture, independent creation is the likely explanation.

The preacher prefers certain of these phrases for whatever semantic, psychological, and metrical reasons, and then uses them verbatim repeatedly. Lacy, for instance, had only two or three; Brown had four or five; McDowell and Franklin had several; all of these men frequently used their refrain formulas without variation. Since they come to mind intuitively, they are ideal for giving the preacher more time to think of what comes next. Some preachers use stalls not only to gain time but to establish their rhythm; since their recital can be as much of a reflex as tapping the feet, stalls are well suited for this purpose. Other kinds of formulas are less stable because they are less frequently used (and thus do not get memorized as effectively), and because the metrical and semantic contexts in which they are used vary, and cause the formula itself to vary accordingly. "I tell you" for instance, may be drawn out to "I want to tell you" or even "I want you to know this evening" according to the demands of the moment. In the very strictest sense we may have two or three different formulas involved, one growing out of the other. However, an academic analysis of formulas is not the most important element in understanding how the preacher composes; what should interest us is the psychological and linguistic process involved in phrase creation and in the relationship between similar phrases.

A second kind of formula is a stimulant to the congregation. Often the stimulant cannot be distinguished from the refrain because both are frequently used unreflectively. For example, the Reverend Mr. Franklin's question above, "Do you know what I'm talkin' about?," occurred several times during a sermon, and the reaction it elicited from the congregation was neutral enough to suggest that it was not meant to get a response. Another of his formulas, the quite similar "I don't believe you know what I'm talkin' about" did seem to get some response, however. Lacy's "Ain't God all right?" was so exclamatory that no one responded to it as a question. But J. J. Freeman, for instance, timed his hortatory formulas so as to evoke a response, and he used them only when the congregation was in fact listless: "Gettin' quiet (in here) (again) isn't it?" The audience laughed and the intensity immediately picked up. When it let down again momentarily a little later, Freeman again chided them and again they picked up. To this very brief list of hortatory formulas one might add Franklin's "Listen if you please," which was probably the most effective of such exhortations.

Three other kinds of formulas are involved in storytelling within a sermon. One introduces dialogue, another introduces narrative, and the last advances the narrative once it has begun. These formulas characterize sermon dialogue:

> The Bible said to me
> I heard Jesus say the other day
> Saint Peter said the other day

They are very popular: any name can be substituted for "Saint Peter," giving the pattern flexibility within the structural framework. A slight variation of this—"I heard John say the other morning [night]"—is also widely used and gives the immediacy of a face-to-face confrontation with sainted names that is dramatic, authoritative, and emotionally compelling: "[personal pronoun] said [message]." And, from the same mold: "David said to Saul, 'Let me go.' "

Beginning a narrative is a counterpart to "Once upon a time." The preacher is likely to say, however, "Every now and then" or "I want to call your attention to the fact that. . . ." The sermons also have characteristic phrases for advancing the narrative:

> After a while
> I want you to know what he said
> By and by

The syntax as well as the incidence of enjambment present no surprises to anyone familiar either with English or with the oral style. The former is almost always straightforward subject-verb-object English with few inversions or convolutions. Most inverted sentences result when the preacher stumbles over words or can't think of what to say next. This is to be expected with pulpit messages, economically expressed in simple language, a lexicon, as it happens, of the everyday speech of the pastors and one by which they hope to communicate with their congregations. Too many distractions get in the way of verbal communication as it is: singing, shouting, emotion, and the preachers' diction. If the syntax were not simple, much less would be communicated.

Enjambment occurs frequently, as in other oral styles. Long sentences are broken up to fit the meter of the sermon, so enjambment is inevitable. Even when the sentences are short the preacher is likely to break them into even shorter units, as in this passage from Lacy, composed mainly of brief utterances:

> And God
> Made the Father
> Son and the Holy Ghost
> Ain't God all right?
> 5 And Mister Hoyle
> Made a three-spot
> And called it a trey
> God from Zion
> In Matthew Mark
> 10 An' Luke and John
> Mister Hoyle
> Made a four-spot

One—but only one—of the reasons enjambment occurs is the frequent use of nouns, noun compounds, and substantives in apposition.[13] The above passage has no such examples; the closest is the lines "Made a three-spot/ And called it a trey." Whatever its effect on the audience, the use of appositives gives the preacher more time to think about what is coming after. In the above example, once Lacy had mentioned the "three-spot" he associated it with "trey," which comes next. The narrative had not been advanced any by the second line, and since it came unreflectively to the speaker he did not have to labor over it, and so could use his time and mental energy to anticipate the next lines.

Periodic sentences almost never occur; this confirms Parry's findings with the Yugoslav *guslars*.[14] Clarity is important, and the easily processed sentence is much easier to formulate. Preachers do not have time to alter their syntax under the pressure of sermon delivery and they do not know how to utilize the poetic effects of such inversions. Occasionally such a sentence does occur: "An' if we don't forgive nobody, we are hell-bound now." This sentence, like nearly all of the periodic sentences encountered, came during the early parts of the sermon before the preacher had begun to chant. Those opening moments, to repeat, are prosaic; metrics, and consequently the length and number of syllables in a line, are ignored. The preacher is often talking casually to the congregation, as in fact Lacy was when he uttered the above sentence. There is no rush to think of the next line and if periodic sentences are spoken, they are most likely to be spoken then. The syntax of the sermons of American spiritual preachers reinforces what we know generally to be characteristic of the oral style.

For many of Parry's disciples the phrase "regularly employed" came to mean "repeatedly employed." For Lord, Magoun, Duggan, and others, formulas became an indisputable mark of oral composition.[15] And we all now concede that the most marked trait of oral narrative is repetition—of some sort. Yet there is no universality of opinion about those aspects of the formula that must be repeated in order to qualify; metrical, syntactical, semantic elements have all been considered, but these phenomena vary among oral narrative traditions. Even the length of the putative formula has been challenged: linguist H. L. Rogers questioned the failure of literary scholars to define with satisfactory precision any of the components of Parry's formula.[16] Joseph Russo argued that a fuller and more rigorously analyzed sample of Homeric verse might not support the claims for a higher formula count in the epics, and that the presence of formulas might prove to be little greater than that assumed for literary texts.[17] Further research has not borne out Russo's suspicions; and despite all the modifications and reservations expressed about the oral formulaic theory, Milman Parry did make us aware of that characteristic of oral narrative, the repetitive formula, however and in whatever way repetitive. Repetition may not be the "touchstone" of oral poetry,[18] but it does occur with such regularity that Ong can meaningfully speak of "the oral drive to use formulas."[19]

Formulas, of whatever sort, are memory aids almost entirely. Too much has been made of the aural audience's liking for familiar language (and language patterns) because of its comforting qualities; it is more likely that aural participants in oral narrative performances like formulas and familiarity with the plot because they enable them to participate more than passively. They are not active performers, but neither are they as merely receptive as modern hushed audiences at a poetry reading.

NOTES

1. As defined by Albert B. Lord, *The Singer of Tales* (New York, 1965), p. 30: "A group of words regularly employed under the same metrical conditions to express a given essential idea."

2. Ibid., p. 68: "Groups of ideas regularly used in telling a tale in the formulaic style of traditional song."

3. This is now a matter of some controversy, but the original conception of "formula" depended upon repetition; in the matter of verbatim repetition of phrases the sermons are even more formulaic than any epic Parry or Lord recorded.

4. James Weldon Johnson, *God's Trombones* (New York, 1948), p. 5.

5. Also observed by Johnson, *God's Trombones*, p. 11.

6. Lacy, like most preachers, built toward an emotional climax timed to arrive near the end, and a denouement closed it out. However, J. Charles Jessup's climax was usually near the middle of the sermon—a structure popular in ancient Greece—and he descended gradually from that peak.

7. This compares favorably with the ratio of formulas found in *Beowulf* by Magoun: 74 percent of the first fifty lines occur elsewhere in the corpus of Old English verse and "at least fifteen percent of the verses of the poem are to all intents and purposes repeated within the poem." See Francis P. Magoun, Jr., "Oral Formulaic Character of Anglo-Saxon Narrative Poetry," *Speculum* 28 (July 1953), 449–50, 454.

8. Donald K. Fry, "Old English Formulas and Systems," *English Studies* 48 (June 1967), 193–204.

9. Milman Parry, "Studies in the Epic Technique of Oral Verse-Making. I: Homer and Homeric Style," *Harvard Studies in Classical Philology* 41 (1930).

10. H. L. Rogers, "The Crypto-Psychological Character of the Oral Formula," *English Studies* 47 (1966), 89–102.

11. Lord, *Singer of Tales*, p. 37.

12. Donald K. Fry, "Old English Formulas," p. 203.

13. Old English heroic poetry also uses this technique.

14. Milman Parry, "The Distinctive Character of Enjambement in Homeric Verse," *Transactions of the American Philological Association* 60 (1929), 200–220.

15. Ruth Finnegan, *Oral Poetry* (Cambridge, 1977), p. 69.

16. Rogers, "Crypto-Psychological Character of the Oral Formula," pp. 89–102.

17. Joseph A. Russo, "Is 'Oral' or 'Aural' Composition the Cause of Homer's Formulaic Style?" In *Oral Literature and the Formula*, ed. Benjamin A. Stolz and Richard S. Sherman (Ann Arbor, 1976).

18. Finnegan, *Oral Poetry*, p. 130.

19. Walter J. Ong, *Orality and Literacy* (New York, 1982).

6

Sacred Themes

Descriptive formulas appear in clusters. In a hortatory art such a cluster is likely to have great functional flexibility; so it does here. For instance, Brown was likely to say "so many times" in various nonnarrative contexts, or "I'm wondering," a phrase he shared with McDowell. An extended demonstration will better illustrate this point. In the following passages, taken from various sermons of the Reverend Mr. Brown, the repetition, especially of "same man," always seems to be used in a characteristic way within its context, and always with a similar galaxy of ideas and formulas around it. The first was recorded in June of 1967:

> He left the church with us in the hands of a man
> He left the gospel in the hands of a man
> Am I right?
> This same Jesus
> 5 This same one that stopped over at Bethlehem
> The same one that had concourse with the lawyers and doctors
> The same man
> That had—gave—told 'em to fill up a pitcher with water
> Same man gave sight to the blind
> 10 Same man
> Said I'll need somebody
> To treat the world after I go home

Half lines indicate only a half pause during which there was no response from the audience. The passage has to do with Jesus' miracles, and the descriptive "This same man [Jesus/one]" comes up again and again in this particular context, almost always related—in Brown's sermons—to the miracles. Lacy also used it, but simply as a refrain. The following passage of Brown's was recorded a month later, in July:

> Go now lawyers and talk to this man Jesus
> We heard! We heard a man now heal the sick
> We heard He give sight to the blind
> Open up the dumb ears
> 5 He start the crippled to walkin'
> Same man!
>
> . . . . .
>
> Same man!
> Same man!
> Is comin' back one of these days
> 10 Same man this evenin'!

At another date in July, Brown recited the following:

> Talkin' with the lawyers and doctors
> Same man!
> Same word!
> He stopped over at the well of Samaria
> 5 Set down there at the well at Samaria
> I want you to fill these water pots up . . .

And on August 6, 1967, Brown preached the following in a sermon on "Paradise:"

> Same man
> Same man
> That got up off of the world Sunday mornin'
> That said all powers
> 5 Inhabitin' the earth
> Is in my hand
> I want to tell you, ladies
> Tell my brethren
>
> . . . .
>
> Stayed here thirty-three long years
> 10 Same man got on the cross and got hung
> Same man

Same man that . . .

A year after the above examples were recorded Brown was still reciting the same sequence of lines. The following passage was performed in Corcoran, California (May 24, 1968), as part of a sermon entitled "He Is the Preparation":

> This same Jesus
> That was carried off in the wilderness
> Same man
> Is comin' back again
> 5 Same Jesus
> That walked the mile brethren
> He walked the sandy deserts
> That many men believe in Him
> He healed the sick
> 10 And raised the dead
> Gave sight to the blind
> Ohh one day
> He went on home

Obviously, Brown associated the formula "same man" with particular events in the life of Jesus, and this particular descriptive passage associatively called this formula, and its variants, out of Brown's word-hoard. In certain psycholinguistic situations the reverse may be true: the formula calls forth the theme. When Brown wanted to describe the miracles or to emphasize Jesus's superiority to the "lawyers and doctors"—the intelligentsia—this ready-made formula was available to him. And in Brown's case particularly I am sure that part of the attraction of this formula was that its brevity allowed him to sing it, to draw it out and dramatize it, by putting his rich, deep voice on display.

But if this was characteristic of Brown's descriptive language, it also evokes the question of where the formula ends and the theme begins. One would not be likely to think of the above as Lord thought of themes[2]—in terms of narrative events—but rather as linguistic entities, sets of formulas that are consistently used to describe certain events or scenes, such as the arming of a knight or of a horse, a council of war, or the description of a castle's battlements. We must again alter the inherited definition to fit the demands of this particular tradition: the sermon theme is a sequence of formulas, nearly memorized, used to describe recurrent scenes, ideas, or actions within the sermon. For illustrative purposes, Brown's recitals are perhaps too brief and too disorganized. A better example is Lacy, who discussed St. John in the same semantic context at two different times; the first passage was taken from a sermon on "Dry Bones" delivered on July 16, 1967:

John was a young man
When he started out
About twenty-some odd years old
Like him now, make a conclusion to the book of Revelation
5 Way up yonder, in his nineties
I said in his nineties
Fixin' to go home
But yet he never had sat down
And—uh—discharged his debt
10 He might have got to the place, brother pastors
Where he didn't shout as much as he used t'
And do evangelistic work as he used t'
But at this particular time
He was sitting down in the city of Ephesia
15 Pastoring a church
That Timothy—Bishop Timothy—
Ahh—had founded a long time ago
Tryin' to say to you we can't give up, as ministers of the gospel

A week later, in a sermon on "Revelation," Lacy used the following series of formulas:

John was young then
But he's an old man now
[3-line elaboration of his old age]
He's not doin' no evangelistic work 'mount to anything
He's the only 'postle livin' follow Jesus
Even the 'postle Paul came on the scene very late
After the death of Jesus Christ
10 'Postle Paul has went and become beheaded yonder at Nero's choppin' block in Rome
And God rest the other 'postles; John was yet here
He's a old man

And at this particular time in this mornin's text
He's pastorin' now, not evangelistic work
15 But he's pastorin' the city of Ephesia
That's in Asia
Ephesia is the capital of that country
He's pastorin' this church in Ephesia where this same Paul
Had organized the church long time ago
20 And put his son Timothy there as bishop over that church

These are similar models from the same mold, yet that mold is twenty lines long. Lacy had not completely memorized the passage, though he nearly had, and in both versions he had gotten the essential points across: John was a young man then/ but an old man now/ he's not doing evangelistic work/ he was in Ephesia/ as pastor of a church/ that had been founded a long time ago. The details of this message are in the same order in both passages.

The sermon theme has a specific relationship to the formulas that comprise it; the theme is a series of related ideas, images, or actions, expressed by the relatively stable sequence of formulas. It is related to its formulas as is the entire edifice to its component bricks. Although the relationship between particular formulas and their order in the theme is often close, it is not memorized verbatim: the same theme may be expressed in several (similar) ways, since it is only as stable as the memory of the one who remembers it and the circumstances of retrieval.

The difference between the two performances above can be explained most accurately by the relationship between preacher and audience during the different sermons. At the time the first passage was recited, Lacy was breaking into a chant. The congregation was beginning to warm up, and its response to him aided Lacy in regularizing the lines. But he had not yet become fully metrical, and as the text shows, several lines are so hypermetric that they could not be compressed. Nevertheless, Lacy's pace is somewhat faster here than in the second passage, which was recited before a less responsive audience. In the latter sermon the pace is more conversational and unhurried, and because the tempo is slack, more details, especially descriptive details, enter. The intended theme—the wording that was closest to Lacy's "ideal" of the moment—is the first illustration; the second is an elaboration of it, in this case an unfortunate elaboration because Lacy's wordiness cost him his rhythm and thus the opportunity to stimulate the congregation. And sensing that the audience was not with him, he became self-conscious and stumbled over his words, and finally began to lose his conciseness. The idea expressed in four lines (14-17) in the first performance—that John was pastoring a church in Ephesia that Timothy had founded—in the second passage has taken seven lines (14-20).

Lacy did not, of course, realize that both passages would be transcribed and compared and so did not vary or try to keep the themes stable; at another time I was able to get an even better illustration of the extent of memorization of themes. On July 9, 1967, Lacy delivered a sermon on the very popular Twenty-third Psalm during which, strangely enough, he suddenly recited a forty-seven-line descriptive theme of the four horsemen of the Apocalypse. Those lines are noted below in the left-hand column of the page. Several weeks later (August 6) I asked him if he knew the passage well enough to recite it to me by heart: my excuse was that I had not gotten it clearly on tape the first time. Lacy was willing, and recited the same theme to me while we sat at the kitchen table in his home; the "kitchen table" version appears to the right of the sermon performance:

They tell me	In the mornin'
In the mornin'	When the saints of God shall
When the horses	rise
Begin to come out	When they all get together
5 And the riders on the horses	they'll be standin' lookin'
Want 'em to come out	Some'll be standin' lookin'
God from Zion	5 For the general that they
Riding a red horse	fought for
There's somebody gonna say	You know a general in the
10 Is that the general	army's a powerful man
That I was fighting for	They'll be standing looking for
And I heard another cry	the
Saying no-ooo	general that they been
That's not the one	fighting for

¹⁵ That you been fighting for
Another one rode out
Riding a black horse
Is that the man
That I been fighting for
²⁰ I heard another voice say
No, no-oo
That's not the general
That you been fighting for
Another one rode out
²⁵ Riding a pale horse
Is that the general
That we been fighting for?
A voice said No
That's not the one
³⁰ That you been fighting for
Another one came out
God from Zion
Riding a white horse
Rainbow round his shoulder
³⁵ Hark Hallelujah
Dressed in raiment
White as driven as the snow
From his head down to his
feet
God from Zion
⁴⁰ In his—from out of his mouth
Come a two-edge sword
Cuttin' sin
Both right and left
I heard a cry
⁴⁵ Is that the man
That we been fightin' for
They said yes

Out come a red horse
Somebody said
¹⁰ Is that the general I was
fighting for
No that ain't the one
Out come a black horse
Is that the general I been
fighting for
Some say
¹⁵ No that's not the general you
is fighting for
Out come a pale horse
Is that the general I been
fighting for
No
That's not the general I been
fighting for
²⁰ Still standin' an' after a while
he looked to see one
Come out on a white horse
With the rainbow round his
shoulder
Out of his mouth
Come a two-edge sword
²⁵ Cuttin' sin
Both right and left
Dressed in raiment as white as
snow
Head down to his feet
Eyes like balls of fire
³⁰ And his feet like polished
brass
Somebody cried out
Is that the general I been
fighting for
Yes that's the man you been
fighting for
I'm ready to go home in peace

³⁵ I seed the general that I been
fighting for

The method of comparative transcription chosen here may be
misleading: the kitchen table recitation (to the right) appears to
be twelve lines shorter, while actually it is temporally longer.
Many of the single lines ("Is that the general I been fighting for")
are chanted as two formulas during the pulpit performance. But
without the pressure of having to come up with the next line
rapidly, Lacy could develop some descriptions in his kitchen that
he forgot or didn't have time for during the sermon. "They tell
me/ In the mornin' " gets elaborated into seven lines when the
preacher is at ease, and several new ideas are added. Once into
the segment of the four horses "coming out," however, he is
structurally consistent, and adds nothing of note until the end
with the sequence, "Eyes like balls of fire/ And his feet like
polished brass." These descriptive elements, as well as the sen-
timent about going home in peace now that the speaker has seen
the "general," are part of the foundation of the theme; they were
also left out. The description of the white horse's rider is jumbled
in the church performance: at home it is (1) rainbow (2) sword
(3) raiment (4) eyes (5) feet. But under the pressure of performance the eyes and feet formulas are left out and the order becomes: (1) rainbow (2) raiment (3) sword.³ Descriptive formulas
quite often get scrambled, as their order is usually unimportant;
Lacy probably did not have any set pattern for the elements of
this description, but did have five—in whatever order he happened to use them—at his command.

Also absent from the kitchen table version are the stall formulas. During the pulpit performance Lacy used "God from Zion"
three times (lines 7, 32, and 39) and "Hark Hallellujah" once
(line 35). This was to be expected. Since their function is solely
for the preacher's benefit (to pause momentarily during the performance to decide what to say next), stall formulas would not
appear when the conditions had been relaxed: there was no congregation and no press of time. In this particular theme, Lacy
made it easy for himself through a largely repetitive structure:
in the pulpit version the red horse sequence (lines 8-15) is nearly

identical structurally with the black horse segment (lines 16-23); the pale horse segment is "missing" one line (it runs from lines 24-30). Such repetition of the structure of sections also aids memory.

The relative positions of the stall formulas show that their occurrence is not arbitrary and not without significance. Since their purpose is to give the preacher time to formulate the lines to come, they are unreflective utterances that can be spoken without hesitation while further speech, which will require more thought to construct, is being planned. The stalls occur within Lacy's four horsemen theme just at the moments when one would expect him to be facing the widest choice of material. When the oral performer, like the conversational speaker, has to make a selection based on information content, he will pause. In a metrical sermon pauses are unacceptable, so the preacher fills in with a stall formula.

The seven- or eight-line sections describing the emergence of each horse seem to be memorized for structure: no stall formulas occur among them. But one does occur just before Lacy brings out the first horse (line 7). Three horses and their riders then come out faultlessly, but just before the final horseman emerges Lacy stalls again. Here, the theme's regularized pattern has been disrupted and for the first time in several seconds (and over twenty lines) Lacy has to concentrate on what to say next. His choice has been dictated by the necessity of having to think of new syntactical structures and new diction, and perhaps even new content. He can no longer merely repeat the same syntactic patterning, and so he stalls: "God from Zion." Lacy mentions the "rainbow round his shoulder" but stalls again—descriptive themes not having a fixed order—until he decides to utter "Dressed in raiment/White as driven as the snow." When that simile is completed he pauses again, and again for the same reason: he cannot immediately decide what to say next. Further evidence of this appears in the next line, reproduced above as Lacy misspoke it: "In his—from out of his mouth."

These conjectures about the occurrence and frequency of stall formulas were confirmed by several experiments conducted on the relationship of hesitation pauses in speech to their context, to the length and transition probability of certain words preceding and following pauses, and to the information content of such words.[4] Frieda Goldman-Eisler confirmed that aside from psychological blocks that certain individuals might have regarding particular words, pauses in speech are related to word selection, choice of thought, and the framing of syntax. Hesitation occurs during situations of uncertainty, and usually that uncertainty is the result of too many rather than too few choices. Hence, pauses of this kind are of interest to us because of their relation to the sentences and formulas among which they appear. Hesitation is likely to occur before words of low transition probability when the forthcoming word choice is great, and is directly related to transmissions of potentially high information. Short words, especially articles and pronouns, often precede pauses while—again as would be expected—longer words tend to follow. These observations were borne out in the sermons.

Goldman-Eisler's experiments also help us understand why the preacher prefers to use traditional themes in the construction of sermons. When a sermon is in the early stages of its development, the preacher has not yet formulated the best way of expressing it. This weakness will be true of precise descriptions and even more so of abstractions. Generally speaking, the more concrete the utterance, the faster it will be learned and become automatic. Once a formulary portion of a sermon—a theme—has been learned, it becomes ideal for the preacher's purposes: its unreflective utterance allows recitation almost without flaw, that is, without pause, as well as allowing time for dramatic gesture, which will reinforce the effect of the words and, finally, provide a chance for formulating the ideas and language to come. In the first moments of most sermons stall formulas and themes seldom occur: the pace of delivery is deliberate and leisurely, much as is conversation, giving the preacher time to encode ideas easily, without the aid of stalls.

One of the curious aspects of the recitation of this four horsemen theme is that it was performed as part of a sermon on the Twenty-third Psalm; it was, in other words, an ideological irrelevance. Lacy's reason for using it makes it interesting. The sermon on the Twenty-third Psalm was going badly: the congregation did not respond and soon became restless. Lacy detected their boredom quickly and tried several means to overcome it:

he shouted, pounded his fists, exhorted his flock. After several minutes he was able to get some response, but this soon faded. Just before the spark died out completely, Lacy then broke into his well-rehearsed theme, the rhythm immediately caught on, and the sermon was saved.

Later I asked Lacy why he had chosen these lines and he replied that it was "all in the Bible." But later he said that he thought he used the passage so that he could pick up the rhythm. This answer may have been merely in response to my suggestion to that effect, but conscious or unconscious this theme's employment was purposeful. Because it was nearly memorized Lacy did not have to concentrate on what to think of next. All his mental energies could be put to getting the theme across; his mind was released from the urgency of composing and he concentrated on gesture, expression, intonation, and perhaps most important, rhythm. The diction and syntax were no problem, and he was free to work on the other aspects of his performance. It did not matter that the four horsemen had little to do with the Twenty-third Psalm; what did matter was that the horsemen theme could be performed successfully and could save a flagging sermon from failure and a lusterless congregation from boredom. The performance was the thing. When the same sermon was recited a year later to a livelier audience, the four horsemen theme was not used.

There are at least five other themes in this particular sermon: David's anointing, his fight with Goliath, his flight to the cave, the conversation between David and his mother, and the recitation of the psalm itself. Any element could be used elsewhere if the need arose, just as the horsemen them was used here. In this demonstration we can see something of the process of sermon composition. The theme plays a large role in sermon structure, thus making it easier for the preacher to compose. In some sermons, themes may be the core of the entire composition, as with "The Deck of Cards," where all else is prologue and epilogue to the one cards theme. In the "Twenty-third Psalm" sermon Lacy intended to use several relevant themes before he started, but their placement within the sermon shows that the structural economy was not built around them. The use of themes has great flexibility; they can be either necessary or ornamental elements within the sermon, and they can be brought in as the immediate situation demands.

Sometimes a theme that has been memorized in outline will be decomposed and then expanded. A sequence that would normally consume about twenty lines may be dilated to three times that number. Such expansion is usually the result of the dramatic failure of the preacher; one of the expected benefits of such dilation is the arousal of the congregation by the lucid performance of fluent, metrical lines. But the conditions are not always right, and even this technique may not save the situation. It is hard to say why. The sermon may have reached an ideological point when a particular theme is mandated. The preacher has planned the sermon a certain way and for various reasons may not want to change those plans. But when that point is reached, the listeners may not be sufficiently excited; yet the preacher goes ahead anyway. Why some preachers are not able at such a point to launch into a metrical theme is a problem I must leave to someone with more knowledge of psycholinguistics; I only know that it happens. Rubin Lacy has made such slips. The following theme on the four beasts of the Apocalypse was taken from a sermon of his delivered on July 9, 1967:

> John said
> I . . . I
> I saw four beasts
> One with a face
> 5 Looked like a calf
> Representin' patience
> And endurance
> 'Nother beast I saw
> Had a head like a lion
> 10 Representin' boldness
> And confidence
> 'Nother beast I saw
> A face like a man
> Representin' wisdom
> 15 An' he had knowledge
> 'Nother beast I saw
> Looked like a bald eagle

Ain't God all right?

Three weeks later (July 30) Lacy used the same material, but the circumstances had changed considerably. The audience was not responsive now. Attendance was poor (fewer than fifteen), the morning was very hot, and the children were particularly restless. The sermon was going badly, but for some reason Lacy decided to use the four beasts theme anyway; this time not even a memorized passage could help. Lacy, whose timing had been poor all morning, continued to stumble:

I said Amen
One of those beasts had a face like a lion
Representing boldness and confidence
Ah, bold—Amen—as a lion
5 Harmless as a dove
Conquer anything you go up against
There be wars and rumors of wars
Tryin' to fight to get into—turnin' over in the hand of God
I heard God say to Moses, standing on the banks of the Red Sea
10 Tell the Israelites God will fight for you
And you just hold your peace
The next beast—Amen—face like a calf
Representin' patience and endurance
Every child of God oughta have patience
15 Be willin' to endure hardness as a good soldier
If you can't take nothin', you can't bear no—wear no—crown
If you can't bear no burden
Umm-hmm
You can't wear no crown
20 God from Zion
I heard Jesus say the other day—umm
If you wanna follow me
Amen
First thing you do
25 Deny yourself, and then take up your cross
And follow me daily
Ain't God all right?
Seed Him went on and said
The third beast

³⁰ Amen
   Had a face, like a man
   Representin' wisdom and knowledge
   And understandin'
   Heard Solomon talkin' with God
³⁵ When he was a young man

Occasionally one or two of the four beast theme lines will appear in other sermons without the rest of the theme; they are, after all, formulas that can be used separately as the situation demands. But in the passage above Lacy retrieves groups of lines rather than individual lines. As soon as he says, "One of those beasts had a face like a lion" he immediately thinks of the next one: "Representin' boldness and confidence." In the expanded theme several lines will intervene before he comes to the next animal, but when he does he will give all the lines "necessary" for its description—here, the calf, representing patience and endurance.

Lacy also thought in terms of grammatical units, not only of metrical ones. Even though in the expanded theme the meter is quite different from the other theme recitation, certain diction is repeated. The words in this passage were what had made the deeper impression on Lacy.[5] When conditions were right he could break up the line "representing boldness and confidence" into two metrical lines:

         Representin' boldness
         And confidence

Again we see an aspect of the ability to compose metrically during performance; Lacy's genius lay in his flexibility, his ways with the Word.

He was by no means unique in this theme wielding. The Reverend D. J. McDowell, whose sermon on "The Christ of the Bible" is included below, admitted that the series of lines that incorporates "You may not be a geologist, but you must tell them that He's the Rock of Ages," is just such a device. In an interview, the technical terms "formula" and "theme" were not used. But McDowell understood the principle involved, and said that he had recited this particular theme in other sermons: he used it in "The Christ of the Bible" because it "fit." McDowell was one of those men who relied on a note card, as already mentioned; but his card on this particular day contained only the allusions to and epithets for Christ in various biblical passages: he had nothing in writing about the geologist theme. It came to him while he was performing, he thought that it would be effective, and so he used it. It was quite effective, though McDowell had so much ability that almost anything he did would "move the Spirit of God" within his congregation.

Like the words "formula" and "system," "theme" has acquired a connotation of something formal, rigid, and inflexible. But as the preachers use this device it is characterized by flexibility. Some themes may be largely memorized; most are not. Themes often occur in expanded form, and parts of them may be used in other contexts. Although they are primarily a mnemonic and histrionic device, they often fail in their purpose. They are seldom necessary to a sermon and often appear in seemingly irrelevant contexts; they float as freely as the preacher's mind. The themes are probably the greatest of the preacher's memory aids, even though their nature allows substantial variation. Themes give a great deal of coherence to the message of a sermon; preachers depend on them to hold their sermons together and they use them as departure points. Without themes and a coherent narrative plot line, most sermons would be structurally (and probably semantically) chaotic; with them the sermon does not become inflexible, but rather just rigid enough to cohere and just flexible enough to allow communication with the shifting moods of the congregation.

NOTES

1. This theme is by no means unique to Brown. In a sermon recited in Charlottesville, Virginia, on March 17, 1968, Elder Jerry H. Lockett recited the following three passages during a sermon entitled "This Same Jesus:"

> This same Jesus
> No other Jesus but this same Jesus
> That give sight to the blind
> Cause the dumb to talk
> [5] Cause the lame to walk

Caused the deaf to hear
This same Jesus

. . .

I'm talkin' about Jesus
I'm talkin' about Jesus
Talkin' about the One
Who brought us a mighty long ways
⁵ We seen a child way up in Jerusalem
Seen Him up there settin' down amongst the doctors
Settin' up there among the lawyers
Settin' up there among highly educated people

. . .

This same Jesus
Told the woman one day
Same Jesus
That give sight to the blind one day
⁵ Same Jesus
Spoke to the dumb one day
Caused them to speak
Deaf to hear one day
That same Jesus

Elder Lockett was adamant in his insistence that "the Lord" gave him the words, and would not acknowledge any other source. Polygenesis seems unlikely, given the amount of details in this theme cluster: Lockett had never been to Arkansas or Bakersfield, nor had Brown ever been to Virginia. "This same Jesus" occurs only once in the Bible (Acts 1:11) but the miracles are not enumerated in this passage. The possible source is a spiritual that Rufus Hays remembered only vaguely, whose first lines are:

This same Jesus
Walked at Galilee
This same Jesus
Made the blind to see

I have not been able to find this song in any of the spirituals collections available to me.

2. Compare this segment with those in Lord's *Singer of Tales*, pp. 68–98. The major difference appears to be the uses to which the Yugoslav and American themes are put.

3. The metaphor is an elaboration of Revelation 1:14–16: "His head and hairs were white like wool, as white as snow; and his eyes were as a flame of fire; And his feet like unto fine brass, as if they burned in a furnace; and his voice as the sound of many waters. And he had in his

right hand seven stars: and out of his mouth went a sharp two-edged sword."

4. Frieda Goldman-Eisler, "Speech Production and the Predictability of Words in Context," *Quarterly Journal of Educational Psychology* 10 (May 1958), 96–106; "Hesitation and Information in Speech," in *Information Theory: Fourth London Symposium* (1961), 162–74; "Continuity of Speech Utterance, Its Determinants and Its Significance," *Language and Speech* 4 (1961), 220–31; and "The Distribution of Pause Durations in Speech," *Language and Speech* 4 (1961), 232–37. Professor Richard Bauman brought these articles to my attention.

5. The tendency of subjects to recall aspects of narrative by word association rather than idea or story element was first noted by F. C. Bartlett, "Some Experiments on the Reproduction of Folk Stories," reprinted in Alan Dundes, *The Study of Folklore* (New Jersey, 1965), p. 249.

7

Getting It All Together

How much and what portions of orally composed, performed, and transmitted sermons are memorized, and how much and what portions are authentically created anew? If these questions could be accurately answered, we would know nearly everything about the composition of oral narratives and the precise relationship between the individual artist and the tradition. However, some preachers rely on traditional, or well-rehearsed, or memorized material much more than others; no generalizations can be made about all preachers. The ratio of memorized/rehearsed/original material continually alters, from sermon to sermon; that generalization is true of all preachers. The factors in this geometry include the preacher's mood, that of the congregation, the subject of the sermon, how well it has been mastered by the preacher, etc. Variations in any of these—and none of them are ever static—cause variations in the performer's creative geometry. Variability is the only stable factor.

The most obvious means of deciding which portions of a sermon are memorized and which are created anew at the moment of performance is to record the "same" sermon twice. The rationale is that if certain segments are repeated verbatim, they are probably memorized. If the same subject—e.g., David's fight with Goliath, the Nativity, Moses at the Red Sea—is described differently (syntax and lexicon considered), then such individual descriptions must be original. Such a conclusion assumes, however, that the performer has only one preferred way to describe an idea or an episode, and that the nonoccurrence of this theme demonstrates originality: this is not true. If two sermons on the same subject are shown to have similar descriptive or ideational passages, can it be concluded that they are memorized? Not with certainty, because we know that the phenomenon of short-term memory differs from long-term memory. If the sermons are recorded a year or more apart, however, repeated phrases and themes are likely to have been memorized; the phrases, verbatim; the themes, in general; the entire economy of the sermon, by gist memory. Two lexically and syntactically different performances of the same episode or idea, a year or more apart, suggest (though not infallibly) that they have been created at the moment of performance. It is possible that between recordings the performer could decide to change the description of an episode or adopt an entirely new one, which when recorded and studied confounds the analyst. This risk, not a very great one, is nevertheless one to be alert to. While the only sure method of comprehending the repertoire of a singer or preacher is to record or hear every performance—an impossible task, of course—comparison of the "same" sermon, performed and recorded a year apart, has provided a working hypothesis for the way the preacher gets it all together in the making of an oral sermon.

Early in July of 1967 the Reverend Mr. Lacy was asked to be the guest preacher at the Liberty Baptist Church in Bakersfield (the Reverend W. G. McRoy, pastor). But, for personal reasons, Lacy did not prepare himself for the day's message; he obviously had not done his homework and had not in any noticeable way readied himself for the sermon. Not that excuses are relevant here, but Lacy had also been asked to preach on the previous Sunday, when at the last minute McRoy had called upon another preacher who had happened to be in the church; Lacy may have anticipated yet another last-minute substitute, though if he did he was disappointed (or elated, depending upon how one looks at it). Although he had not adequately prepared, Lacy had been casually thumbing through a newly acquired copy of Burns's *Master Sermon Outlines*, and he found one to his liking, probably because its theme was a favorite of his anyway: a eulogy of the pastor.

This undistinguished performance—carelessly prepared, poorly delivered, and listlessly received—does help our understanding of the making of an oral sermon. Several days after Lacy's sermon I was able to purchase *Master Sermon Outlines* and so was able to compare Lacy's prose source with his metrical performance. This was interesting enough; yet eleven months later, he used some of the same figures in another sermon, also on the importance of the pastor. This third version is relevant to any understanding of Lacy's art, for in it we can see language and idea as they are assimilated in the preacher's mind a year after he first conceived them. By comparing these three sermons we can see the preacher at first struggling with his source, and then mastering his material so that it becomes a part of his repertoire that he can recite without notes.[1] And we can also see how much outside material—language and ideas that the preacher had been absorbing for many years—finds its way into the performance. Finally, we can surmise how the preacher constructs the sermon —however unconsciously—by evaluating the relative position of formulas and metaphors in terms of their sources.

In this section we examine the process by which many oral sermons are composed, using Lacy's "God's Plowboy" sermons as a paradigm. Examples from the work of others will also be used to illustrate certain techniques, for what we are trying to describe is the process of a tradition and not the exclusive property of one man.

Spiritual preachers use certain scriptural passages to justify their style of preaching the Word. From Luke 24:49 they derive their most important lesson, that the apostles were to go to Jerusalem and wait there until the "power from on high" came to them. Nothing is mentioned in this verse about self-education, about biblical exegesis, or about seminary schooling of any kind. Spiritual preachers believe strictly in the literal Word of God; they are chosen from above and have no control over that choice, except, perhaps, to deny God. This passage from Luke cannot be used to justify sloth and ignorance. Sometimes that may happen, but usually spiritual preachers sincerely believe that God intended them to preach without manuscripts, straight from the soul, lending themselves for the moment to the Holy Ghost. They get these ideas from several people: their own pastors, family and friends, or from preachers heard or seen as they ride through town or appear on local radio. Spiritual preaching is the only way and that way rarely changes, no matter how much education preachers may eventually receive.

The first thing incipient chanting preachers learn that will influence their style is not language but rhythm. This hypothesis may be controversial, in part, because one cannot prove it; it rests, for the moment, as an article of faith. Any portrait of preachers as young children will show them in church on their mothers' laps or beside them on the bench.[2] They will barely listen to the sermon because they can distinguish only a few words, and in any event the meaning is lost on them. But they do respond to the music. Seldom do young children in the churches I have visited bother with the sermons at all. When the preacher begins they get restless and fidgety, play silent games with other children, and sometimes even sleep. But the singing usually elicits an active response, and very often the children sing along with the music and clap their hands to its beat. There is often singing—even organized singing—in the home, but never any preaching there. We can see in such circumstances how children learn rhythm; if the young children eventually become preachers, their first schooling has been in the music of their churches and with their culture.

The great importance of rhythm was demonstrated to me in Oklahoma City, where I encountered for the first time several preachers and evangelists who preached spontaneously, but did not chant, and so produced quite a different kind of performance. As I have pointed out before, the nonrhythmical oral sermon produces syntactical units of greater flexibility than the chanted sermon, but is more repetitive than conversational speech; in this sense it is a kind of transitional performance. The nonrhythmical sermon has very few memorized formulas, and memorized narrative formulas are rare. Anaphoric passages do appear often enough to be noticeable, but they are by no means as frequent as in chanted performances. The following two examples, both taken from a sermon by Dorance Manning of the Holiness Pentecostal Church of Norman, Oklahoma (May 1968), will illustrate this point:

And so they moved their family and sold their land and headed for
    the land of Moab
Now let's turn over to Jeremiah the forty-eighth chapter for just a
    moment
And let's find out what the land of Moab is talking about
What is the land of Moab
5 In chapter forty-eight, if you have your Bible and would like to
    turn . . .

And we find them doing something typical that most of us do in a
    like situation
Instead of them examining the situation and then saying now what
    is the problem here
Why do we not have rain
Why do we not have a place of worship
5 Why has our crops failed and why has this come upon us . . .

The disinterest in rhythm has led to irregular sentence meters,
and formulaic language does not develop. The first passage is
taken from late in the sermon when Manning was far more emotionally involved in his work than in the second. Yet the first
passage is barely parallel in structure ("let's turn over," "let's
find out") and infrequently repetitive ("the land of Moab"). The
second passage, which seems to be more characteristic of the
oral style, developed anaphorically more by chance. Manning
was not thinking about anaphora at the moment either, and his
emotional involvement had little to do with the form of this passage. Even though nonrhythmic sermons may be spontaneously
composed, compositionally a different set of rules apply. In this
book we have to be concerned with the singers of sermons and
the effect of chanting upon utterance formation.

Young preachers (we should recall here) develop in ways
roughly parallel to those described by Lord: they listen and learn
(often in ways unknown to them), they practice short prayers
and testimonies and then, having mastered their material, step
to the pulpit and deliver their own sermons spontaneously. I have
been able to record the sermons of two apprentice preachers;
one of these is included below. The Reverend W. L. Parker
preached the other (May 28, 1968), and because Parker had been

Brown's deacon for many years some interesting comparisons can be made.

One would expect Parker to have sounded like Brown, but actually, aside from one memorized formula, his style was nothing like his pastor's. The same was true of the Reverend William Robinson in his independence of his pastor, C. Earl Williamson. Not only did the young preachers differ from their pastors in their first performances by not using formulas that they must have heard repeated thousands of times, but their rhythms were different; so were their inflections and the music of the few lines they did chant. It remains to be proved to what degree the young preacher reverts, with maturity, to the style of a "master." But the performances of the young men are, in this respect, surprising, and cannot be accounted for except to postulate the obvious: the desire to have an individual style while remaining within the tradition is strong, and the young men worked to develop a sense of their own identity.

If the novices failed to use many of the formulas of their pastors, one is even more surprised to learn that they used few memorized formulas at all. Perhaps the reason lies in the fact that in the sermons by young preachers I have heard, the sense of rhythm is poorly developed; the trouble seems to be that during the first sermons of their careers too many problems intrude: what to say and how to say it. Being so preoccupied with language, with both syntax and semantics, the rhythmical flow is interrupted and the sermon style nearly breaks down. Robinson had had a bit more experience than Parker, and this may explain why he was able to gain some rhythm toward the end of his sermon as he became more sure of himself and of his material. Also, with the finish in sight he could plug in a section that he had used before and knew well, knowing that it could carry him to the end. But not so with Parker; he was "teaching not preaching," as Deacon MacFaddin criticized it afterwards.

As the novice gains experience, style changes markedly. After several years—and of course this varies, depending upon aptitude—rhythm begins to show itself and to shape the language of the sermon. The Reverend D. J. McDowell is a good example: in his forties he was still considered a young preacher because he had been preaching only a few years. McDowell's supply of sermons was limited. He did not yet have enough experience to enable him to break away from prepared sermon structures. Though he worked hard to develop new sermon ideas, he was not yet able to preach spontaneously (in the strictest sense of that word) by blending materials from many sources, but worked with established outlines. The curious feature of McDowell's style (and the style of most young preachers with his limited experience) was that he was heavily dependent upon memorized formulas. I assume this happened because after, say, five years, he knew fairly well what he wanted to say and had sufficient mastery of his material to be able to say it rhythmically. The music was no longer a problem; what was of some difficulty was the phrasing of old ideas in new formulas. This may account for young preachers' great repetitiveness: having learned to regularize the lines, they have some difficulty thinking of what to say next and so must rely upon verbatim formulas to give them a moment to think about the matter.

My theory is that this early phase gives way to one in which both language and music are mastered: Brown, Lacy, Freeman, and nearly all of the other men interviewed and transcribed in this book were at that later stage. They were rhythmical always. They had mastered their message techniques beyond the point of preparing each sermon individually. They may have thought about each sermon, sometimes for several days, beforehand; but experienced preachers have such control that they are able to create new sermons—message, language, structure, and rhythm—as they go along. They continue to use verbatim formulas, as many admit, and use them to stall for time occasionally, but the experienced will not use them as frequently as younger preachers who have to think more often of what to say next. This stage of maturity seems to last the longest and in it preachers are at the height of their creative powers. Only one further plateau can be reached, and this does not seem to happen to all preachers: as they become older many of their powers may deteriorate. Their chanting may become irregular; they may have difficulty in converting prose to metrical verse during the performance; and most noticeable, they will once again rely more heavily on memorized formulas, to compensate for their failing creative abilities.

In Lacy's sermon on "God's Plowboy" we can observe two mental processes at work. First we can see the preacher's spontaneous conversion of prose to verse, and later, by comparing the resulting sermon with one recorded a year later, we can see what happens to the sermon after it has bounced around in his mind and has become fully assimilated in his repertoire. Brown once began with a verbatim reading of St. John and soon turned to his own idiom. And we shall see Goins gradually change Genesis to his own music. For Lacy, on a very hot day in July of 1967, the following passage was part of his written source:

II. GOD'S PLOWBOY MUST FEED HIS MASTER'S SHEEP
The Lord said to Peter "Feed my lambs," and again He said "Feed my sheep." The Lord has no flocks or herds; He was talking about people. The lambs were the newborn babes in Christ and such as had not yet fully developed. He said to Peter twice, "Feed my sheep." He was referring to the fully developed and strong Christians.

But when transmuted through the alchemy of Lacy's brain the passage was recited somewhat differently:

> Let's go on a little further
> God from Zion
> God's plowboy
> Must feed
> ⁵ We're goin' on to the feedin'
> I say God's plowboy
> Must feed
> His master's sheep
> The Lord said to Peter
> ¹⁰ Feed, my lambs
> And then He said unto him
> Feed, my sheep
> The Lord
> Didn't have no flock
> ¹⁵ Didn't have no herd
> He was talkin' about
> God from Zion
> He was talkin' about the lambs
> Of newborn babes

²⁰ In <u>Christ</u> <u>Jesus</u>
<u>Such as had not yet, fully developed</u>
<u>He said to Peter twice feed my sheep</u>
Said to him the last time
Feed my lamb
²⁵ Ain't God all right?
Feed my lamb

(Solid and broken underlining are used in this selection to show which lines were recited exactly and which approximately with relation to Lacy's source text.)

Lacy's performance is faltering at best, and this section is typical of the entire performance. He did not know well the passage he was reading; perhaps he had glanced over it two or three times, but certainly not more. During the performance he obviously could not spend more than a fraction of a second looking for topics; his eye hit upon the capitalized title GOD'S PLOWBOY MUST FEED HIS MASTER'S SHEEP and he read, as metrically as he could, from that section. When he had gotten what he could from the heading he moved on to the next thing that caught his eye. A sure indication that this in fact is the way he composed this sermon is shown from Lacy's line 1 above (line 145 in the entire sermon), "Let's go on a little further." He had just finished talking about the preacher as burden-bearer, and having exhausted his source's ideas, moved on to the next one—"on a little further." Sometimes he was able to regularize his meter, as in lines 12-16, but at other times he was so dominated by the meter of his source that he repeated it exactly and ignored what he was trying to accomplish at the moment. In other words, some of the language could be assimilated into Lacy's style right away, but only a little at a time: it was hard mental work to make this assimilation, and after several lines his style broke down. It may have picked up again, but only for a moment, after which it collapsed once more. Lines 21 and 22, for example, are repeated without regard for meter.

The following three extracts are on the same subject; the first is from Lacy's source (*Master Sermon Outlines*), the second is Lacy's version during that first sermon in 1967, and the last is from a sermon by Lacy in May of 1968 after he had digested his thoughts and language.

1. Take Heed How You Feed the Flock
During a dearth, Elisha's servant set on the great pot and one went
out into the field to gather herbs to feed the sons of the prophets.
Not knowing the food properly, he gathered wild gourds; and
when the food was served, death was found in the pot.

Let's see am I right about it
God
Went up on the mountain
The other day
⁵ To pray
And while He was up there prayin'
Some of the
Laborers
Said I'll be
¹⁰ I'll go out and get some stuff
And feed the people
Because they're hungry
Went out to pick vegetables
And got the wrong kind
¹⁵ Brought 'em on back
Put 'em in a pot
Begin to boil green
Had death in the pot
Ain't I right about it?

Pastor must know how to feed
Just any old thing
Throw in the trough
Just won't do
⁵ Must know how to feed
Don't y' remember
When Moses went off that time
Up on the mountain
Left the boys down there
¹⁰ Somebody cried out I'm hungry
Went out there in the woods
Pulled up the wrong thing
Went on back there
Put it in the pot

[15] Began to boil
Before Moses got back
Some of 'em was eatin' that stuff
Everybody began to die
I want you to know Moses
[20] Umm-hmm
Somebody said death
Was in the pot
Pastor must know
What kind of food
[25] Is to give his children

The tapes would show far more clearly than does the transcription how Lacy's later performance is more uniform metrically. But something else has happened as well: the story has become amplified, the characters have changed, and the language has gotten further away from that of Lacy's source. All of these mutations (which are apparent and need not be itemized) came about because the story was now Lacy's; with each new retelling he would change it more, though with diminishing variations, until its style and even its content were entirely his.

We can, however, profitably examine in some detail a few of the changes Lacy made from 1967 to 1968 to evaluate their quality, and to decide about the effect of those changes on the sermon as oral art. Since the passage we have been discussing on the pastor feeding his master's sheep was selected for thematic reasons, so far as aesthetics are concerned its choice is random and it will do for our purposes here.

Lacy's major achievement with this sermon in the year's time was to blend the parable of the poisonous gourds into the texture of the sermon. In the 1967 version it is clumsily fitted into the exposition with abrupt transitions. A year later the story is more logically connected to the lines that come before and after it.[3] Although the earlier version begins with "Let's see am I right about it," the preceding lines had been jerry-built at best and appear to have been a stall while Lacy groped for the next point in his text. In 1968 most of that has been honed away: Lacy comes right to the point with "Pastor must know how to feed" and concludes the parable with the same message, "Pastor must know/ What kind of food/ Is to give his children."

The 1968 version of the parable is more interestingly and artfully told. Instead of the declarative (and dull) statement, "Had death in the pot," we now have the more vivid "somebody" who "said death/ Was in the pot" drawn out over two lines, the first (enjambed) line ending with the dramatic word "death." The 1968 version also gets more action into the story by alternating its focus between Moses on the mountain (line 7), the "boys down there" (line 9), Moses getting back (line 16), and the pot of death (lines 17 ff.). Instead of straight narrative as in 1967, the most recent version blends elements of conversation, narrative, and exposition.[4] Because the 1968 version contains direct dialogue, it has a greater vitality. This was the difference a year made.

Not all of the major structural elements of a sermon are altered. I recorded Lacy's performance of "The Twenty-third Psalm" on two separate occasions, also one year apart. The 1967 sermon ended with a forty-five-line memorized theme that was irrelevant to the subject of the sermon: a description of the four horsemen. I conjectured at that time that Lacy had used the four horsemen section just because it was memorized and thus he could devote all of his energies to the various histrionic techniques necessary to revive a flagging audience. That hypothesis was proven a year later when Lacy fortuitously recited the same sermon without the four horsemen: a comparison was then possible. And while the language altered in this sermon much as it had in "God's Plowboy," the major ideas and episodes of the narrative remained stable.

To facilitate a comparison of these two performances I have outlined both of them by subject. The 1968 sermon is on the left, the earlier, 1967, version is to the right:

Lines	Subject	Lines	Subject
1-4	Scripture	1-3	Scripture
5-10	Digression on experience	4-22	Digression on preaching
11-17	David as shepherd	23-35	Digression on self, fishing
18-19	Digression on self	36-44	Digression on liars
20-68	David's anointing	45-48	David's experience
69-100	Fight with Goliath	49-60	Digression on St. Paul

101-105	Transition	61-67	Description of David
106-143	David's flight to cave	68-81	David's anointing
144-167	Digression on dangers of being shepherd	82-107	Fight with Goliath
		108-140	David's flight to cave
168-205	David saves lamb	141-161	David as shepherd
206-213	Digression: Lord is shepherd	162-218	David saves lamb; recitation of Twenty-third Psalm
214-222	Digression on personal experience and moral for day	219-260	Digression on coming Judgment
		261-277	Digression on selfishness
223-235	Digression: warning to preachers	278-330	Four horsemen

Considering individual formulas, only the passages from Scripture and the stall formulas remained constant. But the larger elements that remained constant tell an interesting story. Both sermons contain the same four narrative elements presented in the same order: David's anointing, his fight with Goliath, his flight into the cave to avoid Saul's wrath, and the exemplum of David as the good shepherd. One can guess that so far as Lacy was concerned these four tales are essential to his sermon on the Twenty-third Psalm. That the narrative elements are most constant shows that they comprise the frame upon which the siding is mounted. Various digressions are built around these four stories, and in these two versions Lacy used them flexibly. He did not, however, always use them well, something that a further analysis of the text will show.

The failure of the 1967 version and the somewhat warmer reception in 1968 can be explained by a simple line count. During the first performance Lacy took 330 lines to say practically the same thing about David that he said in 235 lines a year later. The importance of those 95 extra lines is the fact that they were spoken at the expense of the narrative stories from David's life—stories whose retention and repetition suggest that they were the chief elements in the sermon. In 1967 only 92 lines were devoted to these four episodes, while a year later Lacy spent 157 lines on them—and in a sermon 95 lines shorter overall. In 1968 only

78 lines, about one-third of the entire performance, were used for exposition and other purposes; the year before, 186 lines were so used, nearly two-thirds (excluding the four horsemen, a thematic excrescence). Including this last theme, 238 lines were devoted to topics extraneous to the four stories of David's life, three more lines than it took Lacy to preach the entire sermon a year later.

Digressions in themselves do not necessarily undermine a sermon; the important factor is the way in which they are used. The digressions in the successful 1968 version are few in number and are related, though often associationally, to the episodes. Consider, for instance, the digression on experience as the best teacher (lines 5-10 and 213 ff. in the 1968 sermon, lines 45-48 in 1967). Perhaps C. L. Franklin of Detroit first thought of the idea or merely made it famous, but it is now a common *topos* for spiritual preachers to dwell upon David's face-to-face confrontation with God. David is alleged to have spoken so personally in the Twenty-third Psalm because of his experience with his Lord. Lacy thought enough of this *topos* to use it in both sermons, but its casual handling and the sparse time devoted to it in 1967 suggest that it was not central to the sermon, but was certainly something that Lacy was reminded of whenever he preached on this psalm. In 1968 it was deftly tied in with other digressions on self-experience, and its impact was not vitiated by the presence of several other digressions.

We can be nearly positive, then, that the four episodes from David's life comprise the core of this sermon around which the preacher established his message for the day. The episodes are the same in both sermons and they were related in the same order. Probably this came about because the first three were taken chronologically from the biblical story of David's life; and the last, where David saves one of his lambs from the wild beasts, was important for showing the hero's devotion to his flock. That, in turn, enabled Lacy to move on to discuss the Lord as shepherd. He did not always take this course, however; in 1967 it was to his disadvantage. In any event, one can see in these four repeated episodes the core of the sermon that Lacy had mentally retained, and one can also see how much (and what) is extemporized.

Preachers seem to retain the narrative; the morals are preached spontaneously and vary widely.

The key to understanding the composition of the oral sermon is an analysis of the preacher's psychological associations. In "God's Plowboy" Lacy retained certain images and ideas that he apparently found striking,[5] and added them to his repertoire, modifying their language and amplifying their details. In "The Twenty-third Psalm" Lacy had retained the core of the sermon from one year to the next by remembering just four episodes from David's life around which he could build sermons of greatly varying lengths. The following analysis returns to "God's Plowboy" and analyzes the sermon's components. The version chosen is the more recent; here the old language and images contained in that one sermon comprise a relatively small part of the entire performance. Several other sources intruded upon Lacy's mind so that the finished product was a very eclectic one indeed. As it happened this performance was smoothly delivered and was well received by a large congregation.

As a guide, capital letters are used to represent the sermon's sources (if they could be identified): P, from a published sermon entitled "The Pastor"; G, "God's Plowboy"; B, material from Lacy's friend Brown; D, original and spontaneous digression; A, amplification of theme or subject; MP, from a published sermon on "Ministerial Promotion"; E, from the sermon delivered by Lacy in 1967 on Ezekiel's story of the "Dry Bones":

Lines	Brief Description	Source
4-15	Scripture	P
16-42	King of England	D
43-69	Preacher's labors	G
70-84	Apostrophe to Rev. W.H. Henry	D
85-102	Pastor as overseer	P
103-122	(Same)	P, A
123-133	Faults of present church	P (D?)
134-157	Pastor as feeder	G, A
158-184	(Same)	P, G, A
185-197	Pastor as friend of congregation	P, A

198-211	Digression on Ezekiel, etc.	E
212-221	Preach the Word	B, A
222-239	The call to preach	P, A
240-253	(Same)	B, A
254-267	Grievous wolves	P
268-286	(Same)	P, A
287-298	Boasters	D
299-324	Joseph	MP
325-330	Closing	D

Lacy had retained the parts and consequently composed this sermon, as with his others, through associational clusters. The borrowings from "God's Plowboy" are within a third of the sermon; those from Brown (Lacy also chanted the lines with Brown's music), from Ezekiel, and from "Ministerial Promotion" are also bunched; the material from "The Pastor" runs throughout. Lacy seems to have had this sermon most actively on his mind throughout the performance.

The subject, one of Lacy's favorites, associationally attracted materials from other sermons to it. "God's Plowboy," "The Pastor," and "Ministerial Promotion" all deal with Lacy's profession. "Dry Bones" is also related: it is about the prophet in the desert, an image Lacy had used to describe himself before. All of the sources can be raided for materials and everything should fit; the resulting sermon does not have a formal structure, but this was to Lacy's advantage in that he could use each idea as it came to him. He had several comparisons to make: the pastor as feeder, as burden-bearer, as overseer, as friend, etc., but he did not need to make these comparisons in any particular order. If he just remembered most of the comparisons he would have enough to say for the morning. Unlike the sermon on the Twenty-third Psalm, where Lacy was aided by the chronology of the story, he had to rely on memory and association here. The pastor as overseer (I would guess) reminded him of the pastor as burden-bearer, and then possibly as feeder. Exactly how it was done will remain Lacy's secret, perhaps it was unknown even to him; that it was done and done well we can appreciate.

Why a preacher retains a certain metaphor or exemplum is a matter for psychological analysis; I can only guess at the obvious, that it is for some reason appealing to him.[6] I have tried on several occasions to suggest metaphors and ideas to various preachers before their sermons, but always without success. On the way to a sermon that the Reverend Otis McAllister (of Bakersfield) was to deliver in Delano, I intentionally suggested several ideas to him. Brown, who was also in the car, quite unconsciously suggested several others as we discussed, in rather general terms, McAllister's sermon for the night. McAllister used none of our ideas; but he did pick up a figure while talking to the host pastor and he used that. Brown has occasionally done the same. It would be interesting to learn whether either McAllister or Brown continued using the same figures after several months or a year. I see no reason why they should not have, since there is nothing essentially ephemeral about spoken metaphors. We can conclude from this "experiment" that preachers are continually open to suggestion from several sources, that sermons can be altered, however slightly, at the very last minute. But what makes language memorable to any particular person, be it felicitous phrasing or soul-stirring idea, I cannot say.

One of the curious phenomena of chanted preaching is that two sermons on the same topic performed during the same day may not be more alike than two sermons delivered a year apart. The statement cannot be made with certainty since I have been able to record such a repetition only once. The Reverend T. J. Hurley, a white preacher, of the Oneness Pentecostal Church, Oklahoma City, spoke on "Perilous Times" on the morning of May 12, 1968, and that afternoon delivered a similar sermon over KBYE radio, Oklahoma City. I classify the sermons as similar and not identical, because of the 483 lines in the (later) radio sermon, only thirty-one—or 7 percent—would be underlined in a formulaic chart. Yet both sermons ostensibly dealt with the same topic and both contained long lamentations about the sinfulness of contemporary society and a discussion of recent mass murders as evidence that we are living in the last days.

As we might by now well expect, the thirty-one lines that were repetitions appeared in the later sermon in clusters: the first group of eleven appeared between lines 2 and 17; a cluster of two fell between lines 48 and 53; four consecutive lines followed line 180; and the last fourteen ran from lines 429 to 442. Though

Hurley remembered in clusters the words he had previously used, several ideas were repeated, and he occasionally used a word or two of the original expression. Several of the preacher's expressions returned for the second sermon, but these involved a different sort of memory since they often came up in new contexts. Actually, aside from the opening lines and a well-developed theme that described recent sensational crimes, the two sermons were hardly the same. Hurley did not rely on narrative particularly, and there was little that was necessary in his sermon. Consequently, we find much the same disorder as we found in other sermons of this kind; the surprising thing is that we should find such a disparity so soon after the first recitation.

Apparently Hurley knew in only a general way what it was he would communicate: he would talk about recent signs that the world was in its last days, but little else seems to have been planned. Only two passages have enough consistency to be thought of as themes. The first of these deals with the Scriptures on which the entire sermon is based, the admonition "that in the last days perilous times shall come" (from 2 Tim. 3:1). In the morning it took all of fifty-three lines to develop; in the afternoon sermon on radio the same idea was encompassed in the first seventeen lines. Several factors are involved in this compression. To begin with, all speakers with a modicum of self-awareness—be they actors, teachers, public speakers, or preachers—try to improve their style in each succeeding performance. Hurley's morning performance was word-bloated; in the afternoon he disciplined himself and said the same thing in about one-third the time and thus had more time for other subjects.

Comparing the underlined typescript of the afternoon performance with that of the morning, what immediately stands out is the spacing of the repeated lines. In the morning performance they are clustered in groups of three and four lines followed by three lines that are not retained, then three or four that are repeated, followed in turn by several that are not. In the afternoon these repeated lines are bunched, eleven of them falling within the first seventeen. Hurley had cut away much of the fat.

In general one should consider other possibilities, though they may not be applicable here. The afternoon sermon was a radio performance, though recorded live in the church before the congregation, and radio sermons mean time limits. Although such limits can affect the length of performances, such was not the case here, since Hurley actually finished preaching about ten minutes before his allotted time was up and had to have the rest of the time segment filled in with church music. However, his voice had begun to give out in the morning. T. J. Hurley was not the regular pastor, and his voice was obviously not in shape for the demands two or more sermons a day make on the throat. His father, T. C. Hurley, (the regular pastor) was called away rather suddenly and T. J. had to fill in at the last minute. On the air T. J.'s voice cracked constantly, and that may have encouraged him to cut short the sermon, but it probably would not have affected the opening passage in any event, since his voice was strong for those lines. There are other possibilities, of course: that this passage was well known by him, got amplified in the morning and then cut back to its original form later. I was not familiar enough with Hurley's style to know if this was actually the case; I can guess that it was not, and conclude that in these performances at least, and in this particular passage, Hurley's style improved.

There will be more to say about the quality and character of repeated sermons shortly; meantime I want to conclude my observations on the tendency of preachers' minds to grasp ideas (and sometimes language) in vague clusters (Parry's "given essential ideas"?) and to build sermons around these amorphous frames. Before Lacy first recited the "Deck of Cards" sermon he told me that he could preface it with any remarks about "heart." And so he did:

> 3 . . . the fool, has said in his heart, there is no God
> 16 Therefore, the hearts of men are wrong . . .
> 23 The hearts of men is far from right
> 41 Whatever is in your heart
> 43 Tryin' to say I'm talkin' about heart . . .
> 46 . . . after God's own heart
> 75 Some of us are too stout-hearted even to confess . . .
> 93 My heart is fixed
> 101 And know my heart
> 117 He's a heart fixer

And so on. Now there is nothing central to the sermon on "The Deck of Cards" in these references to the heart. Admittedly, there is the slight though obvious connection between playing cards and "hearts," but that connection was lost on the several members of the congregation to whom I spoke. Lacy piled up references to the heart in that first performance. The second time such allusions hardly appeared at all; after opening with the psalmist's warning that "the fool hath said in his heart there is no God," he hardly refers to the heart again. Lacy was sidetracked onto some other topic and never returned. The point is that he had demonstrated that he could use an extensive cluster of references, but would not do it all the time.

We see how even the simplest sermon structures are likely to vary by comparing two outlines of "Deck of Cards" performances by Lacy in 1967 and then in 1968. The structure here is so different from that of "God's Plowboy" that it is deserving of a few words by itself. The early sermon is outlined on the left, the more recent one on the right:

1-4	Scripture	1-6	Scripture
5-15	Messiah's coming	7-25	Noah; Messiah's coming
16-36	Selfishness	26-38	Digression: Elijah
37-46	Amplification of above	39-82	God is alive
47-69	David's selfishness and repentance; our lack of same	83-91	God's return
70-101	David's repentance; our conscience	92-97	Noah's days
102-118	Te Deum	98-134	The end of the world
		135-139	Scripture; transition
119-249	Deck of cards	140-205	Deck of cards
250-278	Conclusion	206-273	Conclusion

What has remained the same is what Lacy predicted: the basic structure and the relative placement of the deck of cards theme near the end, where it would be most effective.

But much else has changed. Even the phrasing of the deck of cards theme, which Lacy must have known quite well, was varied somewhat. The passage on the left is, again, from the 1967 version; that on the right from 1968. Each passage occurs near the middle of the sermon:

Ain't God all right?
And, God
Said there's two ways to go
Heaven
5 Or either hell
Mister Hoyle
Made a two-spot
He called it a deuce
God from Zion
10 And put it in the deck
And God
Made the Father
Son and the Holy Ghost
Ain't God all right?
15 And Mister Hoyle
Made a three-spot
And called it a trey

And Mister Hoyle knew God
    had two ways to go
Either heaven an'—or to hell
Mister Hoyle made a deuce
God from Zion
5 That—hmm—that meant either
    heaven or hell
And Mister Hoyle knew there
    was a three-Godheads
God the Father Son and the
    Holy Ghost
And he made a trey
God from Zion

Lacy's timing was poor in the second performance. He had poor musical rhythm that evening in 1968 and consequently his verbal rhythm was thrown off. He should have alternated between God's actions and those of Mister Hoyle: God makes a heaven and a hell, Hoyle makes a two-spot, etc., and when Hoyle makes a three-spot the formulaic construction should be similar:

Mister Hoyle
Made a two-spot
He called it a deuce

And Mister Hoyle
Made a three-spot
And called it a trey

Both of these passages are from the 1967 version quoted just above; they demonstrate the regularity of phrasing that aids (or perhaps results from) a regularized meter. In the 1968 version there was neither.

These characteristics of memory as well as the symbiotic relationship with the congregation must be accounted for in terms of the personal situations of the preachers at the times of performance. Lacy had good retention on the Four Horsemen theme when I asked him to recite it five weeks after its sermon performance. In his kitchen the meter was different, but he did have time to think about what he was going to say; one sure sign of Lacy's calm was the absence of the stall formulas. However, a year later, after three heart attacks and before an audience that did not inspire him, retention of the deck of cards section was less "accurate." The fact that it was still more repetitive than the two sermons of T. J. Hurley was due, I feel, to the latter's youth and his failure to fully master any of his sermons: Hurley simply did not compose sermons by the extensive use of traditional themes; his sermons were more amorphous, and when he did use themes they were not as well retained. In the two lines below we can see two of Hurley's syntactical variations of a single day:

> What is it that makes a man climb to the top of a tower and kill
>   thirty-two people in one day

> There's somethin' wrong
> When a man goes to the top of a tower
> In Austin Texas
> And murders thirty-two people in a matter of hours

The placement of these thematic lines also varied, the first example occurring near the beginning and the second near the end of the sermon. Typical of Hurley's use of metaphor is a traditional cluster that also appeared, as it happens, in the "Perilous Times" sermon on the afternoon of May 12; all have to do with the "armor of God":

> 340 The armor of God
> 480 The girdle of truth
> 532 The breastplate of righteousness
> 570 The sandals of preparation for the gospel of peace
> 623 The shield of faith
> 632 The helmet of salvation

As the line references show, the individual metaphors are widely scattered throughout the sermon, a suggestion that Hurley knew this metaphor sequence well. This time he undoubtedly did. Unlike the Texas tower murder theme, which he had himself thought of recently, the armor of God cluster is hundreds of years old and is likely to have been known by Hurley since he was a young boy. One is certain that it was memorized so thoroughly that it could be dissolved at Hurley's discretion and spread amidst 300 lines.

This examination of the fluctuations in the preacher's art over the course of a year may now conclude with a few remarks about the quality of repeated sermons. Unlike the ballad or the medieval romance, the sermon seems to have no rule governing its length in repeated versions. The Anglo-American ballad, we know, tends toward compression of episode; the romances frequently grow longer each time they are retold, owing to the inclination of medieval authors to amplify their stories with philosophical matter. But whether a sermon will be compressed or enlarged depends entirely on the immediate circumstances of the performance. We have seen the Reverend Mr. Hurley shorten a theme by more than half in a second performance as though he were "perfecting" it, yet another traditional complex of metaphors, the armor of God, was widely scattered. Lacy and Brown did the same things often; if their rhythm was erratic, or the audience dull, or the preacher uninspired, a brief theme could acquire a lot of fat and grow quite flabby.

The immediate circumstances will also determine the aesthetic quality of the sermon; there is just no telling how well any particular sermon is going to be performed. Lacy's favorite sermon, "The Deck of Cards," was beautifully performed in 1967, but was mediocre a year later. On the other hand, "God's Plowboy" was a failure when first performed but a success later. If any principle can be drawn from this it is that while preachers gradually improve the style of individual themes and sermons, they are subject to temporary failures and reversals at any time. These failures need not indicate a general trend; to determine that, we should have experience with a preacher's performances over the course of several years. During that time, even while improving, a preacher will still have poor days, just as one whose powers are failing will have occasional outstanding performances. The folklore of the preacher never deteriorates, but the level of performance may degenerate, as will be the case with a baseball player, an airline pilot, or a heroic baritone. Likewise, the texture of the preachers' folklore tends, if anything, to wax richer as they encounter and reflect upon more of the world, and this will be reflected in the richness of their sermons. But more noticeably, they will improve their techniques if they truly have the calling.

NOTES

1. Several experiments have been performed with repeated reproduction: F. C. Bartlett's is perhaps the best known (especially pp. 63–94 of *Remembering* [Cambridge, 1932]). But Bartlett did not use stories that were native to his subjects, who were in any event university students and not members of a homogeneous folk group. Most important, Bartlett's subjects read their material and then wrote it out so that their transmission was likely to be quite different from oral transmission. The informal experiments of Walter Anderson were also conducted in writing. And Albert Wesselski (*Versuch einer Theorie des Märchens*, Prager Deutsche Studien [Reichenberg, 1931]) used young girls rather than adult storytellers. The comparisons of the sermons in this study were of adult bearers of their own tradition orally transmitted. Bartlett allowed his subjects about thirty minutes between reception and transmission; the comparisons here were made, for the most part, eleven months apart. For a discussion of the achievement of fluency and the relationship of it to content and initial performance, see Frieda Goldman-Eisler, "Continuity of Speech Utterance, Its Determinants and Its Significance," *Language and Speech* 4 (1961), 220–31.

2. William Faulkner's description in *The Sound and the Fury* is quite accurate (New York, 1946), pp. 310–13.

3. A type of self-correction similar to Anderson's "Law." See also Goldman-Eisler, "Continuity of Speech," pp. 229–31.

4. F. C. Bartlett, "Some Experiments on the Reproduction of Folk Stories," reprinted in Alan Dundes, *The Study of Folklore* (New Jersey, 1965), p. 249, remarks that "relations of opposition, similarity, subjection, and the like, occurring in the original, are very commonly intensified. This forms one illustration of a deep-rooted and widespread tendency to dramatization." One might supplement Bartlett's observation by citing Axel Olrick's "Epic Law" of the tendency to polarize characters and their qualities in oral transmission—also reprinted in Dundes, pp. 135–37.

5. Bartlett, "Some Experiments," p. 249, found visual imagery readily retained and often intensified.

6. Cf. ibid. pp. 249–50: in repeated reproduction, elements that are forgotten are called "under potent"; the "normally potent" are repro-

duced; and the "over potent" will gain in importance. This is tauto-logical and merely supplies pseudo-scientific terms for what is observed, as though naming the phenomenon somehow explains it.

8

Pleasing as Well as Edifying

Every listener who has ever heard a traditional song or tale, from Heorot to Bosnia, from Ireland to India, has an idea whether the performance was a good one or a bad one. At the very least we can say that the audiences of traditional performances respond differently to those they like and those they don't, such aesthetic considerations are involved in the humblest rendering of an Appalachian folksong, in the *pjesma* chanted in Novi Pazar, and in the folk sermon.

The sermon's ostensible purpose is to edify, and that is the professed objective of every preacher I interviewed. However, aesthetic satisfaction is an important element of the recital, manifest in the performative style of many spontaneous, oral preachers, and in the responses of their congregations. Once into the sermon, the preacher accelerates the rhythm, and accentual stresses become distributed throughout the line as in singing (not a typographic line, of course, but acoustically, an utterance framed and punctuated for metrical purposes by the preacher: in a transcription it looks like a line established for print). Often a tonal center emerges. Preachers gradually increase rhythm and vocal intensity—occasionally pausing along the way while seeming to regain strength—until they are singing (or chanting melodically). At some self-determined emotional climax they will break off, reverting in their concluding remarks to normal, or near-normal, conversational prose.

The Reverend Otis McAllister did once state in an interview that the preacher must entertain as well as educate (the Renaissance ideal); unfortunately, he did not elaborate on his concept of entertainment. But certainly the aesthetic quality of chanted sermons is noticeable; after listening to a particularly poor sermon one afternoon in Bakersfield, poor in that the preacher's language never became metrical and was never chanted, a deacon remarked that the speaker was "teaching, not preaching." The sermon's message was a sound one, though conventional, and was delivered with clarity; but the preacher was "teaching" a message, and because his sermon had no aesthetic form, he was not—in the particular sense of the congregation—"preaching." Rev. Rubin Lacy summed up his idea of the sermon's form in two sentences: "You want to make the people glad twice: glad when you get up and glad when you sit down"; and, "When you've said enough, sit down."

Lacy was here reflecting on the architecture of the sermon. He was aware of the impact of gradually mounting rhythms and increasing vocal tensions in his sermon, and how they could be manipulated to fulfill a congregation. When an emotional climax was reached, Lacy had "said enough" and he would (one hoped) sit down. If the preacher's timing has been aesthetically correct, the congregation will have been satisfied aesthetically: they will be "glad." And thus, in anticipation of the preacher's next sermon, they will be glad when he gets up again to preach. Now to a certain extent this may seem abstractly unreal to the reader who has never experienced such sermons; specifically, the preacher's rhythm and timing and the emotion of the congregation. Unfortunately, there is no substitute for the real performance. On paper the reader (quite a different subject from the listener) will never experience what happens during performances of chanted sermons, and may question, for instance, that Rev. Mr. Lacy really meant what has been claimed. For this disbelief there is no evidence and little proof that print can provide: aside from immediate experience the matter must rest on descriptions and analyses of such sermons elsewhere and perhaps on fictionalized descriptions, such as the remarkably accurate one in Faulkner's *The Sound and the Fury*.[1]

The preachers' craft is no mean skill. We have seen how they develop sermons with great care, always with the congregation's emotions and emotional level in mind. But this is only one aspect of their aesthetic sense. Rhythm, the meter of a single line and its harmonious relationship to the lines of its environment, is perhaps the most important aspect of the preachers' musical talent. It is perpetuated with care in that it must be sustained. It must be consistent with its rhythmic environment; yet it must be used flexibly throughout the sermon to be effective. Preachers sustain, even develop, their rhythms to deepen their congregations' involvement in the performance; but they must have sufficient control to deflect or retard or even to smother the emotional response they have themselves largely created should they deem it necessary.

Only a few of the most talented performers can sustain the rhythm of their own delivery regardless of the congregation and its mood. There is an intricate symbiotic relationship at play during the performance of oral sermons, and preachers may often have to struggle to bring the audience to their emotional level—whether actual or desired—rather than descend to its. When sermons are chanted, the syntax and even the diction are largely determined by rhythm, and when the latter is faulty many other problems ensue.

The above considerations ignore the most obvious creative task facing preachers of spontaneous sermons, that of composing language. While they are sustaining rhythms or changing them, while they are considering the mood of the congregation and their relation to it, they are uttering more or less meaningful messages. The preachers' verbal tasks are remarkably difficult, and perhaps could be appreciated only by someone who has tried to deliver a lecture in iambic pentameter, singing most of the lines. As we know of all oral performers who recite rhythmically, the need to compose the next line is felt the very instant that the line of the moment is being uttered. And as we know from psycholinguists, preachers subjectively formulate not only the immediate line but perhaps the ideas and even the phrasing of several lines to come. Meanwhile they are encoding the ideas of the minute into a coherent syntactical unit, having already made several lexical choices.

But it is the audience and its response to the art of the folk preacher that is our chief concern in this chapter. The services of many Baptist and Methodist churches in the South are antiphonal, but such one-word descriptions are misleading. "Antiphonal" suggests that two entities are responding to each other, as might actors in a dialogue. It would be more accurate to say that in the services under study, congregation and preachers are not only responding to each other, but to themselves and to God. The preachers not only strive to move the congregation, they are moved by it. They may have to struggle to avoid falling to the dulled level of a listless audience. But when the congregation is "high" and the Spirit of the Lord has taken hold of the preacher, each becomes more withdrawn within his or her own experience. There is a point during the most successful services where manipulation or stimulation is no longer an issue, when the congregation has given itself to religious ecstasy, and is hardly aware of the preacher at all. In religious terms we say that at such moments the congregation has been consumed by the Spirit, and this is the avowed aim of the preacher. At such moments the congregation is not responding merely to the preacher, nor vice versa: they are both responding to the Holy Ghost. This is likely to assume various forms: shouting, clapping, dancing, foot tapping, and even speaking in tongues. The catharsis of classical literary theory occurs; and at the sermon's end the congregation will rest, nearly exhausted, exhilarated, thoroughly purged, their sins "washed away."

It is clear that to bring about this state the preacher must use what in secular terms may be called an aesthetically acceptable form for the presentation of the subject. In the chanted folk sermon the medium is nearly the message, and that message is almost entirely the rhythm. When oral performances are transcribed, the reader (who is no longer a listener) is confronted with a different medium. The language may appear lucid, though often simple, as was the case with sermons by Bakersfield's Rev. D. J. McDowell or Detroit's C. L. Franklin; often they were agrammatical jumbles, such as one often found in the sermons of Rev. Mr. Lacy. We murder to transcribe: in print the sermon does not seem to have rhythm, and certainly lacks the music and the cries of the congregation. If in this art the medium is the message, that message is in many ways nonverbal. James Weldon Johnson recalled that in his youth he attended services where the congregation was "moved to ecstasy by the rhythmic intoning of sheer incoherencies."[2]

One gets an entirely different viewpoint from the preacher, who insists that the sermon expresses an idea, or a series of them, and that it presents a rational point of theology. However, from my own observation of hundreds of services of oral, spontaneous preachers, there is more matter here than is dreamed of in the preacher's philosophy. The optimum mode for the presentation of data, theological or spiritual, in the case of the preacher, is prose. For clarity, precision, and explicitness prose is best suited. For one thing, chanting presents language too rapidly for the assimilation of logic, while prose allows the preacher time to develop ideas thoroughly and to clarify the message for the day. Since informational content is seldom interesting when repeated, the manuscript preacher must search weekly for new topics, or at least for novel ways of presenting traditional ones. But preachers who chant are much less concerned with new data: their messages are ever on the gospel, a point of pride with most Fundamentalists, and though they will vary their texts from day to day, not only is the number of biblical texts limited (and the favorites even more limited), but the number of moral themes that may be derived from them is decidedly restricted.

An audience raised with traditional literature is less concerned with data, with information, than one concerned with originality in art. In fact, in many tradition-oriented cultures novelty and invention are suspected of being unauthentic. The traditional audience does have certain expectations, however, and the native performer will avoid narrative surprise in order to exploit the listener's anticipations. Therein lies the artistry of the traditional performer. The congregations of the folk preachers come to church well prepared in several respects. Primarily they have read their Bibles and they know them well. The facility with which most churchgoing Fundamentalists can quote Scripture is amazing. Many of the congregation are deacons and Sunday school teachers, and a few may even preach occasionally themselves. In the Baptist and Methodist churches (at least) most of the congregation will have had experience in rendering testimonies, and so will have had experience not only in public performance but with the materials of edifying literature, particularly the exempla. With such an audience the preacher can also expect another vital element, an a priori preparation in subject matter, an interest—which is usually intense—in their religion and in the proceedings of their church; and one knows that they will have certain stylistic preconceptions about the performance of a sermon before they ever settle in their seats. Most people in the United States expect fairy tales to begin with "Once upon a time" and end with "They all lived happily ever after." Analogously, preachers know that they can stimulate certain conventional anticipations in the congregation: their opening remarks, their quotations from Scripture, the form and the melody of the entire piece and its parts, even some of the language itself.

In any traditional art where the narrative content and especially the ending are known, the performer relies heavily upon the aesthetics of form. James Weldon Johnson had listened to "sheer incoherencies"; yet the congregation was moved to ecstasy: in effect, the incoherencies were uttered successfully, and in all probability that meant aesthetically. Kenneth Burke showed long ago the various methods that the artist employs to manipulate the emotions of the audience.[3] The key is to gain a portion of the listeners' assent, to win over a portion of their will, to induce them to empathize with the performance, a skill that involves much more than a simple empathy between audience and artist. When this takes place, a portion of the listener assents to the will of the artist, giving the artist a great tactical advantage. If preachers, through chanting and rhythm, can induce the congregation to tap its feet, to clap hands, to nod heads and to sway to the rhythm, they have gained an important measure of persuasion—nonverbal to be sure—over it. When the congregation sways in unison, it has already given its leader a measure of its belief and of itself; in church, where the intellectual content—the doctrine—is already an established matter of faith, and that usually unassailable, the preachers' information content will not be nearly so important as their rhythm.

When the performance is viewed as an interaction between preachers and their congregations, the oral sermon may be said to be an ego-manifestation in that the preachers are striving for the assent of the audience: they want to impose their will upon it, and this act is thus antisocial. However, their activity is expressed within the confines of a "controlled" situation; the preachers' emotions are not controlled (quite the contrary), but limited by the direction the aggression takes, namely an attack on the devil, or wickedness, or merely "bad" people. It is both ironic and fortunate that the preachers' success in their sermons tends to nullify their influence over the audience in that the audience too is at first responding actively (aggressively); but when the Spirit moves the people, the influence of the preachers wanes. The preachers too may become less concerned with the audience in the later stages and with imposing their will on it: they will already have gotten it "high" and may tend to withdraw into their own ecstasy. Meanwhile, the audience has been exerting influence, guiding the rhythm, calling out responses that indicate its responsiveness, and its mood will often influence not only the preachers' language (as in such formulas as "Gettin' quiet in here, isn't it?"), but the length and quality of the performance. Thus the congregation's aggressiveness is also channeled through proper outlets and becomes socially acceptable.

The congregation also assents to the preacher's melody, and becomes a part of the service by that much more. Each preacher has a personal style of music: at the most intense moments of performance chanting becomes markedly melodic, and can be so notated. Certain lexical collocations of which the preacher is particularly fond may be consistently sung to the same melody, indicating that the preacher often makes a close identification between specific verbal units and certain lyrics. Congregation members anticipate their minister by a second or two, often singing a brief melody that the preacher has not yet begun. In this anticipation as well is the congregation committing a further portion of its belief to its preacher.

In traditional art, we have said, there is no suspense and no surprise. The auditor is satisfied aesthetically because of a sense of the logic and justness of procedure, the inherent dignity of it, and because of the final fulfillment of traditional expectations. Those expectations can be satisfied on the level of narrative, as when the master finally returns and casts out the lazy servant who merely buried his talents. Kenneth Burke suggests the scene in which Hamlet dallies with Guildenstern about the latter's "game-playing" with the prince, and then hands him the pipes to play upon.[4] To this one might add the retardation and thwarting of the lyric in Wagner's *Tristan and Isolde* until the final scene when the full melody is finally presented though the lovers are now dead; or the rescue of the Russian secret agent in Hitchcock's *Topaz*, when the escape is several times thwarted only to succeed at the last moment and under the most adverse circumstances, with time running out and the NKVD moving in. Such dramatic moments also occur in sermons; and as an illustration a passage from a sermon delivered by the Reverend C. L. Franklin is used. Moses and the Jews are at the Red Sea, but for Franklin their goal is not the physical crossing: it is rather the recognition that the power to overcome adversity lies within the individual. Here that individual is named Moses:

> And here they were standing on the brinks of the Red Sea
> Here they were, when they looked behind them
> They heard the rattling of the chariot wheels
> Of Pharoah who had regretted/ his decree of deliverance
> 5 And decided to recapture them/ and lead them back/ into the
>   oppression of Egypt.
> When they looked on either side/ mountains prevented their
>   escape
> When they looked before them the Red Sea/ and its perils loomed
>   large/ before their imagination
> I don't believe you know what I'm talkin' about
> And the very same folk who had praised Moses
> 10 For his valor and for his bravery
> For his courage for his insight
> For his great victory of deliverance
> Began to complain
> And Moses said to them stand still
> 15 And see the salvation of the Lord
> I don't believe you know what I'm talkin' about
> Stand still
> Sometime you know we can get in not only our own way
> And everybody else's way
> 20 But it seems sometime we can get in God's way

Stand still
My God I heard Him say the thing you need
Is in your hands
I don't believe you know what I'm talkin' about
²⁵ The instrument of deliverance
Is within your hands
It's within your possession
The-the-the way out
The powers that need to be brought into exertion
³⁰ Is within you
Good God
What are y' cryin' about Moses
What are y' lookin' for
What do y' think that y' want
³⁵ Why the rod of your deliverance is in your own hands
Stretch out the rod that's in your hand
I don't have a new rod to give y'
I don't have a new instrument to give y'
I don't have a new suggestion for y'
⁴⁰ I do not have a new plan
Your course has already been charted by destiny
Stretch out the rod that's in your hand[5]

The plot is simple: about to make good their escape, the Jews, who are trapped, complain to Moses, who is in turn exhorted by Franklin to seek within himself the strength to overcome this new adversity. But within these forty-two lines Franklin thwarts our expectation for an easy solution again and again, turning this way and that, presenting physical obstacles and verbal, gradually building up our anticipations and our suspense over formal considerations (since we know that Moses and the Jews must escape).

Line 1 and the first clause of line 2 briefly set the scene: from the preceding portion of the sermon we know who "they" are. The next lines further describe the situation and somewhat build suspense in speaking of the approach of Pharoah, who has brought his army to recapture the Jews, whose escape is blocked by the water in front of them and the mountains on either side.

The next nine lines (9-17) describe the situation in the Israelite camp. The Jews panic; those same people who had previously praised Moses for his many virtues now begin to complain of their plight. But Moses merely orders them to "stand still/ And see the salvation of the Lord." Franklin has here reached a lesser climax, for in a sense the action of the plot is over, culminating in the exemplum's message. More than mere written language can show, Franklin's intonation indicates this climax.

But he moves on; the next twenty-three lines (18-40) discuss over and over again the spiritual advice of the preacher in such situations, all the while retarding the action, while the congregation awaits Moses' next move. Of course they know what it must be eventually, but they do not know what Franklin will say has caused Moses to act, or when he will finally act, or how long the preacher will withhold that information. And while this other kind of suspense is developing within them, they will come to look at the retardation not as a hindrance to pleasure but as something pleasurable in itself.

This passage of Franklin's also contains within it a felicitous instance of fulfilled form, giving the sermon one of its lesser dramatic consummations within the larger framework of the entire performance. Such momentary peaks within oral sermons are frequent, because many experienced preachers work toward fruition through a series of them rather than directly. Line 36 ("Stretch out the rod that's in your hand") is the culmination of the preceding fourteen lines. In the performance as Franklin recited it, the line also relaxed the tension somewhat, though that was to be immediately resumed. The bridge to the next line, "I don't have a new rod to give y'," is provided by "rod." With this line a new anaphoric sequence begins, which gradually rises in intensity to line 39, "I don't have a new suggestion for y'." The argument that new formulas are created by analogy with old ones looks formidable in this series.

Although the three anaphoric lines (37-39) scan differently, Franklin's interpretation renders them nearly identical in tone and meter. By doing so he establishes a metric pattern that arouses an anticipation in the congregation that is largely fulfilled in the hypometric line, "I do not have a new plan." The line, as chanted, and as its break in the pattern established by the previous lines indicates, closes out the sequence. But Franklin is not satisfied to end on an abrupt note, and so he adds a denouement to this sequence that relaxes the tension that the anaphoric lines developed, "Your course has already been charted by destiny." Then he concludes by returning to the language of line 36: "Stretch out the rod that's in your hand." Again, the transcription is important to express the finality with which this line is uttered, but the semantic fulfillment—the answer to Moses's problem—is communicated.

Lines 18-21 are Franklin's commentary on the panic of the Jews and perhaps on the implied hesitation of Moses: sometimes we get in our own way, everyone else's way; sometimes we even get in God's way. The right way is the way of faith, it is (how unlike contemporary society) to stand still. Now Franklin shifts his attention directly to the congregation (lines 22-30), explicating the previous few lines and then applying them to daily life. And finally, in another apostrophe, he again shifts focus and addresses Moses, giving him the ultimate command, further elaborating his message, retarding the action for yet another instant. The last two lines summarize the advice, and repeat the call to action. Now Moses is allowed to save his people.

Audience participation and anticipation also occur on the level of rhetoric and the individual line. For instance, when the Reverend J. Charles Jessup begins his defiant challenge, "Take it," the audience expects the concluding, "or leave it." So with "Like it" and "or lump it." Expectations here are based on the frequency with which this pattern and these particular words are used in ordinary speech. The reaction will be the same when Rev. Rubin Lacy says that God "Know all about you"; the congregation will have an inkling that "Seed everything you do" (or some line closely approximating it) will follow. And the latter having been uttered, the congregation will, however unconsciously, expect the next line; in an aesthetic sense they will actually demand it: "Hear everything you say," or else their sense of balance and proportion will be upset.

Much the same expectation will be found in such extended series as that of Rev. T. J. Hurley:

> He said oh Lord
> It's not my will
> It's not my way

It's not my thoughts
5 It's not my ideas
It's not my opinion
It's not my theories
It's not what I think
It's not what I do
10 It's not what I say
No God it's Your will be done

The expectations of the congregation for a denouement are developed in more than one way in this series. "It's not my will" may evoke a slight anticipation for the following line, which, properly, retains the same syntax, changing only the most important word—suitably placed last—by substituting an alliterative. Experiments suggest that we retain the rhythm of language even more readily than the words, and we may speculate (not wildly therefore) that the rhythms of such series as "It's not my will/ It's not my way" involve the audience as much as the lexical anticipation. The length of the entire series may vary somewhat without substantially altering the demand that the series end with the assertion that "No God it's Your will be done." Aphoristically, then, rhythm creates belief, further involving the congregation in its own religious experience, an experience that is essentially metrical, not semantic.

What we have just said is similar to an observation made years ago by William Butler Yeats on the role of rhythm in symbolic poetry (quoted above on p. 65).[6] Yeats sought to communicate symbolically with his audience; preachers seek to gain the assent of their congregation so that eventually it may commune independently with its God.

The well-preached sermon intensifies steadily, sometimes with appropriate moments of relaxation, both in tone and rhythm. The emotions of the congregation determine the form of the sermon. More than with the telling of a folktale or the chanting of a heroic song (the Yugoslav "epics" are folktales chanted metrically with an instrumental accompaniment), the aesthetic goal of the sermon is not merely an arbitrary break in its linear development—when the congregation is appropriately "high"—but the climax is its culmination, its fruition.

At the moment of denouement in the chanted sermon the congregation is purged of its tensions, or if you will, is at peace in the bosom of the Lord. If preachers gauge the reactions of their flocks aright, they will break off. As Lacy put it: "When you've said enough, you ought to know when to sit down." The same sense of aesthetic timing holds true, at least on the level of individual lines, for the Yugoslavian *guslar*, for European tellers of tales, and presumably for other transmitters of oral art. In the way in which performers interact with their audiences we can ignore the tremendous difference in the surface structure and texture of narrative: the deeds of Marko Kraljevic differ vastly from those of John the Bear or King David, but in the recounting of each of their stories the performer will be appealing to similar psychic patterns within the audience.

NOTES

1. See Bruce A. Rosenberg, "The Oral Quality of Rev. Shegog's Sermon in William Faulkner's *The Sound and the Fury*," *LWU* 2 (1969), 73–87.

2. James Weldon Johnson, *God's Trombones* (New York, 1948), p. 5.

3. Kenneth Burke, *Counter-Statement* (Berkeley, 1968), especially the essay, "Psychology and Form."

4. Ibid., p. 35.

5. Chess Records "Sermon Series" 19. Recorded at New Bethel Baptist Church, Detroit, Mich.

6. W. B. Yeats, *Ideas of Good and Evil* (London, 1903), pp. 247–48.

9

Concluding Thoughts

Amidst a dense technology, the sermons of some American preachers are composed with the aid of syntactical units that resemble in conception the formulas and themes used by other oral performers around the world. The oral tradition of composition, far from dying out under the relentless "disease" of literacy, actually flourishes alongside learning in one of the most highly literate countries in the world. In fact, in several ways this oral tradition exploits literacy. The ability to read and write does not seem to hinder the oral tradition at all. For instance, by far the most popular preachers are now in urban areas: the late C. L. Franklin's Detroit congregation (whose literacy is presumably higher than people in rural mountain regions) numbered over one thousand. More and more revivalists visit the major cities of the Northeast and Midwest more frequently each year. But specifically, literacy seems to have little to do with the sermon style of the men observed during this research. Lacy did not have more than a year or two of formal education. Brown got through grade school in Arkansas; Hanner, in Virginia; and Ratliff, in North Carolina. McAllister had been to a seminary; and Manning attended classes at the University of Oklahoma. But the most heavily formulaic sermon recorded was that of McDowell, who had college training, with two years at the Linda Vista Seminary in San Diego.

The Reverend Mr. McDowell was born in Giddings, Texas, and had an extensive singing career that included stints with the Alabama Blind Boys. At one time he formed his own group, the Southland Singers. These are the details of his life that along with his early interest in and frequent attendance at church are most relevant to his sermon style. Like nearly all the ministers interviewed, McDowell "fought" serving God, in his own case for seventeen years. At ten he wanted to be a singer; and his singing ability was not wasted in the ministry. That McDowell wrote, that his study was lined with books (which he read), was irrelevant to his sermon style; it was irrelevant to his formulaic composition. What was pertinent was that McDowell's congregation demanded that his sermons be metrical, that he grew up amidst the chanted sermon tradition, and that not only was this style an engrained part of his background, but he believed it to be the most effective way to communicate the Word of God.

Although literacy does not destroy this type of sermon, often when sermons or parts of them are read the results are poor. Almost always the rhythm is broken; the reading is usually poorly executed; the preacher's voice lacks conviction, naturally enough, for most writing is unconcerned with metrics; poetry is an obvious exception. When spiritual preachers read a sermon, they have to translate the prose on the page into the metrics of delivery, and with all their other concerns of the moment, the translation is too difficult. We may profit by examining a portion of a sermon delivered by the Reverend Mr. Goins, unaffiliated, of Bakersfield (June 20, 1967), which begins with the preacher reading from Genesis 1:1 ff. (preceded by apologies to the congregation for Goins's poor eyesight). Goins soon breaks into a chant:

> In the beginning God created the heaven and earth
> The earth was without form and void
> And the darkness was upon the face of the deep
> And there wasn't no light to be seen nowhere
> 5 And—uh—God said let there be light and—uh—there was light
> And—uh—God saw the light and it was good
> And—uh—God divided light from the darkness
> And the light He called day/ and the darkness He called night
> And the evenin' and the mornin' were the first day
> 10 And God—God said let dry land appear

And—uh—bent down and scooped up the mountain/ with His hand
And—uh—thought of the sea
And—uh—gathered the water together/ in one place
And gathered the water together/ He called it the sea
15 Umm-hmm now now now now umm-hmm
And God tooken this water together/ into one place
He made the great rivers and He made the fishes uhh-uhh
And put them in the sea
And He made every living creature
20 That creeped upon the earth uhh-uhh
He made the beastes of the forest uhh-huh that's right
He made green grass
And He made green trees
And all the beautiful flowers

After reading a few lines from the text, Goins prefers to tell the story his own way, and so fits the words and the rhythm of Genesis to his own metrical style, one that is in his case much like the camp and cornfield "hollers" (on file at the Library of Congress).[1] In this excerpt we can see (hear!) Goins making formulas spontaneously. He could read, like nearly all of his fellow pastors; but he could not read well while preaching—like nearly all of his fellow preachers. Lacy is an even better example of the way in which the spiritual style deteriorates when the preacher tries to read a sermon, or large parts of it (his sermon on "God's Plowboy" is printed below along with the text from which it derived). The spiritual sermon, then, must be composed spontaneously and is not effective when print-prepared; spiritual preachers cannot mix performative modes in the same recitation effectively. They might write out the sermon in verse—but never do.

Literacy becomes a deterrent to oral recitation only when preachers try to read their sermons; when this happens the effect is often discordant. Almost always the preachers' rhythm within each line becomes erratic and they lose metrical consistency. Spiritual preachers have been recorded who can read aloud effectively, but for the most part such attempts fail: forced to rely on an established text, they cannot make the adjustment between stress for sound's sake and for the sake of meaning. Those few spiritual preachers who occasionally use manuscripts do not write their sentences to facilitate oral delivery, yet their thrust during performance is toward metrics. Hence the failure comes about because the two modes have not been reconciled; literacy, per se, has nothing to do with it.

When spiritual preachers read their sermons, only part of the performance comes from the prepared manuscript. The preachers eventually break away from the printed page and into their "natural" style; Lacy, who was uncomfortable with manuscripts, would begin to extemporize early in the performance, while the Reverend T. R. Hanner, who had more practice with texts, would generally wait until he was well into the day's message. In both instances, however, the chanting emerged toward the end of the sermon, for again rhythm, not merely the words themselves, is necessary to "make the Spirit of God" move in the congregation. Even within the same performance the preacher can both read prosaically and recite formulaically; the reading is usually inferior metrically (but not necessarily so), but nothing in the preacher's literacy level causes a poor reading performance. The trouble in such cases is always that the preacher does not know the text well enough to take liberties with conventional syntax so as to render it metrically. Some preachers can adapt well-known passages of Scripture to their own meters without any difficulty; but for the most part preachers cannot even adapt their own written words simply because they do not know them well enough.

One final example before moving on: so strong is the tendency toward rendering the sermon in metrics that in one instance, though the sermon had been written by the preacher himself for presentation to his congregation, before he had finished he had broken away from his own prose and had begun to chant. The Reverend T. R. Hanner (of Proffit, Virginia) was my unique example, though doubtless the same thing would happen if more spiritual preachers wrote out their material. To Hanner not even his own writing was fixed, and since to him his medium was his message as much as his words, he could sacrifice the meter of his prose to the "Spirit of God." At his home he may have thought in prose, but behind the pulpit he reverted to his traditional metrics. The following prose is from Hanner's holograph:

Then was Nebuchanezzer full of fury, and the form on his face was changed against the three men, so he ordered that they should heat the furnace seven times hotter. And he commanded the most mighty of his army to bind the three men, and cast them into the burning furnace.

Behind the pulpit, however, Hanner chanted the lines:

> I can see the old king when he ordered
> That their furnace be [heated?]
> Or heated seven times hotter
> They tell me that he sent for the three strong men
> 5 The strongest men from his army
> He'd taken these men in and bound them
> Hand and feet

This tradition is a subtle chemistry of the art and the individual talent. As with Lord's epic singers, the tradition of spiritual preaching is kept alive by the constant re-creation of it. But unlike Lord's *guslars*, the preachers have some sacred texts that cannot be altered. That is not to say that Bible stories cannot be told in different ways—we have seen quite an individual version of Genesis—but that David must always slay Goliath, Christ is always the Son of God, and always in the beginning God makes the heaven and the earth.

The tradition is also kept alive in its verbal aspects by the repeated use of shared language. From the Bible preachers get not only their theology, not only their exempla and narratives, but many of their formulas: "You shall know the truth/ And the truth shall make you free." Even "Amen" is used formulaically. Gospel songs and those from the Baptist hymnal, widely sung and long in the public domain, provide many another formula: "I'm glad about it," "After a while," "Am I right about it?" Still others come from the clichéd rhetoric of oratory: "I want to call your attention to the fact that," "I say unto you tonight," or "I want you to know this evening." These seem to me to be some of the most influential sources, though they by no means account for a majority of the preacher's formulas. All these sources are agents of conformity of diction. Within the tradition there is a great deal of freedom and considerable liberty in the sermon's syntax.

The source of most formulas is the everyday speech of the preachers and their world: family, congregation, friends, preachers they hear on radio and in other churches, and songs they sing. Esoteric diction provides only a very small part of the preachers' sermonizing vocabulary: Edmund Blair's favorite refrain formula, "God from Glory," for instance, was (so far as I know) peculiar to him. Lacy claimed to have invented "Hark Hallelujah," and Brown had his own preferences. Such language is not casual or conversational, while for the most part the refrains and stalls arise from everyday speech. McDowell admitted that he had learned something from every man he had ever heard.

The individualizing diction, then, of American spiritual preachers is derived from their own idiolects of American English. The diction is not as varied as is common usage in vocabulary, syntax, or flexibility. It is a specially ordered subgroup of southern American English, specially ordered because of its simplicity, its attention to meter, and its ecclesiastical lexicon. It is, however, contained within the parameters of usage common to most of us.

Yet few of us could stand up in front of one of the congregations in question and deliver an oral sermon for twenty minutes or half an hour. Showmanship aside, most of us do not "speak the language" though we know all the words and all the combinations of words. We do not know, in other words, the special poetic grammar.

To begin with, conversational speech is not concerned with metrics. That, more than any other factor, sets aside the grammar of the spiritual preacher. Lexical concentration on the Bible is heavy, as would be expected; all the words themselves (some proper nouns aside) are of common usage, but some appear more frequently than would be the case in conversation: "church," "God," "preacher," "heaven." Curiously, "love" is seldom used; this is a faith among blacks of endurance and of suffering, but not of love primarily. The gospel songs have contributed much, but again the words themselves are common; it is their combinations, and the frequent repetition of those combinations, that set sermon diction aside: "every now and then," "I want to wear the crown," "I'm glad about it."

Periodic sentences are spoken often enough in English, but they occur less frequently during sermons, because (as has been discussed) of the demands placed on preachers of spontaneous matter. The preachers utter a line at a time; one line is quite enough for them to handle, and in most periodic sentences a subordinate and a main clause are involved. In oral recitation governed by metrics the preacher is on safer ground with non-periodic sentences. Among the men recorded the tendency was also away from Latinate words and polysyllables. In some instances the cause was quite simply a weak vocabulary. One suspects this to have been the case with Lacy, for instance, and even though such a word as "redemption" was used once in a while in his sermons, it is likely that its importance as a doctrinal word had caused its retention. Polysyllables are avoided, again, not only because of a modest vocabulary, but because such words are more difficult to handle in the metrical context. McDowell and Franklin (and many others) were well educated and knew—and used—polysyllables in conversation, but for the most part kept their language simple on the pulpit. If questioned about it, preachers say that it is easier to communicate with their congregations in monosyllables since they have to speak the language of their flocks.

For the spiritual preacher the ocean is the ocean, not the "swan's road" or the "linnet's bath." David is a king, not a "giver of rings." And Herod is a tyrant and not a "thrall maker." Yet we can say that the oral preachers' language is distinctive enough to speak of a special diction. There are no dawns painting the East with rosy fingers, but neither in Homer is there a Judas "crooked as a barrel of snakes."

As concerns the formula, whatever implications this study may have for other oral literatures, of this fact we may be certain: the great individual talent of American spiritual preachers lies not in their memorization of a special diction or of thousands of formulaic systems, but in their ability to compose spontaneously the vocabulary at their command to fit their metrical patterns. The Bible, gospel songs, and the English of the American South provide most of the basic molds; the preachers fill them as the need arises. They rely, of course, on certain retained stall and stimulant formulas, and even on certain ways of introducing narrative and of carrying it along, but for the most part what they say is structured by the grammar of their community. Transformational grammarians can formulate the structures of English; a less complicated, but entirely compatible, equation could be devised for the oral preachers. As for their vocabulary register, one begins again with the English language, and gradually reduces the register with successive overlays: southern dialect/black English (if applicable)/ministerial lexicon/and the limits imposed by meter.

In view of what has been said about the frequent repetition of refrain and other formulas, any theory about their spontaneous creation needs further clarification. Many such formulas as "Ain't God all right" and "I want you to know this evenin'" seem to be memorized; their function—that of allowing the preacher time to think of what he will say next—depends upon their unreflective delivery. Yet the vast majority of phrases within most sermons are not refrain formulas: McDowell used a limited number of syntactic patterns, but Lacy, Brown, Freeman, and most of the others studied used far more. Often syntactical patterns are repeated but it is questionable whether the syntax is repeated or whether what is "memorized" is an abstract pattern of English grammar. I have opted for the latter.

We should be skeptical of the argument that if many more of, say, Brown's sermons were available on tape, or on paper, and were compared with a far greater sample of his preaching, even seemingly unique phrases would be found to be "formulaic." This is hypothetically possible, of course, but what would such an exhaustive study prove? Only that the English language is finite in the possibilities of its syntactical structure, and that the preachers, because of their often limited education and the further limitation imposed on them by the metrics of their art, are thus limited in their syntactical possibilities.

Any formulas that one claimed to be unique might be variants of those not yet collected: the theoretical possibility must be admitted. In the following passage the Reverend Rufus Hays of Virginia was preaching on the One Hundred and Sixteenth Psalm when he erred and referred to the psalmist David. He was able to correct himself without changing his meter or rhythm; I find it unbelievable that such self-correction of a spontaneous error could have been planned or that Hays had memorized formulas to cope with such a situation:

David
I gotta move on
As he uttered these words
He lay upon a sickbed
5 Oh I don't mean David I mean
The psalmist
If I don't make it correct me
The Bible didn't say it was David
I'm just sorta used t'
10 The greatest psalms of David
When I got on the Psalms I almost
Go right on—carryin' on about David
But seventy-three psalms
Is credited by us to David
15 And many other psalms in the Samuels
And the other Scriptures about David
But this was just another psalmist

We have seen above an instance of the Reverend Mr. Goins reading from Genesis and translating the prose of the Bible into metrical formulas as he read. Nearly all of the preachers could do the same with greater or lesser proficiency. The point is that such ability is a further demonstration that formulas are creations of the moment to a great extent, and that the spiritual preachers' genius lies in their ability to intuitively recite metrical lines. That ability is the most important lesson they learn about preaching.

The content of their preaching is stabilized because their texts are sacred; the preachers' individual styles, their preferences for particular melodies, rhythms, formulas, and themes continually recreate the tradition within a Christian framework that is very much alive today.

Both preacher and congregation respond (often to each other) alternatively throughout the sermon, but the latter's is not a wooden response to an aloof high priest, nor are the roles played by each party equal. In the most effective sermons both preacher and congregation are responding to each other and influencing each other, while ultimately they are identifying with the Spirit. In these sermons there is an intimate symbiotic relationship between pastor and flock: that the preacher leads them—by selecting the subject of the sermon and to a certain extent by the proficiency of the performance—is obvious. What needs to be emphasized is the active role of the audience in such performances. We have seen how it determines the length of the sermon: if it is bored, the sermon is likely to be cut short; and if the audience is caught up in the passion of the moment, it may induce a preacher to extend the moments of ecstasy. Further, the congregation can improve the quality of the preacher's performance by its active participation in the service: it urges on, encourages, and infects the preacher with its cries, its clapping, its tapping.

The situation is not quite the same as Melville Jacobs found among the Clackamas.[2] Brevity to the extent that he found is not desirable here; nearly all of the congregation know the stories from the Bible and the traditional exempla that the preacher is going to recite, and they are familiar with many of the sermons. Obviously they like hearing these stories over again, just as the preacher likes them and makes them the focus and the structural basis of sermons, and they no doubt are comforted by the moral implicit (or explicit) in each tale. There is comfort not only in familiar and reassuring stories, but in familiar words ritually intoned to well-known music, all of which must immediately stimulate feelings of solace and release because of many years of association with such phenomena in the church. Repetition alone does not comfort, but repetition of the meaningful does. Often the congregation knows what words are coming next, or if they do not know precisely they are not surprised, as with all oral literature. Occasionally they can anticipate, as I have pointed out, even the music of the line to come.

A great deal of the appeal of this kind of service is that it frees the minds of the audience from concern with what language, music, or story element is to come next, and so they are freer to involve themselves with the rhythm and the music and the emotion of the performance. Consequently, the audience is freer for active participation in the service, participation that is expressed in cries of joy, in clapping, in dancing, or whatever. Both the knowledge of the performance and the freedom to participate in it thus allow the congregation members to participate in the service and the sermon individually while they are expressing that individuality publicly; through their own singing, shouting, and clapping, the church members are to a certain degree creating their own service. Not only are they, by their active participation in the service, influencing the preacher in several ways, but they are creating a personal religious experience and expressing it while the rest of the congregation are creating theirs. They are all a part of the sermon, and every bit as much as the preacher. The preacher leads, it is true, in providing the subject for the day, and is the most influential member in the church's rhythm, but often the music of the congregation is individual, as will be their cries of joy.

Self-expression aloud in public is always implicitly (and sometimes explicitly) encouraged; singing and toe tapping are acknowledged as a sign that the worshiper is sincere and certainly "got the Spirit." Reticence, thoughtfulness, or emotional reserve is always somewhat suspect; the quiet person is not thought to be "moving with the Lord." The good sermon, then, the effective one, is the sermon that moves and that best allows the congregation to partake of the Spirit of the Lord with the preacher.

And as long as good sermons can be preached there is hope that the tradition can survive. After listening to spiritual preaching for several weeks, one can easily and without mental strain judge a good sermon and a bad one. The congregation will also intuitively judge; they will know infallibly because in a sense they are the ultimate arbiters. If the congregation is not moved, the sermon has failed. It is almost as simple as that. And a congregation is moved, as most of us are, to great excitement by the gradually increasing rhythm and intensity of words movingly spoken. The response of a black congregation is the learned response of people who live with a rich heritage of rhythmic music and rhythmic sermons. They are musical because they have been brought up with music. As long as mothers bring their children to church each Sunday and bounce them on their knees in time with the preacher one would expect the heritage to perpetuate itself.

Repetition not only comforts, of course, but it adds to the mounting emotional intensity nearly as much as does rhythm. Lord has pointed out that the need to formulate the next line is upon singers before they have finished the line of the moment;[3] thus they are more inclined to build their narratives in patterns

of sequences, called the parallelism of oral style. So it is from
the preacher's point of view; the effect on the other side of the
pulpit can be just as striking. Idea builds upon idea, image builds
upon image as a series of incremental repetitions increases in
emotional pitch.[4] As an illustration I quote first from a radio
sermon by J. Charles Jessup on the crucifixion; his extremely
rapid delivery urges him toward parallel developments:

> Oh my friends upon that cross of Calvary Jesus died for you and
>   me
> While blood flowed from His hands
> While blood flowed from His feet
> While blood flowed from His sword-pierced side
> 5 While blood flowed from His forehead
> While blood flowed down upon that rocky crag of Golgotha's heel
> . . . .
> The sun hid His face
> The moon blushed in kind of total darkness
> The rocks were rent in twain
> 10 The veil in the temple was rent

And to give a better idea of the parallelism of the chanted
sermons I would like to quote once again the section from the
Reverend C. L. Franklin's famous sermon "Moses at the Red
Sea":

> And here they were standing there on the brinks of the Red Sea
> Here they were, when they looked behind them
> They heard the rattling of the chariot wheels
> Of Pharoah who had regretted/ his decree of deliverance
> 5 And decided to recapture them/ and lead them back/ into the
>   oppression of Egypt
> When they looked on either side/ mountains prevented their
>   escape
> When they looked before them the Red Sea/ and its perils loomed
>   large/ before their imagination
> I don't believe you know what I'm talkin' about
> And the very same folk who had praised Moses
> 10 For his valor and for his bravery
> For his courage for his insight
> For his great victory of deliverance

Began to complain
And Moses said to them stand still
¹⁵ And see the salvation of the Lord
I don't believe you know what I'm talkin' about
Stand still
Sometime you know we can get in not only our own way
And everybody else's way
²⁰ But it seems sometimes we can get in God's way
Stand still
My God I heard Him say the thing that you need
Is in your hands
I don't believe you know what I'm talkin' about
²⁵ The instrument of deliverance
Is within your hands
It's within your possession
The-the-the way out
The powers that need to be brought into exertion
³⁰ Is within you
Good God
What are y' cryin' about Moses
What are y' lookin' for
What do y' think that y' want
³⁵ Why the rod of your deliverance is in your own hands
Stretch out the rod that's in your hand
I don't have a new rod to give y'
I don't have a new instrument to give y'
I don't have a new suggestion for y'
⁴⁰ I do not have a new plan
Your course has already been charted by destiny

Parallelism occurs in clusters. In line 32 Franklin asks Moses
a rhetorical and expository question ("What are y'. . ."), then
follows it with another question that uses the same syntax and
the same first three words. The third question begins to break
the pattern, retaining only the first word: "What do y' think."
Line 35 is a transition, though retaining the syntax and much of
the diction of lines 25-26; the questions of the preceding three
lines are answered and new elements are introduced: the rod and
the fact that Moses has the power to deliver himself. Line 37

carries through on both of these new elements: "I don't have a new rod to give y'." The next two lines follow the same syntax, retain much of the diction, and convey the given essential idea. Line 40 begins to break the pattern, especially as concerns diction and syntax, and line 41 has broken completely and moved on to a new idea. In this passage we can see the formulation of parallelism and the creation of new formulas from extant systems. The oral tradition is alive so long as the preacher's imagination is alive, as long as he can continue to create within the existing limits of that tradition.

Rev. C. L. Franklin's narrative serves as an excellent illustration of one tenet of oral composition: that at least as important as the formula and the theme is association, creating new formulas by adjusting the patterns of the old. The trend in Old English scholarship is away from concentration on the formula to an understanding of the formulaic system, the mold from which various related formulas are formed. This study rejects the contention of some scholars that all lines within sermons are formulaic,[5] and suggests instead that they may actually be recreated anew for each performance. To be specific, I cite lines 25-27 from Franklin's sermon on "Moses at the Red Sea":

> The instrument of deliverance
> Is within your hands
> It's within your possession

Now the line, "It's within your possession" is formed by analogy, and doubtless its use at this particular moment, its diction and syntax, in a word the distinct qualities of its creation, were largely dictated by the context and especially by the preceding line. Semantically it is similar to (though a generalization of) the line before it, "Is within your hands." It is very hard to believe that once Franklin had uttered line 26, which in turn completes the sentence begun in line 25, he had not paved the way, in however slight the microsecond, for line 27. Even supposing that line 27 was a memorized formula, it is hard to think of it in its relative position isolated from the preceding line, which is so similar.

At work here is the psychological association of many factors: diction, syntax, and the logic of the sermon. In these lines Franklin tells us that Moses holds the power of his own deliverance;

the next three lines in the sermon (28-30) say nearly the identical thing—that the necessary powers are within Moses:

> The-the-the way out
> The powers that need to be brought into exertion
> Is within you

The associative link between these three lines and those that preceded it is thematic: they express the same essential idea. But Franklin has used different language in saying it. He did not do so simply in order to vary his phrasing and so please his congregation, but rather, because his mind, like those of others of whatever genius, is nevertheless finite and could not advance at once along every front: semantic, syntactical, lexical. By retaining the meaning of the preceding three lines, he is more easily able to concentrate on changing his syntax and diction. Here, meaning provides a bridge. Thus the oral style's leisurely pace ensures the listener's comprehension as well as aids the preacher.

Franklin's construction provides the key to spontaneous oral composition, a principle to which our theories of formula and system may be subordinated. To understand oral composition we have to go beyond the level of formula creation and somewhat beyond the Parry-Lord theory. Once more, the experiments of Professor Goldman-Eisler on the context of spontaneous speech are helpful.[6] She distinguishes between "subjective" speech, in which thoughts are encoded into words, and the planning of the content, grammar, and diction in the physical utterance of "objective" speech.

The context of the oral performance bears upon speakers—preachers or otherwise—in at least two ways, for while they are objectively uttering sounds, they not only have recall of what they have already said, but they are subjectively forming the ideas, and though somewhat vaguely, perhaps the syntax and the diction ahead. This subjective preparation of future lines may not be very precise—one has no way of testing how vague or how specific such subjective composition may be, but certainly the speaker has at least a general idea of what he or she intends to utter shortly. Goldman-Eisler conducted predictability tests on both forward and reverse guessing; and while all the guessers thought that forward guessing would be easier, guesses in both directions were found to be about equally accurate. Many words of poor predictability were readily predictable when the context ahead was known, even though their predictability was poor when the subjects had knowledge of the previous context. The speaker's subjective anticipation of the utterance to come is, then, at least as important to the construction of the moment as is what has already been said.

This distinction in speech production makes it easier to understand how the future context is being conceived at the moment of utterance. Thus preachers anticipate themselves by using immediately some words and constructions that they will also utter later. In literary texts the author's intentional signals prepare the reader for the action to come, but such anticipation also occurs in oral performances, though for these quite different reasons. Since the relationship of context to the lines of the moment works both forward and backward, we can also see how formulas derive from systems already uttered, yet form the basis of those that are several minutes away from acoustic speech.

This explains the frequency and relative placement of stalls, and most important, the symbiotic relationship of formula and context. It is fragmentary and artificial to think of the formation of a single line in isolation. Without that single line's context we really do not know very much about the way oral narrative is composed and nothing of the way by which it progresses from line to line. Oral literature is, after all, a sequence of interrelated lines, and not the mere amassing of individual and discrete formulas. The Parry-Lord theory—as significant as it is—tells us little about the way in which a single line is formed. Unless we are familiar with the particular performance and the context of that single line, we think of formulas as memorized or analogously manipulated entities—which was not Lord's idea—and instead of a creating artist we have a computer.

We are, unfortunately, stuck with the nouns "formula" and "system," whose connotation is of something precise, mechanical, and above all autonomous. Such an attitude is a concomitant of that philosophy given us by the New Criticism, which implied that works of literature were not the personal products of human authors intimately related to those works, but autonomous artifacts that the critic knew as much about as did their creator. An analogue is to be found in the prevailing attitude toward the formula and the system; we have not tried to see their creation as related to the other formulas within the same composition (except in terms of memorization), or as something closely related to the life of the singer. The resulting concept of the formula is rigid, memorized, and somehow apart from the forgetful, sometimes careless, occasionally faltering, and altogether creative human singer who composes it.

From the preachers' point of view, however, this is not the way sermons are composed at all. Everything comes from God. The entire sermon is divinely inspired and everything in it is an expression of God's will; preachers simply lend their voices to God at those moments so that He may express Himself. If the preacher has been reading up on a particular passage in order to prepare for a sermon, God has given the thought in the first place. When preachers think about several passages in the Bible that may be relevant to a main idea, or if they mark several passages in Scripture for use in a sermon, God will come to them at the moment of performance and select for them the proper passages. Association and context in the psycholinguistic sense has no meaning to a spiritual preacher. Lacy said that he could begin his "Deck of Cards" sermon with any biblical passage having to do with "heart"; but he would deny that his eventual choice was inspired by less than the Divine. This process has been described in a taped conversation by the Reverend Rufus Hays:

> You don't always have the time to use the access of Scripture that you have referred to in your particular study, simply because at the time of your communication of preparation of sermon material where the spirit of inspiration might relate to you certain passages of Scripture that would blend in with the text verse that has been given to you. You don't always have the time to refer to this in particular simply because of the lack of time here, but at any normal time for sermon material, or sermon for instance in your church, at the time that you would enlight upon any particular passage of Scripture or a number of passages of Scripture, there is an outburst of spiritual inspiration that is spurred by the edification of the Spirit of God at that particular time; in other words

this is the—in the unknown—unbeknownst to us inspiration of God that He would have related to the congregation at this time. I certainly believe, distinctively believe, that any time that the ordained minister—the appointed minister of God—is administering, it is God actually doing the speaking—we are only vessels: our lips, our tongue, our mouths, our mind, our thoughts; and if we will be submissive to this leading and this guiding, God can use us. If we be contrary or stubborn or resistant in any way, He would not be able to get His point over to the congregation.

This transcription not only articulates the preacher's point of view on why he chooses a particular passage from Scripture for his text, but also shows how the repetitive, adding style appears even in his conversation. Now, it must be admitted that this was not conversation of the marketplace; the situation was similar to that of preaching, in that Hays was trying to educate me. It was a quasi-formal public context. Nouns get repeated ("ordained minister—the appointed minister") though little new has been added, because "appointed minister" is in apposition. The syntax of the phrase has been repeated; sentence patterns recur: "You don't always have the time to. . . ." Word leads to word, phrase to phrase, sentence to sentence, all the while that idea leads to idea. The basis, as Hays himself suggested, may be in Isaiah 28:10–11: "For precept must be upon precept, precept upon precept; line upon line, line upon line; here a little, and there a little. For with stammering lips and another tongue will he speak to his people." Nevertheless, Hays's conversation was not as repetitive as his preaching.

The most "special" part of the Preachers' diction is that it is a limited register of English. Within such a register, of course, certain words and phrases are likely to appear more often than outside, thus giving the appearance of a special diction. In Old English the situation is different, as those compound nouns, the kennings, do not appear in the prose. But whether the kennings developed as magical word-avoidance synonyms or as a language to be used only in poetry, further examination of special dictions could be fruitful. Lacy did not use "Ain't God all right?" when sipping his breakfast coffee, yet there is nothing mysterious, exclusive, or special about any word in the expression.

An oral tradition—composition, transmission, performance—thrives in the midst of literate, industrial America. Not a trivial tradition, either, but one that transmits a culturally important and spiritually supreme message complex. The first edition of *The Art of the American Folk Preacher* attempted to deduce the principles of oral composition by comparing the American oral performances with those of Yugoslavia and elsewhere. That effort has not been entirely successful, probably because no one theory will account for all oral compositions worldwide. Too many different traditions, in too many different cultures, whose poetic traditions are too different, are involved. Our deduced principles, which may adequately describe the oral performers of one culture, are usually irrelevant for others.

The American preacher's art does not produce the same kind of narrative as did the *Beowulf* poet, the *guslars*, or Homer. The Old English manuscripts show a poetry that is not as free, metrically, and that had a greater inherited selection of formulaic metaphors—the kennings. None of these has a meter as demanding as the meter of Homeric verse. A kind of narrative is produced on the pulpits of spiritual preachers; but it is not close enough to those other traditions for us to be able to formulate a solitary set of rules that will account for scop, *guslar*, and folk preacher. In each cultural tradition we find too many exceptions to any previously formulated rule—in this case Parry's. His original definition can be expanded, and made more vague, to account for all of the exceptions; or it can be used as a nebulous model (a given essential idea itself) on which to fashion other descriptions for each new body of narrative as it is found and analyzed. A unitary principle will not describe all; localized, contextualized theories dealing with each tradition within each culture are not as satisfactory aesthetically, but are the most accurate way of proceeding.

In African praise poems (*izibongo*), as in American sermons, formulas are useful but not necessary to composition.[7] This is an important point considering Lord's later thoughts on the subject, that a formula is not necessarily a repeated utterance but describes only those constructions used in oral generation/performance.[8] The Xhosa praise poets seldom use narrative formulas, though repetitive lines and line clusters (of praise) occur commonly. The *imbogi*, like the preacher, like the singer in other traditions, uses formulas—often they are commonly uttered phrases of the native language—to create "new" lines by analogy with well-known ones.[9] Xhosa eulogies frequently are the result of free improvisation, as are those segments of American sermons that link gist-memorized passages.

The findings reported here differ with those of Parry and Lord in only minor ways, and are not important enough to argue for a major overhaul of oral-formulaic theory. The singer's literacy is at the center of one of the disagreements. Parry and Lord thought that illiteracy was one of the essential requisites of the oral singer: "There seem to be two things that all our singers have in common: illiteracy and the desire to attain proficiency in singing epic poetry . . . it is the first, namely their illiteracy, which determines the particular form that their composition takes, and which thus distinguishes them from the literary poet."[10] In the American tradition literacy is not a factor in sermon style; and though the few singers whom Lord interviewed could not write a poem as fluently as they could recite the same piece (though this is a level of literacy), further interviews might have uncovered others who could. More important for a comparison with Old English verse, Lord was not looking for a literate singer who had been impressed with the desirability to write metrically or who had been trained to do so. As most Old English scholars now believe, there is little reason to think that the *Beowulf* poet or any of his colleagues was necessarily illiterate; the evidence from the text suggests just the opposite,[11] and analyses of modern sermon formulas support the view that our oldest English epic was composed by a literate person writing in the traditional for-mulaic style. On the basis of sermon analysis, one should have no difficulty believing that the authors of Old English lyrical and narrative poems were learned, since their education would not necessarily interfere with their "oral" style.

Certain cross-cultural comparisons may be ventured. We have seen in detail how preachers allow themselves time to formulate future lines by the use of stall formulas. Although stalls are oc-casionally used in Yugoslavia they are not pleasing to the audi-ence and so the singer tries to limit their use. Nevertheless, the *guslar* (as well as his central Asian counterpart, the *akyn*) also needs time for his composition. We get an idea of the *guslar's* stall in his leisurely pace and especially in his incremental, adding style. The following selection is from song number 8 of Parry's collection: "When Mujo was a shepherd, he used to tend cattle with the shepherds; he used to go out with the shepherds. He was weak and the shepherds beat him; they beat him and tormented him. The unhappy Mujo was walking along the mountainside and he found the young of a Vila, the little children of a white Vila, in a thicket on the mountain."[12] Not only are key words carried over from line to line, but many phrases merely repeat the previous phrase without advancing the narrative: "he used to go out with the shepherds" is a rephrasing of "he used to tend cattle with the shepherds," thus giving the singer time to think of "He was weak and the shepherds beat him," a new idea.

Much the same technique is used by those little-known (to the West) oral epic singers of central Asia, the *akyn*, Kirghiz traditional performers:

> When he grew to be a prince, he overthrew
> princely dwellings;
> Sixty stallions, a hundred horses,
> He drove thither from Kokand;
> Eighty mares, a thousand kymkar
> He brought from Bokhara;
> The Chinese settled in Kashgar
> He drove away to Turfan;
> The Chinese settled to Turfan
> He drove yet farther to Aksu.[13]

Stall formulas as the American preacher knows them do not appear in these oral epics, so the *guslar* and the *akyn* construct their poems in other ways in order to effect the same result. The *guslar* may occasionally use a stall just as the preacher resorts to the adding style, but for the most part each device is characteristic of its own literature, which has in turn derived from the demands of the audience and the singer. This incremental adding will be retained to a large degree when the *guslar* and the *akyn* write down their texts, as Lord has observed, even when the performance is in other ways substantially changed.[14] But the preacher's stalls do not occur except during performance; thus, in at least this one aspect, what is paramount is the performance and not merely its transcription from a casual interview.

As concerns the printed text of *Beowulf*, we may see oral residue in this poem, but we cannot treat it entirely as oral art. That *Beowulf* is formulaic is without doubt, but as we know all language is formualic in that it is grammatical. An analysis of the sermons suggests, however obliquely, that *Beowulf*'s formulas are not all memorized, but that certain repetitions were likely to occur given the structure of Old English grammar and the further restrictions placed on that grammar by meter and alliteration. These restrictions do not rule out the likelihood that most of the half lines were re-created during performance rather than memorized.[15] The findings of Russian ethnologists in their study of the central Asian epics support this view: "Yet it is not a case of passive memorizing and mechanic reproduction of verses learned by heart, but of a creative memory which, in the process of recital, reproduces anew and recreates the contents of a poem already familiar in its outlines to the singer."[16]

One of the most important leitmotivs—"litanies" would be a more appropriate metaphor—of this book has been the insistance that the sermons and the services being writen about will never be adequately understood on the printed page; that folk preaching, like folklore, is everything in the performance that does not get copied down in writing. "You've got to have been there." And yet, in one important way, all of my readers have "been there." Everyone remembers hearing, or has heard of, or seen, videotapes of Rev. Martin Luther King, Jr.'s "I have a Dream" speech. That morning—August 28, 1963—he preached his memorable sermon, though it was received by the more than 200,000 in the audience as a civil rights speech—which it also was. King knew how to give a speech when he wanted to, and (to point up the obvious again) he knew how to preach. His speech to the Fellowship of the Concerned (delivered on November 16, 1961) is a model of a well-reasoned, precisely organized statement on behalf of "Love, Law, and Civil Disobedience." King began,

Members of the Fellowship of the Concerned, of the Southern Regional Council, I need not pause to say how very delighted I am to be here today, and to have the opportunity of being a little part of this very significant gathering. . . . I would also like to express just a personal word of thanks and appreciation for your vital witness in this period of transition which we are facing in our Southland, and in the nation, and I am sure that as a result of this genuine concern, and your significant work in communities all across the South, we have a better South today and I am sure will have a better South tomorrow with your continued endeavor and I do want to express my personal gratitude and appreciation to you of the Fellowship of the Concerned for your significant work and for your forthright witness.[17]

This speech outlined the philosophy that controlled the nonviolent civil rights demonstrations in America, detailing its chief features and manifestations. King concluded in the same tone of irresistibly sweet reason:

That is the basis of this movement, and as I like to say, there is something in this universe that justifies Carlyle in saying no lie can live forever. We shall overcome because there is something in this universe which justifies William Cullen Bryant in saying truth crushed to earth shall rise again. We shall overcome because there is something in this universe that justifies James Russell Lowell in saying, truth forever on the scaffold, wrong forever on the throne. Yet that scaffold sways the future, and behind the dim unknown standeth God within the shadows, keeping watch above His own. With this faith in the future, with this determined struggle, we will be able to emerge from the bleak and desolate midnight of man's inhumanity to man, into the bright and glittering daybreak of freedom and justice. Thank you.[18]

He was teaching, not preaching, almost; the repetition of parallel syntax in the clauses beginning with "there is something" has the stamp of the pulpit. At the Washington Monument in late August of 1963 the teacher was subordinated to the preacher. "Five score years ago, a great American," he began, "signed the Emancipation Proclamation." The preaching style soon commanded this speech:

But one hundred years later, the Negro still is not free.

One hundred years later, the life of the Negro is still sadly
    crippled by the manacles of segregation and the chains of
    discrimination.

One hundred years later, the Negro lives on a lonely island of
    poverty in the midst of a vast ocean of material prosperity.

One hundred years later, the Negro is still languishing in the
    corners of American society and finds himself an exile in his
    own land.

So we have come here today to dramatize a shameful condition.[19]

No American who was alive in 1963 will forget this preached
oration's peroration:

So I say to you, my friends, that even though we must face the
    difficulties of today and tomorrow, I still have a dream.

It is a dream deeply rooted in the American dream that one day
    this nation will rise up and live out the true meaning of its
    creed—we hold these truths to be self evident, that all men
    are created equal.

I have a dream that one day on the red hills of Georgia, sons of
    former slaves and sons of former slave-owners will be able to
    sit down together at the table of brotherhood.

I have a dream that one day, even the state of Mississippi, a state
    sweltering with the heat of injustice, sweltering with the heat
    of oppression, will be transformed into an oasis of freedom
    and justice.

I have a dream that my four little children will one day live in a
    nation where they will not be judged by the color of their
    skin but by the content of their character.

I have a dream today.

I have a dream that one day, down in Alabama, with its vicious
    racists, with its governor having his lips dripping with the
    words of interposition and nullification, that one day, right
    here in Alabama, little black boys and black girls will be able
    to join hands with little white boys and white girls as sisters
    and brothers.

I have a dream. . . .[20]

The conclusion of King's remarks were pure oral sermon:

So let freedom ring from the prodigious hilltops of New
    Hampshire.

Let freedom ring from the mighty mountains of New York.
Let freedom ring from the heightening Alleghenies of
Pennsylvania.
Let freedom ring from the snow-capped Rockies of Colorado.
Let freedom ring from the curvaceous slopes of California.
But not only that.
Let freedom ring from Stone Mountain of Georgia.
Let freedom ring from Lookout Mountain of Tennessee.
Let freedom ring from every hill and molehill of Mississippi, from
every mountainside, let freedom ring.
And when we allow freedom to ring, . . .[21]

The Washington Monument speech called for rousing oratory,
not for finely reasoned philosophy. The subject was basically a
religious one, though heavily freighted with patriotic cargoes.
Situation and subject called for just such a sermon; the formulas,
the repetitive syntax and phrases, were produced by a highly
literate and sophisticated man, whose speech to the Fellowship
of the Concerned was appropriate to his audience; and his message showed that he could adjust his style of address according
to the needs of the situation, and do it with great effect. He was
a great speaker, but those of us who remember the Washington
Monument speech know also what a great preacher he was. And
we know, too, which style had by far the greater impact on the
emotions, the spirit, of the audience.

Though King is dead, we have by no means heard the last of
the oral sermon style; we have not been deprived of its great
emotive power. At the 1984 Democratic presidential convention
in San Francisco, Rev. Jesse Jackson delivered one of the preliminary speeches, which the Knight-Ridder reporter called "an
emotional, triumphant valedictory address for the 42-year-old
Baptist preacher who brought out both the best and worst in
people in his eight-month campaign for self-respect and dignity
for himself, blacks and the disadvantaged." Describing the speech
in more detail, the reporter wrote:

For 50 spellbound minutes, the noisy Democratic Convention came
to a stop last night as Jesse Jackson—a descendant of slaves who
became this country's first major black presidential candidate—

talked of the dream, passions and frustrations that inspired his historic bid for the White House.

Tears, cheers and chants of "Jesse, Jesse, Jesse," greeted Jackson, who came to symbolize the hopes of millions of black Americans.

Thousands of delegates joined hands and rocked from side to side to a soothing gospel hymn when it was over.[22]

When it was over—the next evening—television reporter David Brinkley was not overly moved or impressed, pointing out that after all, Jackson was a Baptist minister and had been doing that sort of thing for years. One's inference has to be that Baptist ministers all have the ability to move their congregations (which is obviously not so) and that we ought not to be impressed by a preacher's skill in rousing the Spirit. But no churchgoer could agree with this evaluation, which slights this great talent. It is all the more surprising coming from a professional media commentator who has over decades established a substantial career by his speaking voice.

Jackson's speech began conventionally enough: "Tonight we come together bound by our faith in a mighty God, with genuine respect and love for our country, and inheriting the legacy of a great party—the Democratic Party—which is the best hope for redirecting our nation on a more humane, just and peaceful course." It began conventionally enough (except for the mention of party) for a sermon, which it was in part. Not yet well into his performance, Jackson evoked heightened emotion when he apologized:

> If in my high moments, I have done some good
> Offered some service
> Shed some light
> Healed some wounds
> Rekindled some hope
> Stirred someone from apathy and indifference
> Or in any way helped someone along the way
> Then this campaign has not been in vain.[23]

He continued:

> If in my low moments

> In word, deed or attitude
> Through some error of temper, taste or tone
> I have caused anyone discomfort
> Created pain
> Or revived someone's fears
> That was not my truest self.
>
> . . . .
>
> I am not a perfect servant
> I am a public servant doing my best against the odds
> Be patient
> God is not finished with me[24]

This political sermon invokes the message of C. L. Franklin's "Stand still, and see the salvation of the Lord." In this parable Jackson places himself in a position analogous to that of Moses at the Red Sea. Like that other public servant, he too is not perfect; his followers should be patient; God is not finished with him. These passages are not only replete with parallel syntactical constructions, but internal rhyme and alliteration as well. This sermon/speech was probably not composed with that poetry as a conscious compositional element in mind; rather it occurs unreflectively in the recitation of the oral performer of this tradition, one of whose most skilled practitioners is Jesse Jackson. "Suffering breeds character," he told the convention at the close of his sermon:

> Suffering breeds character
> Character breeds faith
> And in the end faith will not disappoint
> Faith hope and dreams will prevail
> We must be bound together by faith
> Sustained by hope
> And driven by a dream
> Troubles won't last always
> Our time has come
> Our time has come
> Our time has come[25]

"Thousands of delegates joined hands and rocked from side to side to a soothing gospel hymn when it was over."[26] Jackson's use of the folk sermon style—not, in this case, spontaneously composed—for a political speech demonstrates the form's adaptability. Martin Luther King's "I Have a Dream" sermon/speech was on behalf of a cause that evoked deep religious feelings; Jackson's performance was more secularized, but not entirely. He asked for forgiveness, pleading that he still had a divinely inspired mission to fulfill: God was not finished with him yet. While it might be counterargued that those of such backgrounds might well justify almost any of their actions with scriptural support, their sermon/speeches demonstrate the close similarities between effective orations and moving sermons. In both instances, the minds of the audience were arrested and their emotions engaged. King and Jackson prepared manuscripts carefully, but realized that people are not always moved by reason alone; logic penetrates deepest in quiet chambers, by and by. The green in front of the Washington Monument, the Democratic convention hall—like a church full of expectant worshipers—required another approach. The sermons that have moved millions since 1800 are thus shown to stimulate a response more fundamental than mere emotion, with more breadth than Protestant Fundamentalism.

NOTES

1. Especially the recordings of such chants made for the Library of Congress by Charley Berry, Thomas J. Marshall, and Iron Head: LC Albums L8 and L59.

2. Melville Jacobs, *The People Are Coming Soon* (Seattle, 1960), pp. x–xi; and *The Content and Style of an Oral Literature* (Chicago, 1959), pp. 268–69.

3. Albert B. Lord, *The Singer of Tales* (New York, 1965), p. 54.

4. A word needs to be said about the effect of anaphoric passages on the congregation and the preacher's attempt to exploit these effects. Parallelism of this type can have a profound cumulative dramatic impact. Perhaps the reader will have heard sermons by the Reverend Martin Luther King, Jr., or the Reverend Ralph Abernathy, and will have felt this impact personally. The Reverend Mr. King's "I Have a Dream" speech, though written, is rich in anaphoric development. Yet nearly all of the preachers interviewed for this study were unaware of creating such parallel passages, and claimed to have been concentrating exclusively on the problems of composition. However, in the case of

Dr. King and other preachers of comparable learning who preach spontaneously, it is hard to believe that they were not aware of the effect on the audience.

5. Actually Lord makes this point, though it is often overlooked: "I believe that we are justified in considering that the creating of phrases is the true art of the singer on the level of line formation, and it is this facility rather than his memory of relatively fixed formulas that marks him as a skillful singer in performance": *Singer of Tales*, p. 43.

6. Frieda Goldman-Eisler, "Speech Production and the Predictability of Words in Context," *Quarterly Journal of Educational Psychology* 10 (May 1958), 96–106.

7. Jeff Opland, *Xhosa Oral Poetry*. (Cambridge, 1983), p. 165.

8. Albert B. Lord, "Homer as Oral Poet," *HSCP* 72 (1968), 15.

9. Opland, *Xhosa Oral Poetry*, pp. 165 ff.

10. Lord, *Singer of Tales*, p. 20.

11. See Larry D. Benson, "The Literary Character of Anglo-Saxon Formulaic Poetry, *PMLA* 81 (1966), 334–41.

12. Milman Parry, *Serbocroatian Heroic Songs* 1 (Cambridge, Mass., 1954), p. 116.

13. Nora K. Chadwick and Victor Zhirmunsky, *Oral Epics of Central Asia* (Cambridge, 1969), p. 31.

14. Lord, *Singer of Tales*, p. 127; but Lord does not mention what happens to stall formulas when a song is dictated at leisure.

15. It is the thesis of Alan Jabbour of the American Folklife Center that *Beowulf* is neither formulaic (in Lord's sense) nor improvised, but entirely memorial. Chadwick speaks of a strong tradition of epic memorization in central Asia (pp. 17–18), and analysis of the sermons suggests that Jabbour's thesis is possible. His theory thus accounts for the absence of all stall formulas in *Beowulf* as well as the presence of certain repetitions (*paet waes god cyning*). The contemporary parallel might be the actor who remembers by heart all of Shakespeare's tragedies, or the symphonic conductor (such as Sir Thomas Beecham) who has memorized the entire score of an opera: see Jabbour's "Memorial Transmission of Old English Poetry," *Chaucer Review* 3 (Fall 1969), 174–190.

16. Chadwick and Zhirmunsky, *Oral Epics*, p. 326.

17. Roy L. Hill, *Rhetoric of Racial Revolt* (Denver, 1964), pp. 345–56.

18. Ibid.

19. Ibid., pp. 371–75.

20. Ibid.

21. Ibid. I have restructured the sentence and paragraph format for emphasis.

22. Reported locally in a Knight-Ridder syndicated article headlined "Jackson Asks Forgiveness, Vows Support." Providence (R.I.) *Journal*, July 18, 1984, p. A1.

23. AP dispatch, July 18, 1984. Format my own.

24. Ibid.

25. Reported in the Providence *Journal*, July 18, 1984, p. A1.

26. Ibid.

PART II

Formulas of J. Charles Jessup

The following illustrations of the use of formulas in characteristic semantic contexts were taken from several sermons of J. Charles Jessup at various times during the summer of 1967:

1.

    I'll tell y' a lot of these seminary preachers
A lot of these big-wig intellectuals
That stand up on Sunday mornin'
And depend on their literary education
To lead people
I want you to know
They need some more prayer and fastin'

2.

    Brother let me tell y' this
Not many high and mighty
Not many intellectual big-wigs
Not many money people
Are willing to pay the price
And order themselves and go to heaven
But I'm gonna tell y'

3.

    The altars have been taken out of the churches
And with sugar-coated and white-washed and bargain-countered and
    streamlined and wholesaled and bargain-counter religion

To the public today

4.

How many of you will stand by a preacher
That won't compromise or sugar-coat the gospel

5.

We're livin' in a compromisin' age
When religion's been put on the bargain counter
When the altars have been taken out of the churches
When "Do the best you can" has been our modern theme

6.

I want you to know that there are some people in this good old
    United States of America and our sister countries
That still appreciate a man that'll roll up his sleeves
And preach the Bible and the truth of God's holy Bible without fear
    or favor of man
If you want a compromisin' sugar-coated and bargain-counter gospel
Then you don't need to hear J. Charles Jessup of Gulfport,
    Mississippi
There's been some of these intellectual big-wigs and some of these
    modernists
Have been writing to me and saying that you make God a monster

7.

An' if preachers that go to rollin' up their sleeve
An' preachin' sin black hell hot
There's certain judgment shoulda
An eternity long
We'd save this generation

8.

No it's not what I say
It's not what you say
It's what God's black-back holy Bible teaches
I'm gonna tell you the Bible said
Ye shall know the truth

9.

How many of you people out there listenin' to God's humble
    servant

Are still sincere enough
That you love to hear the old-fashioned black-back Bible preached

10.

You keep writing to me you hypocrites
You keep writing to me you fault-finders
I'm gonna preach the truth whether you like it or lump it
You can take it or leave it
The Bible said ye shall know the truth

11.

Praise Allmighty God
Like it or lump it
Take it or leave it
Get in or get out
Put up or shut up
We've got a boministic modernistic hand-shakin' jack-jawin' world
 today

12.

But do you know that in all the cities of Sodom and Gomorrah and
 the plain
They couldn't find ten holy dedicated separated consecrated people
That were walkin' before God and living a holy life

13.

God will call
His separated dedicated (unintelligible) Christian people

14.

How many of you are willin' to live a holy consecrated life

15.

We've got to get the power of God in our lives
The Spirit of God in our hearts
And it can only come
Through the medium of consecration and dedication and separation
From the world

16.

Brother let me tell you
You've got to live a holy consecrated dedicated life
If you wanna get to heaven

You can't drink on Monday
And gamble on Tuesday
You can't play cards on Wednesday
You can't commit adultery on Thursday
You can't paint the town red on Friday and Saturday
And go out to church and have the kind of religion
That's a holy religion

17.

It's gonna take a clean holy consecrated sanctified dedicated
    separated life
Hidden away with Christ in God
To be among that number

The Sermons

The following sermons were transcribed using an individual system and so may require explanation. They are very lightly punctuated, since punctuation is a form of editorializing. That policy in itself is a form of editorializing, but it is a less obtrusive one. Nearly always preachers and their congregations punctuate the performance. The latter regularly call out "Amen," "That's right," "You tell it," "Lord, Lord," and the preachers pause momentarily to honor their expressions. These pauses are metrically regular, and help break up utterances into formulas; preachers also pause to gasp for breath, clearly audible in most performances. When the congregation is not punctuating the performance, the ministers are punctuating it themselves.

Edson Richmond told me, after hearing a tape recording of a sermon performance, that once again he appreciated the old truth that folklore is everything that gets left out when the live performance is transcribed. The following sermons have been transposed to print with one formula or metrically punctuated utterance occupying each line as though it were a sentence prepared for print. My intention was to convey the sermon's rhythm and metricality.

When punctuation was unavoidable the following rules were followed: a virgule (/) is used at the metrical juncture when I was uncertain whether one word set should be rendered as one formula or two. Missteps in performance induced either nonsense utterances or pauses; these are indicated with a dash (—). Some nonsense sounds are uttered that occur in absence of meaningful statements—ah, ahh, uhh, etc.—and they are rendered much as they were performed, since their audible performance influenced the meter of their context. "Amen" is often used as a formula and is printed that way; usually when it was sung it was stretched (though it was sometimes spoken briskly) in keeping with the established rhythm, or in syncopation with it. Solid underlining in selected sermons whose preachers were frequently recorded serves to designate verbatim formulas; and broken underlining, formulas from systems found in other performances, a convention used by Parry, Lord, and Old English scholars.

The sermons printed here (from the more than one hundred collected during this research) are included for a variety of reasons. Some were felt to be representative of those heard by black Fundamentalists and popular with their preachers. Comparisons with other versions performed by other preachers, and repeated performances by the same minister were thus facilitated: "The Eagle Stirreth Up Its Nest," "Dry Bones," "The Twenty-third Psalm," and "Preach the Word." Other sermons are typical of the individual style of their preachers, such as Brown's "Mindful of Man." Lacy's "God's Plowboy" is included here because such a large part of it was read from a source with which the oral performance could be compared. Rev. Jerry Lockett's "This Same Jesus" has many similarities with Brown's of the same title, though the influence is indirect, even remote. Young and relatively inexperienced pastor (in 1970) William Robinson showed the work of an apprentice in the formative years. The originality and novelty of Rev. J. J. Freeman's "The Postage Stamp" merits inclusion, as does the beauty and piety—not to mention the high formula density—of Rev. D. J. McDowell's "The Christ of the Bible."

Pseudo-phonemic attempts to reproduce the dialect of Southern blacks are almost unavoidably condescending, and are for the most part avoided below. "Over there I saw the man park the car" would sound substantially different if spoken by John F. Kennedy or Lyndon Johnson or Sir John Gielgud, but printed quotations of their speech make no attempt to account for their dialectical characteristics; why should black ministers be treated differently? When I do attempt to depict dialect, it is to maintain the sense of the preacher's performative rhythm. A slurred utterance such as "I'm gonna tell y'- " is briefer than "I am going to tell you," which is really not what was said anyway. The original speech relates a sense of the compression actually used in performance, and for this reason is rendered in print here.

Other sermons have been recently collected in Gerald Davis's *I Got the Word in Me and I Can Sing It, You Know* and are mentioned throughout Jeff Titon's *Early Hometown Blues*. An important discography of sermon records (but cut off at 1942) is to be found in John Godrich and Robert M. W. Dixon, *Blues and Gospel Records* (London, 1969).

THE DECK OF CARDS
Version 1

Recited by the Reverend Rubin Lacy, June 20, 1967, in Bakersfield, California, this sermon was well received; the congregation responded readily and consequently a good portion of the text is metrical. Lacy told me earlier in the day that the sermon could begin in a number of ways so long as it had something to do with "heart." Hence line 3: "the fool, has said in his heart, there is no God"; line 16: "the hearts of men are wrong"; line 22: "peace come when the hearts of men is right"; and lines 37, 39, 40, 41, 42, 43, etc. With "heart" in mind, Lacy was able to stock his sermon with its frequent use. Otherwise the structural plan was simple: to dwell on our sins and on our consciences, and when the time was right—when the congregation was "up"— to bring in the deck of cards theme (Thompson Type 1613). A partial chant begins at line 77; by line 83 music has taken over the rhythm and meter completely, which is sustained until line 249. At this point sung lines, spoken lines, and lamented lines are juxtaposed arbitrarily. Lacy ends by singing "Jesus," lines 275-77.

We're gonna talk short tonight,
    if we can
Watching, watching, close to
    the Psalms

Now, it read like this: the fool,
    has said in his heart, there
    is no God

All right, the fool has said in his heart, there is no God

5 Book says right here, they haven't got the strength—history repeats itself

That has been said before Christ come

Your, prophets had said He was comin'

Men wiser than the prophets had said He wasn't comin'

Been sayin' that for years, for hundreds of years—got to see it yet—sayin' He's not comin'

10 They're saying the same thing now

First Jesus died, they say He's not coming back, been dead yet two thousand years and hasn't got back yet

He'll be back but they don't believe He's comin' yet

That's natural—history repeats itself people had the same mind today that they had in those days

Jesus said when I came back, just like it was in the old days

15 So it will be when I come again

Therefore, the hearts of men are wrong, have a wrong heart

How can men get peace in the world

We are the men goin' around here talkin' about peace

that ain't even been born yet

Runnin' from seaport to seaport, flyin' through the air at two thousand miles an hour

20 Talk about peace

But Jesus said there shall be no peace

I'm trying to say to you peace come when the hearts of men is right

The hearts of men is far from right

We're selfish, every man is for himself

25 I think every man should be named Ahab

Because the word Ahab means selfish

Everybody is for himself

Nobody looks after the things of his friend

Ahh—ahh—and as long as we's selfish we can't get no friends

30 I don't care how you boot[?], how you grow, how good you say you are, nearly everybody else is sayin' nothin'

In the eyesight of God

I heard Jesus say the other day, when you think you're something you're nothing

I heard Him say that

He who exalts himself shall be abased

35 I heard Him say that too

We have to be mindful along
these lines
David here says the fool has
said in his heart
There is no God
I'm tryin' to say to you this
evenin', that out of the
heart pours the issues of
life
⁴⁰ Don't let nobody fool y', that
your heart can one thing
and your life another
Whatever is in your heart
I heard Jesus say the other day
where your treasure is,
there is your heart
Tryin' to say I'm talkin' about
heart—in your heart
This same David Amen
⁴⁵ Was born and God's only man
in the world ever was born
by a woman an'—was near
and was after God's own
heart
Only man, that was ever born
by a woman, after God's
own heart
And goin' up the road, after he
become king hmm?
He got selfish
And wanted everything he saw
⁵⁰ That that belonged to him and
that that didn't belong to
him
And he committed the crime of
murder
To accomplish his deeds
Hmm?

But one thing I like about
David
⁵⁵ He didn't get too high to fall on
his knees
And call out all of his servants
And close the door of his office
Got on his knees and asked
God to forgive him for it
The trouble about some of our
bad hearts these days
⁶⁰ We do these things but we're
too stout-hearted—Amen—
to ask somebody to forgive
We just don't need to askin'
God, unless you ask the
one that you ain't done
wrong to
So many of us tries to go to
God, to straighten up our
heart
Amen, and then give our
brother or our sister Hail
Columbus
Am I right? But you can't cut
no air away [other way?]
⁶⁵ You got to come by God first,
Amen
He said the other day ahh—in
the prayer—he said 'give us
our debts, as we forgive
those, that we are indebted
to
Amen
An' if we don't forgive nobody,
we are hell-bound now
Think I know what I'm talkin'
about
⁷⁰ Ahh—we must fix our heart—
the same David—Amen—

after he had done so badly
wrong
Uhh-huh and after he'd been to
God
God had forgive his other sins
Heard God say the other day if
you confess your sins, you
don't have none
That's another thing wrong
with us
75 Some of us are too stout-
hearted even to confess
that we done wrong
Ahh—David went to God
Just to be satisfied
As long as that sin was resting
upon him
You heard me talk about your
conscience condemning
you
80 Paul say when your conscience
condemn y', you is
condemned already
When your conscience's
condemned, don't care
what nobody say about y'
No man is condemned, unless
his conscience condemn
him
An' when your conscience
condemn you
You better go in bed
85 Oh yes he is
An' after David, had went to
God
This same David
I said this same David
After he'd went to God
90 Got up one mornin'

An' walked out in the breeze
Said my heart is fixed
My heart is fixed
Uhh-huh, my mind is made up
95 My heart is fixed
Umm-hmm, y' know why?
Nobody tells somebody
Heard it said one day
Be sure that you're on the right
road
100 Said to God search me
And know my heart
God got a search-warrant
God from Zion
These days are searchers
105 Search all day and all night
Know all about you
Seed everything you do
Hear everything you say
I heard him say the other day
110 I heard it before you opened
your mouth
Get ready to come back to God
When you done done wrong
God sees you
When y' get t' get ready
115 He knows y' mind
He's a mind regulator
He's a heart fixer
God from Zion
Mister Hoyle
120 Tryin' his best
To compare with God
Look this evenin'
God made a heaven
And God made a world
125 Mister Hoyle decided
That he here
Could compete with God

That he might draw
Disciples from God
130 Look this evenin'
Men are always
Tryin' t' equalize God
So God
Made a earth
135 A world
With three hundred and sixty-
   five days
In the year
Mister Hoyle
Made a deck of cards
140 With three hundred and sixty-
   five spots
In the cards
Ain't I right about it?
And God
Made a year
145 With fifty-two weeks in the
   year
Mister Hoyle
Made a deck of cards
With fifty-two
Cards in the deck
150 Ain't God all right?
And, God
Said there's two ways to go
Heaven
Or either hell
155 Mister Hoyle
Made a two-spot
He called it a deuce
God from Zion
And put it in the deck
160 And God
Made the Father
Son and the Holy Ghost
Ain't God all right?

And Mister Hoyle
165 Made a three-spot
And called it a trey
God from Zion
In Matthew Mark
An' Luke and John
170 Mister Hoyle
Made a four-spot
Put it in the deck
God from Zion
Jesus, the lamb of God
175 Dyin' on the cross
Dyin' of wounds
In His body
Two in His hands
One in His side
180 And two in His feet
Mister Hoyle
Made a five-spot
Placed it in the deck
Ain't God all right?
185 Mister Hoyle
'Membered it took
Six days
To make the earth
Heaven and the earth
190 Mister Hoyle
Put a six-spot in the deck
An' he remembered
That God rested on the seventh
   day
Mister Hoyle
195 Made a seven-spot
And placed it in the deck
God from Zion
Then God
Saved Noah
200 And his brethren
In the ark

Eight people
Saved in the ark
Mister Hoyle
205 Put a eight-spot in the deck
God from Zion
And then
They put a nine-spot in the
  deck
Representin'
210 Hangin' from the sixth
To the ninth hour
Hangin' on His cross
God from Zion
And then he put
215 A ten-spot in the deck
Representin'
The ten commandments
God from Zion
Thou shalt not steal
220 Thou shalt not commit adultery
Thou shalt not bear false
  witness
God from Zion
Not over yet
And Mister Hoyle
225 Put a queen in the deck
Representin'
The Queen of Sheba
Ain't this a good story?
One day
230 Lookin' over God's children
Not only that
Said the half had never been
  told
Ain't God all right?
Mister Hoyle
235 Put a king in the deck
Representin'
King Solomon

Wisest man that ever lived
And Mister Hoyle
240 Put a jack in the deck
Representin' black horse—that
  death
That rides from home to home
And from house to house
Then y' see what he did then
245 After a while
He put a ace in the deck
Representin' the high card
The Lord Himself
Ain't God all right?
250 Ohh, He's my friend
I say He's my friend
He's my company-keeper
When I get lonesome
He keeps me company
255 All night long
You know what I'm talkin'
  about
He's a good friend
I said He's a good friend
He's closer than m' brother
260 Sometimes a friend
Will put y' down
Yes he will
Sometime
Y' don't want to be around
265 Every hour in the day
[Singing]
I got my hand, in God's hand
He scoop down, and pick me
  up
God from Zion
I don't want you to see me fall
270 But you can't see me get up
Sometime I get up
Feignin' dead

Flat on my back
All alone by myself
275 Jesus!

Jesus!
Jesus!

THE DECK OF CARDS
Version 2

Recited by the Reverend Rubin Lacy, May 19, 1968, in Corcoran, California, this was Lacy's favorite sermon, although on this occasion it was poorly delivered and badly received. But it is interesting for several reasons: it shows how flexible the form is and how different messages can be attached to the same "story"; comparison with the earlier version shows the flexibility of structure in oral literature (discussed in chapter 7); and we get an excellent example of how metrics affects even memorized passages. The 1967 cards portion was metrically performed, but notice the difference in 1968 when Lacy's meter failed. Only those lines that appeared in 1967 are underlined.

In the Fifty-third Psalms and
    the first verse it reads like
    this
The fool has said in his heart
    there is no God
The fool has said within his
    heart there is no God
I repeat that
5 Fifty-third Psalm and part of
    the first verse
The fool has said there is no
    God

We living in the last days
In Noah's days people didn't
    believe there was any God
    or at least they didn't
    believe there was any
    savior coming
To redeem the world—the
    people they didn't believe
    that
10 That thing had been heard ever
    since Adam broke the law

And nations and generations
   had come on the scene
And people were still listening
   to their prophesy
First one thing and another
   about the messiah would
   come to redeem the world
They had heard it so long until
   didn't anybody believe it
15 Fact of it they heard that thing
   four thousand years
And didn't nobody believe it
When you hear a thing so long
   it goes in one ear and come
   out another
If you ain't got mighty strong
   faith
For about four hundred years
   there even the prophets
   stopped talking about it
20 Hmm? yeah the prophets
   stopped talkin' about it
But there was somebody among
   the Israelites that didn't—
   that still believed that He
   was coming
There was somebody I said
   among the Israelites was
   still looking for this
   messiah
But the majority of the people
   had forgot about Him
Because they didn't believe
   what they had heard
25 Didn't read the prophets—fact
   of it they had murdered all
   of the prophets just about
   it

Elijah said one day to God said
   they've killed all of the
   prophets
And I am left here only one
And they're seeking my life to
   take here
It was a great mistake that as
   great a prophet as that
   would make as to tell God
   that he was the only one
30 God has always had somebody
   else
If I'm called today from this
   rostrum there is somebody
   to take my place
Is to carry on
You may not know who they
   are
But there's somebody to carry
   on
35 God said to Elijah that day I
   have seven—several
   thousand
That's walkin' around you
   every day
You see with your own eyes
Have never bowed to Baal
I'm tryin' to say to you this
   evenin' that God is not
   dead
40 As you hear them say
These days the people has got a
   great rumor
All over the world/about a dead
   God
They don't realize the things
   that whispers within a
   man's heart
Even when he's on the job

⁴⁵ He hears a voice that talks with
  him even when they are on
  the job
They don't realize the lightnin'
  and the thunder
They don't realize the shaking
  of the earth
What we call earthquakes
It takes a God to do these
  things
⁵⁰ Science is not able to do it and
  they are not able to stop it
Fact of it they're not able to
  tell when it's comin' on
Science has been studying for
  years trying to find out
  when a earthquake and
  where will it occur
But they're not able to do it
God has that secret hid
⁵⁵ Man learns so much and He lets
  him know so much because
  he can know too much
And if he do he'll know much
  as God knows
The devil lied in the garden of
  Eden
When he said you'll just
  become wise
And know as much as God
⁶⁰ Uhh-huh man never has
  knowed as much as God
And never will know
As much as God
He search the earth and now
  he's searchin' the heaven
He's tryin' to search the moon
  and the stars

⁶⁵ But he never will know much
  as God know about it
But I want to tell you today
  that He's not dead
An' there ain't nobody says
  He's dead but a fool
The wise man never says God is
  dead
I don't care how much
  education you've got
⁷⁰ How great a science you is
If you say God's dead you's a
  fool
You're not wise
Solomon said a wise man will
  change
And a fool will continue
⁷⁵ Nobody says—Amen—that
  God's dead that's got good
  sense
We know that God is alive
An' He always will
I think I heard Him say out
  yonder to Moses on Mount
  Hebron one day
You tell them that I am Alpha
  and I am Omega
⁸⁰ That means that I am the
  beginning and the ending
I am He that liveth—told John
  on the island—I am He that
  liveth and was dead but
  behold I am alive forever
  more
Tryin' to say to y' this evenin'
  God is still alive
An' on His way back—the
  reason I know He's on His
  way back I see a great

falling away from the
church
People don't have time with
the church
⁸⁵ Nobody can't tell nobody
nothin'
Everybody has his own law
Everybody has his own way
Everybody got his own religion
An' nobody can tell the other
when things get like that
⁹⁰ It's in a bad condition
Tryin' to say to y' that He's on
His way back
He said so it was in Noah's days
So shall it be when I come
again
In those days nobody would
listen to the Word of God
⁹⁵ He preached—I think the
history said—every time
the hammer would hit on
the head of a nail
The sound of the hammer
would . . . and men would
laugh at old man Noah
But after a while that rain did
come
I wanna tell you it's on its way
back again
But it won't be rainin' water
¹⁰⁰ It will be rainin' fire 'n'
brimstone
He said I won't come with
water the next time—but
I'll come with fire
This fire will burn up the roofs
and the stairways

All sin shall be burned out of
this world
Then I think John said I looked
and I saw a new heaven
¹⁰⁵ And a new earth
Comin' down from God
A new heaven
This old heaven
Will pass away
¹¹⁰ This old earth
Will be passed away
I saw a new heaven
And a new earth
Comin' down with God—you're
talkin' about the King
¹¹⁵ Amen—that's the time, that
Jesus, will take His
kingship
Jesus in the miraculous name of
God
Will come down on this new
earth
Amen—and set up His kingdom
On this earth
¹²⁰ His kingdom means a
government
I mean a Christian government
Where there will be no more
dark
Umm-hmm no more sickness
No more pain
¹²⁵ No more heartbreaks
An' no more cryin'
An' every day
Will be Sunday
And every month
¹³⁰ The month of May
You heard the song about the
flowers

Blooming forever
Amen
That's the time when these
things will happen
135 Said in the language of the
text—Amen
The fool, has said within his
heart
That there is no God
I wanna tell you today again
That there is a God
140 Mister Hoyle
Amen—the man that made the
fifty-two cards
Tried to equalize with God
Amen God had made a heaven
and made a earth
And had made—Amen—the
earth with fifty-two weeks
in the earth
145 And three hundred and sixty-
five days in the year
Mister Hoyle went on about his
business
Said that I will equalize with
God
Hark Hallelujah
Made a deck of cards
150 With fifty-two cards in the deck
Representin' the fifty-two
weeks in the year
And the three hundred and
sixty-five spots on the cards
Represented the three hundred
and sixty-five days in the
year
Mister Hoyle
155 Remembered that there was
sometimes extra games
played in these cards

An' he thought about the leap
year
That had sixty-nine days—
twenty-nine days every
fourth year
An' Mister Hoyle put a joker in
the deck of cards
That you could play—extra card
160 Every now and then
God from Zion
And Mister Hoyle knew God
had two ways to go
Either heaven an'—or to hell
Mister Hoyle made a deuce
165 God from Zion
That—hmm—that meant either
heaven or hell
And Mister Hoyle knew there
was a three-Godheads
God the Father Son and the
Holy Ghost
And he made a trey
170 God from Zion
And Mister Hoyle knew that it
was Matthew Mark Luke
and John
Three—four gospel writers that
wrote the gospel of our
Lord and Savior Jesus
Christ
He made a four-spot
representin' the four gospel
writers
An' he made a five-spot
representin' the five
wounds that was in the
Savior's side—body
175 Two in His hands, one in His
side, two in His feet

An' Mister Hoyle made a six-
spot representin' the six
days man shall labor
An' he made a seven-spot
representin' the seventh
day—was the day of rest
An' he made an eight-spot
representin' the eight that
was saved in Noah's ark
An' he represented and made a
nine-spot
180 Which represented
Hung from the sixth to the
ninth hour
Out yonder on Mount Calvary
And he made a ten-spot which
represented the ten
commandments
Hmm-mm
185 That was handed down from
Moses
Out yonder on Mount Sinai
An' he made a queen which
represented the Queen of
Sheba
Came all the way
From Africa
190 To meet King Solomon
And told him I heard about you
But the half had never been
told
Ain't God all right
Well on then
195 He made a king
Which represented Jesus
The King of the world
Then he made a jack
Representin' the black horse
death

200 That rides to every man's door
That's been born in the world
God from Zion
Then he made a ace which
represents the highest
order
God—that sets high in glory
205 Looks down on a sin-tired
world
I'm tryin' to say to you
In my conclusion
That God
Is not dead
210 God
Is still alive
He's alive
In my soul
He's alive
215 In my everyday walks
He's alive
In my home
He's alive
On my job
220 I'm tryin' to say to y'
He's a teacher to me
He's a guide
An' He's a company-keeper for
me
I wonder do y' know what I'm
talkin' about
225 That same God
Same God
I say that same God
Is a way-provider
When y' don't have a way
230 When y' can't make your own
way
He's a way-provider
He's a rock

In the weary land
And a shelter
235 In the time of a storm
That same God
That met me one mornin'
In the state of Mississippi
I shall never forget the day
240 I shall never forget the time
An' I shall never forget the
        place
One Monday mornin'
That same God
Met me that mornin'
245 And said Lacy
If you don't go
If you don't go
This is your last chance
I never shall forget the word I
        said
250 I said to Him that mornin' I'll
        go
Where Y' want me to go
If it's to California I'll go
If it's to Nebraska I'll go
All the way

255 Ever since that day
I been on the job
I been into many cities
But that same God
Has been along with me
260 I been into many state
But that same God
Has walked by my side
I been into many dangerous
        places
And many dangers and unseen
        dangers
265 That same God
Has been on my side
Has walked along by me
An' I thank Him this mornin'
I wonder is you able to thank
        Him
270 I thank Him
Pretty good things He's done
        me
I thank Him for keeping me
        alive
Door of the church is open

THE TWENTY-THIRD PSALM
Version 1

Recited by the Reverend Rubin Lacy, July 9, 1967, in Bakersfield, California, this sermon was nearly a complete failure, but Lacy managed to pull it out of its nose dive at the last minute. He started off badly because he did not know what he was going to say. Probably it was a matter of relying too heavily on divine intervention and not enough on preparation. The first twenty lines have little coherence; then he got sidetracked on a reminiscence of his childhood, triggered by the metaphor of God as a fisher of men (line 20). Lacy allowed himself to get carried away because the congregation was enjoying the story. But he was not establishing any rhythmical pattern and it soon cost him the attention of the audience. When he tried to get back to the subject he had nothing to work with. The biblical allusions skip around somewhat: line 70 appears to be from I Samuel 16:10 ff., but after that the stories of David are known. The parable of David and the spider is very popular among Baptist preachers; Lacy had probably memorized it. At line 169 he attempts to salvage the sermon by beginning a theme, but that soon fades. At line 193 he begins a second theme, that of the Psalm proper, and this is slightly more successful though at line 230 the congregation is still rather listless. Somewhere around this point he must have decided to use a theme that he could master, that of the four horsemen of the Apocalypse: line 241 anticipates the opening of the four horsemen theme ("But in the mornin'- "), which is repeated in line 278. From that point until the end Lacy was able to devote himself to all the histrionics necessary to getting the message across; the audience responded warmly and Lacy finished strongly.

I'm gonna talk today about the
    Twenty-third Psalm of
    David
The Lord is my shepherd
The Lord is my shepherd, I
    shall not want
I likes that
5 When I was pastoring I uses
    that every Sunday morning
    for the opening of my
    service: the Lord is my
    shepherd
And every now and then I
    preaches it—and I wouldn't
    preach this if I didn't
    believe it
I noticed the deacon prayin' a
    while ago, and I noticed
    when the tears just broke
    out of his eye, settin' there
    thinkin'
You know when people fight
    you 'bout righteousness it
    make you cry sometime
But people have always fought
    folks about righteousness
10 When you hear everybody on a
    man, or on a woman, they
    pretty well standin' up for
    what's right
Paul ain't look like he got all
    that many friends, among
    his kind
Hmmm?

I know what I'm talkin' about,
    he ain't got all that many
    friends among his kind, he
    should have
Ain't nobody give him his,
    Amen?
15 You work hard, sacrifice, get
    anything for it?
But somebody don't like him
Somebody is stealin', if they
    could steal your very best
    members they'd do it
I done heard some of them say
    so
Hmmm?
20 But I think if you wanta do
    what's right, God said if
    you want to 'come
    fishermen of men, why
    don't you get out there and
    get the right kind of bait,
    and fish, catch y' some
If y' ain't got the right kind of
    bait y' jus' can't catch a
    fish
Hmm?
Some people fish all day—
    another thing you gotta
    move about to fish, just
    sitting in one place all day,
    sitting there in the same
    spot, thinkin' the fish's
    gonna come to you—he
    goes in schools in droves

You don't move about to catch
the droves you don't catch
no fish
25 But it's the truth
My mother—I used to go fish
with my mother, she carry
me to fishin' all the time—
all the rest of the children
at home but she carry me
to fishin', I love to fish
But why did she carry me and
both of us was scared of
snakes
I couldn't understand that, both
of us scared of snakes, and
she carried me
As I get older I get a lot more
ways like my mother
30 If you noticed me whenever I
set down in the pulpit at
home anywhere I'm shakin'
that leg all the time
That's a gift from my—I mean a
birthmark
As I get older my head give me
trouble like my mother
And one mornin' it took her
away from me, jus' after
. . .
Couldn'ta told her, son-in-law
. . . where she's goin',
35 So I'm no better than she was,
it may take me
But I—if it takes me I want to
be a truthful man, not a
liar, 'cause God hate all sin
but He abominates a liar
I don't think it says He
abominates anything else
but a liar

But He hates all sin
Hmm?
40 But I think people oughta tell
the truth, especially leaders
If I'da told a man I was gonna
be here I'da been here
I don't care who come to offer
me fifty dollars I'd say I
gotta go to Blair's if I
promised to go
Just like I told a man I'd be
back there tonight—he
know I don't wanna go out
here tonight, but I'm goin'
'Cause I said that I'd be here
45 David said the Lord is my
shepherd, I shall not want
And he couldn't say this until
he got to be up in age
Nobody can talk about God
until he 'come experienced
enough to talk Him
Hmm?
Paul couldn't talk about Him,
he didn't know nothin'
about Him
50 Amen, but after he was stricken
down on the road to
Damascus
He said, in Damascus, I heard a
voice
He never did forget that
When he was talking to Festus
he told Festus I heard a
voice
He was talkin' to Felix he told
Felix I heard a voice
55 When he's talkin' to King
Agrippa he said—I heard a
voice I saw a light

He said the men that was with
    me saw a light but they
    didn't hear a voice
He said the light blinded me
The king said y' gotta take 'im
    outo' here
Said if y' don't take him outo'
    here he'll convert me
60 Paul said not only you, but I
    wish every man under the
    sound of my voice would
    be converted
David said—after he got up—
    ahh—an' he said the Lord
    is shepherd
I shall not want
He began to think about—like
    you and I—how God had
    taken care of him in his
    young days—in his hard
    days
David was a lover of feeding
    things
65 A lover of watching things
From a bird on down
Hmm?
And the other brother was rich,
    loved dressing
Hmm?
70 That's how come Samuel was
    fooled when he went t'
    honor a king
All them big robust and
    dressed-up boys come
    walkin' out seven of 'em
    dressed to death, say I just
    know that was king
But when he drew the oil horn
    it didn't flow

Old man begin to get worried,
    said to Jesse, is you got
    another son?
I know God sent me here, and I
    came but the horn ain't
    holdin' no oil
75 Is you got another son—Jesse
    say yes, the David boy
Said he's the little red-headed
    thing down yonder in the
    hot sun, watchin' the
    sheep, said but I can't sit
    down 'til y' bring 'im here
Talkin' about?
I can't sit down until y' bring
    him
And they brought him on—oh
    yes it's in the Bible—
    brought him on down
    there, and brought him
    there, and David . . .
80 And you laugh and little David
    had been anointed—a little
    shepherd boy, been
    anointed king
Hmm?
Oh my
They had a man from the
    Philistines over there, he
    was a giant, a great big tall
    giant
And every morning he's walk
    out, with his war clothes on
85 And holler somebody send me
    a man
They couldn't get nobody to go
David said one morning I'll go
Say we love you but to go
    David said we want you to

dress up in some of our
army clothes
Put the things on David that
didn't fit
⁹⁰ Hmm?
What you put on somebody
else doesn't fit him, use
what y' got
God want y' to use what y' got
You can't preach like me—
Amen—God want you to
preach with the gift that
He gave you
Hmm?
⁹⁵ Ahh, David told to put off these
things
An', ah, give me my little
shepherd-boy clothes
An', an' ah, give me my sling
shot
Went on down there and
picked him up five rocks
Just five
¹⁰⁰ Goin' against a giant
He comes laughin' at him saw
David comin', he comes
laughin'
Ha ha ha I'm goin' to give your
body to the so-an'-so today
David, he was walkin' up on
him, he done this, one! in
the name of the Father,
'nother! in the name of the
Son, now! in the name of
the Holy Ghost, and then
he really slinged
Walked on up there cut his
head off, and took it on,
away—began to show it

¹⁰⁵ And the women come as
braggin'—women I say
come as braggin'
Don't let women brag on y'
Amen! women do as they brag,
sayin' Saul has killed his
thousands, but David has
killed his ten thousands
Then the news went out
The news went out about
David, and from that day
on, the devil got behind
that boy
¹¹⁰ Amen he had to run for his life
But if he run God run with him
He run when his friends would
tell him sometime why
don't you stop and fight?
David kept running, don't tell
me he ain't got nothin',
somebody said what you
gonna do run all your life
yeah he said if it's
necessary
Hmm? God'll stop me in time
¹¹⁵ Now while he was running
and—ah—Saul was hunting
him, and he was running
and running in, a cave
And—ah—Saul was so close
behind, and was searching
every nook and corner
And God made a protection out
of a black widow spider
Ah—David ran in the cave, God
had the spider to web up
the hole
He put a web there he'll know
that you're not in here

120 'Cause you're not far up ahead
   of 'em
He'll know that the spider web
   hasn't been broken, you
   not in that cave
David lay in that cave
Ain't God all right?
I heard somebody praying a
   few minutes ago said God
   will make a way
125 He'll do that
Ahh—David lay there
Well, I said in the cave
Saul there in the other end
Said let's rest a while, lay down
   and went to sleep
130 When he lay down and went to
   sleep God woke up David,
   and his servant
The servant said looka here, we
   got him now, the Lord has
   delivered him into our
   hands
Watch this closely, the Lord
   has delivered your enemy
   into our hands
David had been like some of us
   would've said sure did
He said let me go up there and
   cut his head off
135 David said no don't do that
Said go up there cut off a piece
   of his garment
And back up—come on back
   here
And then when he wakes up
   and starts down the road,
   I'll have y' show him that,
   and that will let him know

that you had a chance to
   take his life
And just didn't do it
140 Hot dog, just did that
David had something to thank
   God for
I said as a boy—ahh—a little
   shepherd boy
He loved his sheep
And he had a hundred sheep
   and one would go astray he
   would risk his life to find
   that lamb
145 That means that he had the
   staff with the crook in the
   end
If that lamb was down in the
   gutter
He would take the crooked end
   of that staff and reach
   down and pick him up
Go on up and put up on his
   shoulder
Carry him on to the fold
150 He was a lover of the lamb
And he was a feeder
He would lead his lambs—I
   said—into green pastures
By the still waters
By the pretty grass
155 I said he was a feeder
Ahh, he knew what kind of
   food to give those sheep
Ahh, he knew what time to
   take 'em into the fold
And he knew—Amen—who to
   leave at the door of the
   fold
He knew about that

160 Ahh, I'm tryin' to say to y' he
said after he got home the
Lord is my shepherd
One day as he was out there
watchin' his sheep, ahh, y'
know the devil is big
He's always tryin' to throw a
rock in some good place
Amen—the wolf slipped up and
caught a lamb but David
risked his life to take that
lamb from the wolf
165 Oh yes he did I say he risked
his life to take—and—ahh—
he went on and killed—
Amen—that lion,
overpowered that lion,
takin' that little lamb and
carryin' him on back to the
fold
Comin' on home that night, he
was a travelin' musician
Playing something—Amen—on a
twelve-string harp
That night sitting out in his
room
Mother—Amen—tipping across
the floor
170 David was sitting there
Playing on his harp
The Lord is the strength of my
life
Then whom shall I fear
Mother kept tippin 'cross the
floor
175 Wondering in her mind
What had happened that day
Managed to tip back and said to
him son

What's happened today?
He said a lion
180 Got in among my sheep
And taking a lot of my little
lambs
And God enabled me to
overpower him
And then replaced the lamb
back in the flock again
I heard a fellow Oh Lord
185 Is the strength of my life
Then whom shall I fear?
And the Lord is my shepherd
If He hadn'ta been my
shepherd
I'da been gone a long time ago
190 If He hadn'ta been my
shepherd
Door would be closed in my
face
But now it's open in my face
But Lord God
Lead me
195 By the side of still waters
I heard Him say
God from Zion
He leadeth me
In the path of righteousness
200 For His names' sake
Yea though
I walk through the valley
Of the shadow of death
I fear no evil
205 For Thou art with me
Thy rod
And Thy staff
It comforts me
Thou preparest a table
210 Before me

There in the presence of my
  enemies
Thou anointest my head with
  oil
And my cup runneth over
Surely
215 Goodness and mercy
Shall follow me all the days of
  my life
And I shall dwell
In the house of the Lord
I wonder do y' believe me
220 You that been home again
You that burd—bear the burden
In the heat of the day
You
That know
225 That y' met Jesus
One mornin'
Somebody said in Mississippi
Some said in Arkansas
Somebody been in Tennessee
230 Everywhere you go—that same
  Jesus
Is right here today
I said that same Jesus
Is right here today
He's on your barn over there
235 He's on your barn here
But some of us forget about
  that
We got up—for get up in the
  world
And get a suit of clothes
And able to get a car
240 And said we don't need Jesus
But in the mornin'
We gonna need him
I said in the mornin'

When money won't do y' no
  good
245 In the mornin'
When clothes won't do y' no
  good
Oh in the mornin'
When fine home won't do y' no
  good
Oh in the mornin'
250 When good-lookin' furniture
  don't do y' no good
Y' gonna need
Y' gonna need
By and by
I will see Jesus
255 By and by
I will see Jesus
By and by
I will see Jesus
Oh, in that . . .
260 Over there . . .
I don't care what y' say I got
Y' know some people got a lot
  o' clothes, don't think
  about nothin'
But what're y' gonna get—he's
  selfish
I say he oughta be named Ahab
265 Because we got so many selfish
  people
And the big assembly in the
  church
Umm-hmm
They got that way in the world
If a gambler break his buddy
270 He won't let him go home to
  his wife broke
He'll give him a dollar or two

But a church member umm-
hmm
Can break you
And then he'll laugh about it
²⁷⁵ They oughta have sense enough
To save some
Ain't I right about it?
But in the mornin'
I wanna be looking
²⁸⁰ For the man that I been
    fighting for
Umm—if you sold him
You gonna be looking for him
God from Zion
They tell me
²⁸⁵ In the mornin'
When the horses
Begin to come out
And the riders on the horses
Want 'em to come out
²⁹⁰ God from Zion
Riding a red horse
There's somebody gonna say
Is that the general
That I was fighting for
²⁹⁵ And I heard another cry
Saying no-ooo
That's not the one
That you been fighting for
Another one rode out
³⁰⁰ Riding a black horse

Is that the man
That I been fighting for
I heard another voice say
No, no-oo
³⁰⁵ That's not the general
That you been fighting for
Another one rode out
Riding a pale horse
Is that the general
³¹⁰ That we been fighting for?
A voice said no
That's not the one
That you been fighting for
Another one came out
³¹⁵ God from Zion
Riding a white horse
Rainbow round his shoulder
Hark Hallelujah
Dressed in raiment
³²⁰ White as driven as the snow
From his head down to his feet
God from Zion
In his—from out of his mouth
Come a two-edge sword
³²⁵ Cuttin' sin
Both right and left
I heard a cry
Is that the man
That we been fightin' for
³³⁰ They said yes

THE TWENTY-THIRD PSALM
Version 2

This sermon was recited by the Reverend Rubin Lacy, May 5, 1968, in Corcoran, California. Because this is a repeat of a sermon on the same topic as a performance of Lacy's a year earlier, it has great value for the study of variation in structure and language over a year's time. A detailed comparison is made in Chapter 7. Most interesting is the absence of the four horsemen theme that Lacy used a year earlier. When that sermon was first delivered (in 1967) I could only guess that the four horsemen theme was out of place and was inserted by Lacy to arouse his audience. This speculation was borne out in 1968 when Lacy recited the same sermon but omitted the four horsemen. Only those lines that appear in the 1967 performance are underlined (solid or broken) here. This performance was well received though the congregation numbered only about fifteen. Lacy begins to chant near line 87.

Twenty-third Psalms of David
Since it's so late
The Lord is my shepherd, I
    shall not want
The Lord is my shepherd, I
    shall not want

5 We're talkin' tonight from a
    man that is experienced
You know experience is your
    best teacher
I don't care what you learn in
    books, it's fine—don't
    understand me say it isn't

fine, but don't let books
carry you away
Hmm? experience is your best
teacher
David here knew what he was
talkin' about
¹⁰ Because he was experienced
From his youth he had—he
had—been a shepherd boy
He wasn't like his other fine
rich brothers
That didn't believe in nothin'
but dressin' fine in the very
finest of linen
And waiting on the servants as
they wait on them
¹⁵ But David loved the sheep
And he cared for the sheep
I'm tryin' to say to you that
David was a leader from
his youth
Sometime you see a little boy
running around your home
And you watch his appearance
and somebody will say that
boy is a preacher
²⁰ I don't know I don't think
Samuel was able to see that
about his son—I mean Jesse
was able to see that 'bout
his son David
Ah—he rather thought that
some of the boys—other
boys—was more dressed
fine—an'—ah—stayed in
among the big people
would come nearer makin'
a great man than David

Because David stayed in the
field
All the time—'fact he stayed
there so much until his
color—ah—wasn't like his
other brothers
He was sun-burnt
²⁵ An'—ah—his color 'count of this
didn't favor his other
brothers
But we see here that he was
God's chosen man
From the Jews
When the time come—ah—for
the second king to be
anointed for Israel
God told Samuel to go to
Jesse's house
³⁰ An'—ah—anoint a king
Now listen—God didn't tell
Jesse who t' anoint
Jesse had eight boys
You go there an' anoint a king
Ah—among those boys
³⁵ God fools Samuel too
Jesse wasn't the only man
fooled
But Samuel was fooled too
Because these men—no wonder
the writer said the other
day
Ah—God looks at the inward
and man looks on the outer
appearance
⁴⁰ Samuel and also the father of
David were looking on the
outside
Looking at the high—robustest
boy

That dressed in fine clothes
They wasn't thinkin' about that
   boy in the field
But when Samuel begin to draw
   the horn
⁴⁵ It failed to pour
And they passed through until
   seven boys had went under
   the horn
And then old man Samuel
   began to get all uneasy
I know that God don't make
   mistakes
Samuel—listen to Samuel talkin'
   to himself—I know that
   God don't make mistakes
⁵⁰ But there's something wrong—
   all seven of these boys that
   went under the horn and
   the oil had failed to pour
He asked the father didn't he
   have another son
He said oh yes I got another
   little boy but he's in the
   field
Goodness sake I know he's not
   the one
But Samuel knowin' God and
   believed in God said I
   won't set down/don't offer
   me a chair
⁵⁵ I won't set down until y' bring
   him here
And they had to hurry to the
   field and found David
   around his sheep
Found little David with the
   staff in his hand

Found David with his light
   layin' on the altar for his
   sheep
Found David standin' between
   the lions and the bears
⁶⁰ Guarding his sheep
And they said the prophet
   wants you at the house
David went on up there with
   his little bushy head
See him in my mind
And ah sun-burnt face
⁶⁵ Went on up there
But when he walked under the
   horn the oil began to pour
Listen—and the news went out
That little David is anointed
   king
What I'm tryin' to say to y' as
   long David was in the field
   watchin' sheep he didn't
   have no trouble
⁷⁰ Nobody wasn't payin' him no
   attention
But when the news went out
That David is anointed king
Saul got in behind
I hope you see what I'm talkin'
   about
⁷⁵ The devil got in behind
Yes they tried to get him killed
Put him up—Amen—before that
   great giant
And he trusted God
King sent for him and dressed
   him up in a suit of clothes
⁸⁰ David looked at the clothes and
   said it don't fit me

Ahh—gimme my little clothes
    what I had on
And when the sword is not the
    right kind
Gimme my little sling
And my bag
85 David went on and this king
    looked at him
Begin to make fun of him
Talkin' about how he would
    give him the fowl of the air
David just stood there
Reached down and got one of
    his little rocks
90 Placed it in his sling shot
He made three swings
Representin' God the Father
God the Son
And God the Holy Ghost
95 And direct it between/the two
    eyes
Ohh the giant fell
And David walked up and cut
    his head off
And the news went out
That Saul had killed his
    thousands
100 But David has killed ten
    thousand
Ain't God all right?
No wonder
David in his old age
Can say the Lord is my
    shepherd
105 I shall not want
Devil kept on runnin' after
    David
They run him so tired
Sometime he was hungry

He had to eat the short bread
110 He didn't have time to go to
    the store
He had to eat the bread
That the trees issued
God from Zion
They kept on runnin' him
115 They runned him so fast
'Til one day
They was so close behind
God said to David
Run in the cave
120 David didn't argue with God
Went on in the cave
A widow spider
Crept up the cave
Behind little David
125 Saul come by
Looked and saw the web
And said I know
He can't be in here
Went on down the road
130 And went in the cave
And went to sleep
And God
Called David
To go in the other end of the
    cave
135 And found his enemies asleep
His servant said to 'im
The Lord has delivered 'em
Into your hands
But David said
140 He's God's anointed
No wonder he said
The Lord is my shepherd
He was experienced with that
There can't nobody say that
145 But people that's experienced

David was experienced
And then a shepherd must lay
    his life on the altar
A shepherd don't just drink the
    milk
And eat the flock
150 But he lay his life on the altar
In those days
It was dangerous to be a
    shepherd
Because the wolves
The bears
155 The lions
The bobcats
The panthers/and all those
    things/were dangerous
And it was an open range
And men had to stay out there
160 Both night and day
I wonder are y' goin' with me
That's what the men were doin'
The night when Jesus was born
Out yonder on the plains
165 Watching the sheep
David was one of these men
He were out there
One day he was out there
And a lion got among his sheep
170 Come along and grabbed a
    lamb
You know the devil always hits
    the weakest spot
The weakest thing he can find
He don't bother the strong
    things
So the lion come in the flock
175 And saw this little lamb
Hadn't been long born
And he couldn't run

Like a old sheep
And the devil got after the
    lamb
180 And caught the lamb
Little David
Laid his life on the altar
Takin' his sword
And walked up there
185 And takin' the lamb
Out of the lion's paws
Went on home
Sit down that night
Playin' on his harp
190 The Lord is the strength of my
    life
And whom shall I fear
Mama tippin' across the floor
Listen' at his new song
A song she had never heard
    before
195 Jesus
Here come the strain
She said to him son
What happened today
He said mama
200 A lamb
Was got in the lion's paw
And God
Delivered the lamb
Back into my hands
205 Ain't God all right?
I said it takes a man of
    experience
To say the Lord is my shepherd
Oh anybody can say it
You've heard it so much it has
    become common
210 For people to say the word

I read it to y' every Sunday
   morning
The Lord is my shepherd—
   people don't pay that no
   attention
But it takes somebody with
   experience to know that
   God has been your
   shepherd
I remember once some time in
   my life
215 Guns were throwed in my face
By men that was no . . . kin
But they couldn't pull the
   trigger
Because the Lord was my
   shepherd
God bless y'/hope you got
   something out of this/the
   Lord is my shepherd
220 And if He's your shepherd
   there's no need to worry
You know some of us worry
   'cause people don't go to
   church

There's no need to worry
If the Lord is your shepherd
   preach on
Preachers, preach on
225 Singers, sing on
You gonna get your reward
God has given you that gift
You sing on
And God will give you your
   reward
230 Preach if you don't have but
   three to preach to
Preachers, don't be
   'shamed to preach—I
   preach just as hard to
   this—bunch like this as I
   would a church full
Because I think that's the
   church
I'm through
I think that's the church
235 Whoever be's here I think it's
   the church

THE POSTAGE STAMP

Recited by the Reverend J. J. Freeman (of Pixley, California), July 23, 1967, in Bakersfield, California, this sermon appeared to be a favorite of Freeman's, and he had prepared it well. The congregation responded cordially and Freeman was in control of his material at all times. He was giving a guest sermon in the Reverend Elihue H. Brown's Union Baptist Church and was to be followed by a lecture from a local prison officer, the Captain Medlock mentioned in line 8. The reference to a hypothetical police captain in line 33 was provoked by Medlock's presence, as my presence induced the remark about the "recording gentleman" in line 8. Freeman did not sing well but his sense of rhythm was impeccable. He broke into a chant at line 58; and the congregation was receptive. This early start gave him a good deal of time to work with them—to get his message across. At line 173 he reverted to a more normal speech, but at line 193 he broke into singing, which carried the sermon to its conclusion. The text for the day, "Go ye into the world and preach the gospel to every creature," was the most popular scriptural passage among the preachers interviewed.

And He said unto them, go ye
　　into all the world and
　　preach the gospel to every
　　creature

He that believeth and is
　　baptized shall be saved; he
　　that believeth not shall be
　　damned

From the sixteenth chapter of
the book of Saint Mark,
fifteenth and sixteenth
verse
We're going to use the latter
part of the first verse, ahh,
go ye into all the world
⁵ And our thought will be, like a
postal stamp
And down a way you'll find
why I'm choosing the
stamp
Amen
Giving thanks to God and honor
to Pastor Brown and to
all—to–of my co-workers in
the ministry, to Captain
Medlock, this fine
recording gentlemen, and
to Union Baptist as a
whole, and to all our
friends and visitors we
thank God for the
privilege—we deem it
honor that out of all the
fine ministers here you
chose me for this hour
Thinking as I received the
invitation said the
professional program, and I
thought of everything in
the world to bring to you
today
¹⁰ And I wound up with the
gospel of the Lord and
Savior Jesus Christ
I'm using the stamp because
my, follow-up for the

subject would be stay in
your place
Amen
I believe it's a mighty fine thing
to have a profession
It's better when you have this
profession to stay in your
place
¹⁵ Amen
We find that most professions
seemly to stand their
ground and wait, until we
get to the church
Gettin' a little quiet now
Amen
Ahh, the doctor knows his
profession, and one thing
about the doctor, when you
go to him and he diagnose
your case, unless it's your
wife or some close relative,
he won't tell you a thing
²⁰ That right?
Because he's your doctor 'n'
this is an oath, that
whatever is wrong with you
I'm gonna keep your secret
Likewise—Amen—every
attorney knows his field
I call them the liars
'Cause most attorneys have to
lie if he's gonna free you
'specially if you're guilty of
a crime
²⁵ Amen, but he's a profession in
his field
So he goes about it in an
intelligent way

Sometime he make folk lie that
    wouldn't lie ordinarily
But he is after winning the case
But he knows his profession
30 Amen
    I believe that—ahh—in the
    church we ought to know
    our profession
    We ought to know how to stay
    in our place
    Ahh, if the captain should leave
    his post
    Try to walk the beat, Amen
    he's getting out of his place
    if he have man on the beat
    he oughta give him his
    order 'n' leave him alone
35 Ahh, I'm comin' to you now
    Amen
    You're not gonna be quiet after
    a while
    Ahh, an' every profession seem
    to be able to make a mark
    But when it comes to our
    profession
    The preacher
40 The highest office that's in the
    world
    The lowest-paid office in the
    world
    The most talked-about man
    Amen, everybody knows his
    profession better than he
    does
    Don't nobody know how to stay
    in their place
45 When it comes to the church
    Brother Pastor, if I was you

Ha ha—I'd do this and I would
    do that
Brother Pastor if I was you I
    wouldn't let this go on
And I wouldn't let that—but
    have you ever stopped to
    think that have you done
    your duty
50 Have you stood in your
    profession
    Just as a member in the church
    God Almighty I'm sick of folks
    tellin' me what I oughta do
    And then leaving their job
    undone
    Have somebody that don't live
    right
55 Amen, Lord God, you run to
    the pastor and say turn him
    out
    I'm not big enough to turn
    anybody out
    If you do your job you—ahh—
    make the first trip
    I believe this is your Bible
    Say if you overtake you in the
    fall
60 You go to the—you can't get
    reconcile
    You go back and get another
    one
    And you go the third time
    They feel they hear you—then
    they bring them before the
    church
    We don't bring nobody before
    the church
65 There hasn't nobody turned out
    of the church in the last
    twenty years

Amen?
Gettin' quiet in here isn't it?
We—we're—we ought to know
    our profession
Reason why, that I chose the
    postal stamp
70 Ahh, the minister is like a
    stamp
He's a messenger bearer
He's an ambassador to God
Ahh and Jesus gave him a
    commission
Said go ye
75 In—all over the world
And preach the gospel
Yeah?
Sometime they bring us sad
    news
Sometime he's meddlin'
80 Sometimes he makes you mad
Sometimes he makes you glad
But ohh
You oughta listen sometime
Yeah the stamp
85 Around your home
Sometime a stamp'll get lost
Lay around and get a little
    dirty
And lose the glue power
We throw it away
90 But you can use it
If you just try
To help it along a little bit
You clean it up a little
Put a little glue on
95 And put it on the envelope
Oh yeah
And drop it in the box
The postman

Will stamp his approval
100 And send you on your way
A five-cent stamp
That will take this message
Over into Philadelphia
Your mother's dead
105 Ahh—the airmail stamp
Will take the same message
Your mother's dead
A special delivery
Will take the same message
110 Your mother's dead
Oh Lord
I see the three stamps
Standing together
I have heard one say
115 How come you're like you are?
I heard that stamp say
You did a good job
You carried the message
And I brought the same
    message
120 Stamp didn't say well I'm
    better than you are
But it said well
I got a job to do
The five-cent stamp
Will do as much as a special
    delivery
125 It its own category
Say you oughta stay in your
    place
Ohh Lord
If somebody
Was to say to the stamp
130 I don't like your look
The stamp say well
I tell y' what you oughta do
Take it up with my maker

I did not make myself
135 Ohh Lord
Want you to pray with me
Ahh yeah
I see a preacher
On his way
140 Carryin' God's word
Somebody
Say I don't like it
Don't like the way you look
I don't like what you say
145 This is what you oughta tell
    him
If you don't like me
Take it up with my maker
He made me
Just like I am
150 The stamp
Never stands still
Till it got its approval from
    Washington
Then if it's OK
Before it carry the message
155 The preacher
Ohh yeah
Got to get a OK from God
Ohh yeah
I heard a poet sang it a song
    the other day
160 I been sealed
Till the day of redemption
I don't care what happens
The storm cloud may rise
But I been sealed till the day of
    redemption
165 Don't make me 'posin' my faith
But I been sealed till the day of
    redemption
Jesus said go ye to all the world

And preach the gospel
To every creature
170 He that believe, shall be saved
He that believeth not, shall be
    damned
I'm here to tell you, you oughta
    save your place
Those, young man, he was good
    at doing his job
He built him a little boat
175 Storm came and the little boat
    got lost in the storm
Went down town, saw his little
    boat in the window
Went inside and said looka here
    mister, is that boat for sale
The man said yes
Give me fifty cents and you can
    have it
180 Took the boat and walked
    outside
Began to look at it and say,
    yeah, you mine
Cause I know my handwork
And now I wanna tell y'
    somethin'
I own you twice
185 I made you
Now I bought you
And I got a thought from that
Jesus
Yeah, Jesus
190 Say I made you
Went to the cross of Calvary
    for you
How can you say I'm my own
    boss
I heard Paul say the other day
I'm a prisoner of Jesus Christ

195 Ohh Lord
   I can't do like I want any more
   Since I been regenerated—born
      again
   Holy Ghost got a hold o' me
   Every once in a while
200 Gonna turn around
   But the Holy Ghost say you
      can't turn around
   Ohh Lord
   Ohh this evening
   Lord be my home at evening
205 And walk along with God
   Walk and looka here
   I said looka here
   Your pump is so sweet
   I just can't turn it down

210 Walk another hundred years
   Said I've come too far
   Just can't go back
   Walk another hundred years
   They kissed him and . . .
215 Am I right about it?
   If you stay in your place
   God can use you to serve
   Oh what is this
   I can feel
220 Deep down inside
   What is this
   Set my poor, soul on fire
   With an ever ready heat
   Ohh it won't let me [dissolves
      in singing]

THE EAGLE STIRRETH UP ITS NEST

The sermon was recited by the Reverend Rubin Lacy, July 9, 1967, in Bakersfield, California. This popular theme was fairly successful in Lacy's version, despite the preacher's very poor diction and almost incoherent structure. His diction was so garbled, and the response of the congregation so heated, that several lines are inaudible and cannot be clarified even after repeated tape runs (lines 88 and 178). One of the interesting aspects of this sermon is that when it was over Lacy remarked to me that he had forgotten to come back to the main point of the image of the eagle stirring its nest. The preacher jumps around here from passage to passage, one Bible story reminding him of another, which he then proceeds to tell without attribution. Toward the end he uses a favorite theme of his about the "eagle bird" (lines 230 to 301); the relation to the main theme is obvious, just as it is superficial. He then begins another of his favorite themes, on the four beasts of the Apocalypse (lines 326 ff.), comes back to dreams (lines 354 ff.), then reverts to the story of Daniel's dream, which he had used earlier; Daniel's function reminds Lacy of the functions of various members of the clergy in Ephesians 4:11, and on that note he closes. In few other sermons can we so clearly observe the preacher's mind traveling from idea to idea and phrase to phrase through association, possibly because so much material came to mind when he used this old favorite. The chanting begins on line 84 and continues until line 351, where he begins to speak more conversationally. The mention of a "desert land" in line 7 reminded Lacy of Bakersfield.

Reading today from the book of
Deuteronomy, chapter
thirty-two
Remember the days of old,
consider the years of many
generations: ask the father,
and he will show you, the
elders and they will tell
you
When the most high God
divided nations—their
inheritance separation of
the sons of Adam
He set the bounds of the
people according to the
number of the children of
Israel
⁵ For the Lord's portion in His
people
Jacob is the lot of his
inheritance
He found them—watch this—in
a desert land
In the waste howling land
He led him about and He
instructed him
¹⁰ He kept him as an apple of His
eye
Eleventh verse said
And as an eagle stirreth up the
nest
Fluttereth over her young
Spreadeth abroad her wings
¹⁵ Taketh them, beareth them, on
her wings
Twelfth verse said

So the Lord alone did lead
them, there was no strange
god with them
Bible says—our text says—
eleventh verse
As an eagle stirreth the nest
²⁰ I have to jump down to the
twelfth verse
He said that there were no
strange gods
I don't care where Jacob went
How much God stirred him up
You know He stirred him up a
whole lot of times
²⁵ When he was a boy—nothin'
but a boy
His mother might have been
the cause of some of it, but
it was the will of God that
he be stirred up
It could have been through
encouragement of his
mother
Because he didn't know or
didn't desire to do some of
the things that his mother
insisted that he ought to do
What belonged to him I believe
he 'ventually would have
got it anyway should she
waited on him
³⁰ But she couldn't see it like that
Jacob was her favorite son
Hangin' around the kitchen—
uhh—in the house

Practicin'—he made himself a
good cook
He made hisself such a cook
until he could—when his
brother came in hungry
one day
35 And there wasn't nothin' to eat
down, he told him—said—
I'll make you some lentil
soup if you give me your
birthright
All these things was comin'
upon Jacob that he might
become stirred up
So one day he stole his
brother's birthright . . . his
mother
The thing got so bilious and so
dangerous until his mother
then had to lose her son for
a while, have t' lose him
'Cause he had to go to her
brother's home
40 A distant land from that
particular place
And as he went on, runnin'
away from his brother, in a
strange desert land
He lied down one night and
went to sleep, and his
pillow was a rock
And as he was sleeping that
night he saw a ladder let
down from heaven
45 An angel descending on that
ladder
From earth to heaven
He's asleep

An' he woke up the next
mornin' and said, surely
the Lord is in this place
He said and this rock that I
made for a pillow I set over
here
50 It shall be the gate therein
The house of God
I'm tryin' to say that was long
time 'fore Jericho were
built
Amen! That was long time 'fore
Bethlehem was thought of
Long time before Jerusalem—
Amen—was built
55 But keptin' still, Jacob was able
to see these things
That's God—God was with him
though he had done wrong
Amen! A man does wrong don't
let nobody fool y', he's got
to reap what he sows
Ahh, Paul had to reap what he
sowed
I don't care how much God
forgives you, you got to
reap what you sow
60 When a man's forgiven for his
sins looks like it ought to
be all over
But hear, he's got to reap what
he sows
Jacob was stirred up and had to
leave home
Went on over there an' married
Um-hm
65 An' he stayed over there—let's
see, I think he worked for

seven years for a younger
girl
And then, after he worked
seven years for a younger
girl
Old man Laban told him, he
said this, you have got to
work now for seven more
years because the oldest
girl was married first
And there so he worked seven
more years
That mean he worked fourteen
years—Amen!—for those
two wives
⁷⁰ Then when he had to work for
six or seven more years
which made it twenty or
twenty-one years—Amen
In order to get a . . . of cattle—
a herd—Amen
One day, Amen
God had always been with old
man Jacob
But he had to reap what he
sowed
⁷⁵ He went on from there and
God stirred him up over
there
Things got bad, he had to pull
up and leave there
He's on his way back to meet
his brother Esau
Want to hear this treaty, but he
was rich man then
Had a lot of cattle, a lot of
herd, lot of sheep and all
these different things, lot of
camels—Amen—

⁸⁰ Camels worth a whole lot of
money
Amen—started out on his
journey
Makin' his way back to meet
his brother
Shows y' how God kept him
stirred up
Umm-hmm
⁸⁵ He went on back home
Stayed around there a long
time
And, his brother's son was born
Benjamin and Joseph an . . .
Amen! and Joseph got up to be
a seventeen-year-old boy
⁹⁰ He was loved very much by his
father
One day he was sold—Amen—
to the Ishmaelites
Down in the land of Egypt
They take him down there—
Amen—and make a slave
out of him
God begin to stir Jacob up
again
⁹⁵ After a while the well got dry
Nobody could make no wheat,
nobody could raise no corn
And this uh—butler—down in
that country
Told the king, said, I know
about Pharaoh this mornin'
Said, uh, there was a little
Israelite boy
¹⁰⁰ Go down in jails
That interpretated my dreams
Nigh on two years ago

An' I promise that I will tell
   you
To let the little boy out a free
   man
105 That hadn't done nobody no
   harm
But this day said the king
Had dreamed a dream
God from Zion
He said to 'em, tonight I know
   my fall
110 And the king
Told 'em to go get the boy
Had him a shave
Amen! and put on a clean
   raiment
Amen!
115 Put a necklace around his neck
Bring him on up here
Brought him on up there
And get him to interpretate the
   king's dream
He called it the seventh lean
   years gone
120 He saw the dream/ meaning
   seven years of poordom of
   no prosperity
And the seven fat years of corn/
   mean seven good years
And you know about the cows
I said was seven poor cows
Ate up the seven fat cows
125 And they was still poor
God from Zion
The king said to Joseph
If you all that wise
What shall I do about it
130 Joseph said to him
Get a man

God from Zion
To go around
And get all the people in the
   land of Egypt
135 Get 'em more bonds
Ain't I right about it?
Store up their food
Get ready for preparin'
For seven years of famine
140 Went on down there
Ain't God all right?
King said to him
You shall ride
In the second chariot
145 God from Zion
King got the job
Of doin' all these things
I'm tryin' to say to you this
   evenin'
Joseph dreamed
150 Aggrigated [sic] to come true
When he was a little boy
He dreamed
That his mother 'n' father
And his twelve brothers
155 His eleven brothers
Would bow and receive
Ain't God all right
And then he dreamed another
   dream
God from Zion
160 About the sheaf
In the field
But all these sheaves/stood
   upright
All the rest of boys' sheaves
Bowed down to him
165 And Joseph here
Was thirty years old

Before he saw his dream
Comin' true
Hark Hallelujah
¹⁷⁰ God from Zion
Riding in the chariot
Gettin' ready
To do business
Down yonder in Egypt
¹⁷⁵ I saw
A dream give out in Israel
Old man Jacob
. . . .
Been down in Egypt's cell
¹⁸⁰ All those boys together one day
Goin' over the news
Get your sights in your hand
And bring some money out
Put money in your pocket
¹⁸⁵ And get on down to Egypt
And bring some food on here
That the people here don't
 starve
And Egypt's cattle don't starve
I saw the boys
¹⁹⁰ Gettin' ready to go to Egypt
You know the story
God was gettin' ready
To stir old man Jacob up again
God said to him
¹⁹⁵ As the text says tonight
As the eagle stirs the nest
Gotta go over yon
So God
Stirred up Jacob
²⁰⁰ Every land
That Jacob went alone
God was on his side
He didn't accept no strange
 gods

God said to Jacob
²⁰⁵ God had told him
Thou shalt have no other gods
Before me
God from Zion
He held onto
²¹⁰ That thing that he was raised
 up with
Held on to it
Some many of us today
God from Zion
Don't even have a culture
²¹⁵ Am I right about it?
But Jacob held onto
His old culture
Ain't God all right
Goin' on from there—goin'
²²⁰ I saw Jacob
Gettin' ready
To stir himself again
Went on down there
God sent him
²²⁵ As an eagle stirs the nest
So was he further over yon
God from Zion
About a eagle bird
Now let's go on
²³⁰ Eagle bird
Is a mighty wise bird
Sets out yon
Only fit for the mountain
He don't allow
²³⁵ No clouds
No dangerous clouds
To get between him and the
 sun
God from Zion
Eagle has got an eye
²⁴⁰ Look at the sun

The beams of the sun
All day long
Don't have to bat his eyes
He don't turn his body around
245 Jus' set there in one place
Turn his neck around
And watch the sun
As she rise
There as she go down
250 Behind the western drum [?]
Ain't God all right
That eagle bird
Is far-sighted
He seed a long way
255 Seed the end
Before he makes it around
I saw the eagle
Settin' down on the mountain
Lookin' out yonder
260 Watchin' the sun
As it traveled
He saw
The 'mensions of a tornado
Make its way to him
265 Three days
Before the tornado arrive
I saw that eagle
Gettin' ready
To get on its wing
270 Dive down
In the water
Bathe itself
In the water
Fly back to the mountain
275 Shrug itself
Look around at its body
Seed if it have any false
    feathers
If he saw a false feather on him

Take his bill
280 And pull the feather out
I'm back again
Revelatin' God the Father
Son and the Holy Ghost
If he didn't see a false feather
285 On his first flight
He set there and looked
And after a while
He begin to get up
To get on his way
290 Every trav'lin'
That eagle make
He would go higher 'n' higher
Where y' goin' eagle?
How come y' pull the feathers?
295 Out o' your wing
I don't want no trouble
When I get on the wing
I don't want no false feathers
I don't want no trouble when I
    get on the wing
300 I wonder do you know what
    I'm talkin's about?
God from Zion
Look today
In the church of God
We got so many
305 False prophets
So many
False feathers
In the church
So many green trees
310 Don't bear no fruit
In God's church
That eagle was set on the wing
Where y' goin' now?
I'm gettin' on the wing
315 I'm gettin' higher 'n' higher

Higher 'n' higher
And after a while
Get above the clouds
See you down there
320 Storms overblowin'
Come on back
To these dips [?] in the
    mountain
Ain't God all right
Let's see what John said about
    it
325 John said
I . . . I
I saw four beasts
One with a face
Looked like a calf
330 Representin' patience/ and
    endurance
'Nother beast I saw
Had a head like a lion
Representin' boldness
And confidence
335 'Nother beast I saw
A face like a man
Representin' wisdom
An' he had knowledge
'Nother beast I saw
340 Looked like a bald eagle
Ain't God all right?/yeah, yeah
I know He's all right!
Any time a boy
Oughta be wise
345 B' able to see trouble
Know when he comes to it
Any true-born child
Ought be able . . .
If y' can't see trouble
350 There's somethin' wrong

Don't tell me that you—God
    don't have nothin' to loan
    y'
Some time y' don't know what
    it's all about
But you know what something's
    to happen
Some folks say well, I don't
    believe in dreams,
355 I don't believe in visions
Let me tell y' one thing, there's
    somethin' to both of 'em
Just got to be talkin' about
    dreams
Father said young men would
    dream dreams
Old men would see visions
360 I think I'm right about it
Umm-hmm
I know you're all right
Kings have dreamed dreams
I said kings have dreamed
    dreams
365 All the wise men
One day they couldn't
    interpretate it
When they send for the guard
    man [God man?]
That guard man to tell them
    about it
I heard 'vangelist say the other
    day
370 All kings
Don't look to me to
    interpretate your dreams
Look at Daniel
Ohh, I heard
You able to give me to
    interpretate your dreams

375 And I heard
Umm-hmm
Daniel said that
When they had to send—Daniel
    to interpretate the king's
    dreams
He told him
380 I can't do it
I heard you talkin' 'bout healin'
Some—God got somebody to
    heal
Everybody can't do it
I say everybody can't do it
385 I heard it said the other day
    there's some to heal
Umm-hmm
Some to pastor

Some for evangelist
But everybody nowadays
390 Will do what they want to do
It just won't work
In the end [song]
I want to take, take my rest
Lord, in the end
395 When I have done
Done my best
I want to smile
When I have no-thing to hide
Ohh, ohh, Lord, in the end
400 Lord will not grow
On this old battle-field
I want to rest [dissolves in
    humming]

GOD IS MINDFUL OF MAN

Recited by the Reverend Elihue H. Brown, June 11, 1967, in Bakersfield, California, this sermon was a success, as were nearly all of Brown's. He was quite popular in his community and his sermons were almost always well attended. Brown's style was somewhat different from those of the other men collected in this volume; he had a good rich voice whose plaintive tone was quite appealing. And he used his voice to good advantage, singing nearly all of the sermon. The chanting begins here on line 24 and very quickly becomes singing; it would be very difficult to say exactly when. Because nearly all the lines were sung, the transcription may be deceptive in that some lines appear to be short because few words were spoken in them: "He told him" (line 76), for instance. But when this line was sung it was drawn out and may have taken four or five seconds to recite. Brown's lines were slowly delivered, his over-all pace was methodical and deliberate, and more than half the lines were sung. His sermons were almost entirely lyrical, which more than made up for his poor sense of timing: he had no emotional build-up as such, hit a high point fairly early and sustained it throughout; there was no denouement. This sermon includes one of his favorite themes, that of Jesus and the miracles, lines 191 ff.

But one in a certain place
   testifies saying, what is man
   that Thou are mindful of
      him, or the Son of Man
      that Thou visit Him
      Hebrew two and six

God's concern about man

The text is a quotation of the
position of the eighth
Psalm

⁵ The psalmist in the third and
part of fourth verses sayest

When I consider Thy heavens,
the works of Thy fingers,
the moon and the stars
which Thou hast ordained
what is man that Thou art
mindful of him?

I want you to know my
brethrens and sisters that
God's concern for man is
very great

And I never can get myself
adjusted to why that man's
concern is so limited for
God

Considerin' Thy greatness and
the handiwork of the
omnipotent God, who by
His own fingers made the
heavens the moon and the
stars

¹⁰ The psalmist could not
understand how or why He
be in unlimited ability the
power and authority which
noticed such a low being as
man

Man is a low order of creation
but is the greatest that God
placed here on the earth

Why is the man is a little lower
creation because he is a
little lower than the angels

But when he is the greatest
created thing that ever
creeped this soil

God is mindful of man because
He know how He made
him

¹⁵ And He's still mindful of man
today/as He was in the
days that He made—that
He created Adam

Men are born now with the
same heart/the same mind
and the same instruments
[?]

They are developed in human
flesh

They have the same activities
of the limbs we use to lean
against

When he is developed
according to the adoption
of conditions—physically
conditions in good
condition then he's found
with nine gallons of warm
blood that run through his
veins

²⁰ God is mindful of man because
He gave man a little more
brains

That you may think how to
carry on and operate what
my fingers have written

As we read in the Scripture
they said that as God
written with His fingers the
stars they came/and the
moon it came in existence

And the sun came according to
how God ordered it
But He said now listen I want
you man to rule every
creeping thing that creeped
upon the earth
25 I want you to take care of the
cows
Then I want you to be mindful
how you go in and out
before me
Because I made you in my own
likeness
I don't have anything else to
get glory out of except you
But I'm gonna make somebody
for your glory
30 Then He placed man in—out of
sleep
And takin' from his side a rib
And made woman
And this woman was made for
the glory and honor of man
I want you to know dear hearts
you has your glory
35 Whatever you do my brethren
this mornin' I want you to
give God the glory
And after God had made—
created man in His own
likeness and image
Then He provided a home for
him
Over in a little old garden they
call garden of Eden
And placed man in that home
40 And placed his wife in there
with him

He said now after I have given
you the dominion over
everything
I want you to still know
I want you to know my
brethren if you don't be
strong in the Lord
Satan will ease upon you
45 And get you to accept him a
little easier with no faith
Am I right this mornin'
What I'm talkin' about you're
not able to rule your own
house
If you don't let the Lord lead
you
But I said He provided a home
for Adam
50 Out in the garden
Told Adam I want you to rule
and rule well
'Long came the devil, began to
whisper to Adam's wife
And she began to get close to
old man Adam
Well I want you to know this
eve—this mornin'
55 The Lord wants you to hear
Him
Obey and do what He says
And He'll make everything all
right
After listen' to and obeyin' his
wife
He obeyed the voice of the
devil
60 Well I want you to know this
mornin'

Only way that Satan can get in
Union Baptist Church
He must come through by
somebody
If I was you
I wouldn't be so weak
⁶⁵ That I would let Satan crawl
inside by me
I would stand on everlastin'
courage
And hold to God's judgment
I say God is concerned about
man
He trusted a lot of things into
his hands
⁷⁰ He gave a man the knowledge
How to go in and out in this
world
And till the soil for a living
He gave man dominion and
opinion
How that they could come
together and make all of
these habits[?]
⁷⁵ Am I right this evenin'—
mornin'
He told him
Why're you so disobedient
You're gonna have to till the
soil
You're gonna have to live by
the sweat of your own
brow
⁸⁰ I want you to know
He said to the woman why're
you disobedient
You're gonna have to bring
forth fruit

We find now—every now and
then
Somebody began to try to bring
something to tell us
⁸⁵ The constitution don't give no
life
Some way [highway?] we cut
out what God said
You must bring forth fruit
Tell me He said He's all right
O women that take these kind
of pills
⁹⁰ That will not bring forth fruit
But I want you to know this
morning God is mindful of
you
In every walk of life
Don't you know the Lord is so
mindful of man
He wanted man to have
everything that he need
⁹⁵ He gave him five thinking
capacities
One that he could smell
One that he could see
One that he could hear
One that he can taste
¹⁰⁰ One that he can feel
Say now I want you to go
through the land and
country
I want you to see all the good
things
I want you to hear all the bad
things said
That you may be able to turn
with your life
¹⁰⁵ And just listen to my voice

One thing I want you to know
    brethrens
You can't serve the Lord unless
    you let the Lord guide you
Am I right this mornin'
You can't serve the Lord five
    days a week/ and try to
    serve the Lord on the day
    Sunday
110 You're gonna have to live the
    thing y' say on Sunday
To save your soul
Am I right this mornin'
Jesus
Jesus was so concerned about
    man
115 Until He left His richness and
    glad glory
Came down here in this old sin-
    cussed world
Stepped on the train of nature
    with a virgin woman
And brought Himself out an
    infant baby
On the train of nature nine
    months
120 Stepped off the train at a little
    old station called
    Bethlehem
Wrapped over there in
    swaddlin' clothes
Stayed right there
Till God told His father Joseph
I want you to carry the baby
    over to Galilee
125 Keep it right there till I bring
    the Word
God was always concerned for
    man

Proved His concern for man so
I tell you what brought Him
    here as a little baby
Grew up on a man's stature
130 And began to get acquainted
    out on the field of
    acquaintance
At His first stop brethren He
    made after He started out
    on His father's journey
They stopped in the midst of
    lawyers and doctors
I see in her mind she's gonna
    get worried
She got worried about her son
135 As any mother do these days
One thing I want you to know
Mothers love children
Doesn't matter what the world
    may say about the child
Mother say the child is mine
140 One thing between a mother
    and father
Father will do the best he can
But mother will understand
Yes she will this mornin'
Same Jesus
145 That stopped over at
    Bethlehem and got off the
    train of nature
He pull off the detour road
I can hear the mother begin to
    worry about her son
She said where is my son
Who had followed me and be
    with me all of his days
150 Now I can't seem to find my
    son
I see mother and father

They're down to pick up . . .
They go back and see what
    happened to the son
They found Him in the midst of
    the lawyers and doctors
155 Askin' questions askin'
    questions
I can hear the mother say to
    the son
Why you gotten so far behind
    now
He said Mother I must go about
    my Father's business
That may prove God's concern
160 How much God is concerned o'
    man
God is so mindful o' man
I better skip along now
    brethren
Bring it to a close now
I'll tell that to the judge
165 That I left you at twelve years
    old
See Jesus now
Walkin' out on the field one
    mornin'
Stopped over there at the old
    place they call Cana
There was a wedding goin' on
    at Cana
170 Oh hear what He said to the
    servants around there
Whatever He said to do I want
    you to do what He said
See Jesus
He walked on right through—
He said fill up a pitcher with
    water

175 Somebody said Jesus turn
    around that water to wine
But I want you to know this
    brethren He said fill it up
    with water
Fill it up to the brim
I could hear the priests sayin'
    out there
Oh you save the best for the
    last
180 God is still mindful of man
He said—gave them water to
    put it in
That they may have to carry on
    the way to the feast
Then He started on out on His
    journey
Heard Jesus say
185 I'm so concerned about man
    now
I'm goin' home some of these
    days
I must leave the church with
    man
He left the church with us in
    the hands of a man
He left the gospel in the hands
    of a man
190 Am I right?
This same Jesus
This same one that stopped
    over at Bethlehem
The same one that had
    concourse with the lawyers
    and doctors
The same man
195 That had—gave—told 'em to fill
    up a pitcher with water

Same man gave sight to the
    blind
Same man
Said I'll need somebody
To treat the world after I go
    home
200 Walked out along the seashore
Noticed—saw Andrew
Simon Peter
Told Andrew
Simon Peter
205 Lay down your nets now
Come and follow me
I will make you become fishers
    of men
Same man
Still talkin' 'bout the gospel
210 Walkin' on down the river
    brethren
Looked out there they saw old
    man Zebedee's son
Ohh John now
Ohh James
Drop your nets come follow me
215 I'm talkin' 'bout Jesus' concern
    'bout man
God is mindful of you this
    evenin' brethren
He'll follow you
I'd walk a little closer
I started to singin'
220 If you can't sing so well
Just use the words
Use me Lord
In thy service
Well, by the river
225 Every day
God an' man
Has to run

Run all the way
Serve on
230 The Lord is mindful this
    evenin'
Of how we go in and out with
    others
I want to say to the deacon
    board I want you to be
    mindful
I want you to be mindful how
    you serve as a deacon
Because the Lord doesn't have
    to use you
235 I want to say to you brother
    preachers be careful how
    you preach
Because the Lord didn't have to
    have you to preach
Am I right this evenin'?
I'm so glad this evenin'
Cause I know the Lord'll do
    right
240 Am I right this evenin'
Have you tried the man/ on this
    old journey
Do you know He's a doctor
In a sickroom
Ahh, He carry me on a
    stretcher
245 When I be worried
Some time I get tired on the
    journey
He is my strength
He is my prop
When I try to lag on the
    journey
250 There is somethin' to lift me up
Keep on brethren
Few more days

Few more days
This journey gonna be ended
²⁵⁵ Not how fast you run Brother
    Brown
But how long
But how long you run
Not to the swift not to the
    strong, but he that hold out
    to the end
I want you to know that I know
    my brethrens it's not what
    you been doin' but it's
    what you be doin' when
    Jesus comes
²⁶⁰ It's not how you have lived, but
    how you be livin' when the
    roll is called
Ohh when the roll is called
    brethren
I'll be there
I want you to know that God is
    mindful, He trusted
    something in my hand
When He trusted His Word to
    go into all the world and
    preach the gospel
²⁶⁵ Whosoever shall believe and be
    baptized shall be saved
Doesn't matter with me how
    you may feel about what I
    say

When I know I'm right I'll tell
    it all, I'm in your care
Ohh Lord
Ohh I'm in your care
²⁷⁰ Told me every now and then
    I'll be in your care
It's all right children
Tell the Lord sometime I'm in
    your care
I don't know about you
But I'm gonna see the Lord for
    myself
²⁷⁵ Well one year
When I can see the Lord
    brethren
I'm gonna have to see the Lord
    for myself
Ohh in the mornin'
When every belief should bow
    before the judgment bar
²⁸⁰ My mother can't bow down for
    me
Ohh I got a tongue
I'll have to confess with my
    tongue
By and by
I will see Jesus
²⁸⁵ By and by [singing]

THOU SHALT HAVE NO OTHER GODS
BEFORE ME

Nearly a year after the sermon above was recited, Brown used a similar theme in a sermon delivered in Bakersfield on May 19, 1968.

Same Jesus
Same Jesus this evenin'
Was concerned about us so
    much so
Until He left glad glory
5 Came out of glory to this old
    sinful world
Got on the train of nature
Stayed there nine months
Stepped off at the station one
    mornin'
Early one mornin'
10 Stepped off at the station of
    Bethlehem
Wrapped up in swaddlin'
    clothes

Way down in an oxen manger
Stayed right there
Until God wanted Him to come
    on out
15 Stayed right there
Until God wanted Him what to
    do
Stayed right there
And time began to move on
I'm talkin' about thou shalt
    have no other God before
    me
20 God was so concerned brethren
Till He came all the way to this
    sinful world

That you an' I may have a right
  to tree of life
Came in the shape of a baby

Wrapped Himself in human
  blood
[25] Dwelled here thirty-three long
  years

GOD'S PLOWBOY
Version 1

This sermon was recited by the Reverend Rubin Lacy, July 2, 1967, in Bakersfield, California. The idea and a good deal of the language for this performance was taken from a printed sermon, "God's Plowboy." Clearly Lacy did not read well and the sermon was not successful. When he tried to follow the text closely he could not establish a consistent rhythm. The material was unfamiliar to him, and that further caused him to stumble; but he used it because it eulogizes the role of the preacher. Lacy was able to regain his rhythm only when he broke away from the manuscript (lines 138 ff.). From that point on his eye caught only an occasional word of print and he elaborated spontaneously on those few words; that was the only way he could gain momentum. A few lines are taken from the written material (e.g., 147–48, 168, 190, 241–42) and are then expanded with the material from the preacher's word hoard. The chant breaks down at line 311, but resumes again at 320 and continues until the end. Lacy's source, from *Sermon Outlines* (Atlanta, n.d.), pp. 24–29, is printed first.

> . . . *For our sakes, no doubt, this is written: that he that ploweth should plow in hope. . . ,*

I Cor. 9:10.

INTRODUCTION: The text is taken from Paul's letter to the Corinthian church. The plowman mentioned is God's minister of the gospel. It seems fitting here to call him "God's plowboy." The man who plows has many duties other than walking in the furrow behind the plow. God's plowboy likewise has many responsibilities other than standing in the pulpit.

In this message we will consider the minister under three topics: first, as a burden bearer; second, as a feeder of the flock; third, as a plowman of hope.

I. THE PREACHER BEARS THE BURDENS OF THE PEOPLE AND PULLS THE LOAD FOR THE CHURCH.

For it is written in the law of Moses, Thou shalt not muzzle the mouth of the ox that treadeth out the corn. Doth God take care for oxen?

I Cor. 9:9

The minister is here referred to as an ox. The ox is a very strong beast, stands a great deal of abuse and hard labor. He never complains in his suffering or holds any ill will against his punishers.

1. *The Ox Worked at the Will of Others.*

The old ox was not a freewill agent. He worked at the will of his master. He never stopped in the shade when he was tired; he stopped when his master said to stop. He did not eat when he was hungry; he ate when his master fed him. He did not eat what he wanted; he ate what he could get and had time to eat.

2. *The Ox Was a Plowman but at the Reverse End of the Plow.*

The minister usually gets the end where the hard work is to be done. The task of the ox was to plow one-half acre a day. The minister has a job to do and it will require his best and full time to complete his task.

3. *The Ox Was Hitched to Heavy Loads.*

The ox was very stout and his master knew it; therefore, he got little sympathy or mercy. The minister is called upon by his Master, and of necessity by the church, to pull. The true preacher will pull. The minister must never get in his mind that he is being mistreated or that unnecessary loads are required of him. He must not sympathize with himself or solicit the sympathy of others. The minister has no time to feel sorry for himself.

4. *The Ox Was Used as a Burden Bearer.*

Being strong, very heavy burdens were often laid upon the faithful old ox. He may grunt and groan under the load but must not complain. The church may lay upon their pastor unnecessary burdens but there is not much left for him to do but carry them.

II. GOD'S PLOWBOY MUST FEED HIS MASTER'S SHEEP.

The Lord said to Peter "Feed my lambs," and again He said, "Feed my sheep." The Lord has no flocks or herds; He was talking about people. The lambs were the newborn babes in Christ and such as had not yet fully developed. He said to Peter twice, "Feed my sheep." He was referring to the fully developed and strong Christians.

Take heed therefore unto yourselves, and to all the flock, over which the Holy Ghost hath made you overseers, to feed the church of God, which he hath purchased with his own blood,

Acts 20:28.

Paul was speaking to pastors who were feeders of the flock of God. Every pastor must not only feed, but properly feed the flock.

1. *Take Heed How You Feed the Flock.*

During a dearth, Elisha's servant set on the great pot and one went out into the field to gather herbs to feed the sons of the prophets. Not knowing the food properly, he gathered wild gourds; and when the food was served, death was found in the pot.

And one went out into the field to gather herbs, and found a wild vine, and gathered thereof wild gourds his lap full, and came and shred them into the pot of pottage: for they know them not.

So they poured out for the men to eat. And it came to pass, as they were eating of the pottage, that they cried out, and said, O thou man of God, there is death in the pot. And they could not eat thereof,

2 Kings 4:39, 40.

The pastor must know his flock, understand the food (the Word), and know what they need. Many flocks have been poisoned and some have died because of improper feeding.

2. *The Babes in Christ and Weaklings Must Have Milk. As newborn babes, desire the sincere milk of the word, that ye may grow thereby,*

I Peter 2:2

New converts may be considered babes, newly born of the Spirit. They must not be fed strong meat. The pastor must know how to start them off on the sincere milk of the Word.

I have fed you with milk, and not with meat: for hitherto ye were not able to bear it, neither yet now are ye able,

I Cor. 3:2.

The Corinthians to whom Paul was writing were evidently not babes in Christ. Paul had been feeding them, possibly for some time, but they had not properly developed; they were still weaklings. They seemed to be spiritually diseased and still needed to be fed on milk.

It is no honor for the pastor to boast that he has no bottles for any member of his flock. He must have bottles; if he doesn't have, many of his flock will die for the lack of good care.

3. *The Strong Must Have Meat.*
But strong meat belongesth to them that are of full age, even those who by reason of use have their senses exercised to discern both good and evil,

Heb. 5:14.

All members of the family of God do not eat the same diet. Strong meat that would be required for some might kill others; likewise would the strong become weak if they were continually fed milk.

The pastor must know his flock; equally so, he must know his Bible from which he feeds them.

Study to shew thyself approved unto God, a workman that needeth not to be ashamed, rightly dividing the word of truth,

2 Tim. 2:15.

He must know his Bible well enough that he may gather from its contents the very food each member of the flock may require.

III. GOD'S PLOWBOY HAS A RIGHT TO PLOW IN HOPE.

Notice the text, "He that ploweth should plow in hope." It is only right and fair that the pastor should hope to share in the carnal things of his members.

Who goeth a warfare any time at his own charges? who planteth a vineyard, and eateth not of the fruit thereof? or who feedeth a flock, and eateth not of the milk of the flock?

I Cor. 9:7.

In this one verse Paul impresses upon the Corinthians in duplicate forms the righteousness of the minister being supported from the products of his labors. As a soldier he is supported; as a planter he eats of the fruit; as a shepherd he drinks of the milk. Let us consider separately the pastor under each of these three headings.

I. *The Minister as a Soldier Is Dependent for His Expenses.*

No soldier goes to war at his own expense. His government pays the bill. Likewise must the soldier of God who takes up the sword in warfare depend upon God who through the church supplies all his needs, which would be from a reasonable way of thinking the necessary expenses of normal living.

2. *As a planter, the Minister May Eat of the Fruit.*

It is not reasonable to expect a man to prepare the ground and plant a vineyard without hope of enjoying the fruit thereof. Neither does God expect His servant to go out into the world, break up the fallow ground, sow the seed of the gospel and plant a vineyard and not enjoy the fruit. The pastor certainly has a right to share in the fruits of his labors.

3. *As a Shepherd the Pastor Eateth of the Milk of the Flock.*

The pastor is a shepherd of the spiritual flock, and God expects him to share in their earnings, just as much as the farmer would expect to milk his herd. He who feeds has a right to milk.

CONCLUSION: God's plowboy has a big job and many responsibilities. He must be ready and willing to work at either end of the plow. He must carry the burdens, pull the loads, stay sweet, conceal his feelings, and go straight ahead with his work.

For our sakes, no doubt, this
   was written: that he that
   ploweth should plow in
   hope
For our sakes, no doubt, this
   was written: that he that
   ploweth should plow in
   hope
First Corinthians ninth, and
   tenth
The text is written—taken from
   Paul's letter to the
   Corinthian church
⁵ The plowman mentioned here
   is God's minister of the
   gospel
It seems fitting to call him
   God's plowboy, or
   plowman
The man who plows has many

duties other than walking
   in the furrow behind the
   plow
God's plowboy likewise has
   many responsibilities other
   than standing in the pulpit
In this message we consider the
   minister under three topics:
   first as a burden bearer;
   second as a feeder of the
   flock; third as a plowboy,
   or plowman, of hope
¹⁰ While we're emphasizing this a
   little bit—no man break up
   new ground weed garden
   here—in the devil we call it
   death
You do all that work, prepare
   to do all these things, listen
   to it, he does it in hope

He's got faith and hope that
   he's going to reap the
   benefits of it
Hmm?
The hardest thing ever I done
   one year—I didn't tell an[y]
   one 'bout this in
   Mississippi; I was young
   and my bossman was young
15 Promised to give me a cow, and
   a calf to milk; I was
   sharecroppin' for him
I want to emphasize that—
   doesn't take me long to
   preach, 'cause I can talk
An' ahh this is the truth, I was
   through there a few years
   ago and laughin' about it
When time comes to give me
   the cow and the calf he
   give me the cow with no
   calf
I said you say you're gonna me
   a cow and a calf; he said,
   well she's milkin'
20 I said you said you'd give me a
   cow and a calf and this
   ain't gonna work
And we kept arguin', over that
   cow and the calf—the cow
   was milkin', but I wanted
   the cow and the calf
So that broke the treaty
Sharecroppin' for him; fact of it
   I didn't want to stay there
That would've been the hardest
   crop that ever I made in
   my life if I'd stayed there

an' made it—but I didn't
   like it
25 Was sorry—if you don't like a
   thing—the thought of it—
   ahh, you shouldn't joined
   up
No man do these things—roll
   logs, join bricks, tow logs
   unless he does it in hope
It's the hope of reaping
   something more than he's
   putting out
Hmm?
The preacher bears the burden
   of the people and pulls the
   load of the church
30 I don't know whether you want
   to believe that or not, but
   it's true
Lot of times you don't want to
   do it, but you can't keep
   grumblin' about it—I'll get
   to that later—I say y'
   can't—I'm talkin' about
   preachin' today
He can't even grumble too
   much about what he does
He can't even have no fiftieth
   point set [?]
All right, let's see am I right
   about it
35 Paul is backin' me up as I travel
   through this desert land—
For it is written in the law of
   Moses thou shalt not
   muzzle the mouth of the ox
   that treadeth out the corn.
   Do-eth God take of the ox?

I want you to answer me
somethin'
Do-eth God take of an ox?
The minister here referred to
as an ox
40 The ox is a very strong beast—
stands a great deal of
bruises and hard labor
He never complains in his
suffering or hold any ill will
against his punisher
Watch where you's goin'
The ox worked—not worked—at
the will of others
The old ox was not free—not a
freewill agent
45 He worked—ahh—at the will of
his master
He never stopped in the shade
when he was tired
He stopped when his master
said stop
He did not eat when he was
hungry, he ate when his
master fed him
He did not eat what he wanted
to eat, but what his master
give him, to eat
50 The ox was a plowman, but at
the reverse end of the plow
stood a man
Ha ha, who do the hardest
work?
I say at the reverse end of the
plow stood a man
The minister usually gets the
end where the hard work is
to be done

The task of an ox was to plow
half an acre in one day
55 The minister's job is to do an',
to do—his job is to do and
will require his best and
full time—don't have no
time for nothin' else
Folks say why don't you go to
the field an' chop cotton,
why don't you pick cotton,
why don't you cut some
grape—he doesn't have
time to do but one thing
Umm? Jesus said to Peter, an'
John, an' Andrew, and
James on the lake--ahh
drop your net and follow
me
You fishin' for yourself, I want
you to fish for me
C'mon an' follow me
60 Peter said to Him, I'm not
educated, I'm just a—ahh—
high school scholar—ahh—
can only read and write my
name
I'm not able to follow you Jesus
said, follow me
Hear my cause, hear my cause
[calls?]
Hmm? Follow me
The guys these days don't think
they're a preacher unless
they go into the seminary
65 Tryin' to put the seminary
before they're being a fool
The same 'postle Paul said the
other day I count all my
education nought

I become a fool he said to gain
    Christ
Didn't he say so?
I had to become a fool to gain
    Christ
70 And to speak fourteen different
    languages
Man—ahh—that was able to
    speak to anybody
And we, ain't got that kind of
    learnin' these days, are we?
No!
A Mexican could come in here
    right now—and speak some
    about—wouldn't know what
    he was saying
75 Hmm?
What I'm tryin' to tell you what
    Paul could do that
Ahh, but he said I had to
    become a fool
They're not lettin' you say it
He said the letter will kill dead
80 Grace of God will make alive
Didn't he say so?
Ahh, he didn't eat when he
    wanted to eat
But he ate when he—ahh—had
    the opportunity, by his
    master
An' then he—the minister
    usually gets the end where
    the work is the hardest
85 The task of the ox is half acre,
    the task of the minister is a
    continuation
Amen! everyday, even some
    nights on his bed

Lyin' down at night, can't be at
    ease, there's somethin'
    wrong in the church
That pastor's layin' there, all
    night long
Thinkin', study what to do,
    prayin' to God to give him
    wisdom an' understandin'
90 How to do these things, Amen
The ox has hitched to heavy
    loads
Uhh-huh, the ox was a very
    stout, uhh, beast Amen and
    master knew it
Therefore he got little
    sympathy, or mercy
Umm-hmm
95 By the church any man know
    that the pastor—the
    preacher—is the strongest
    man—should be the
    strongest man in the
    church
They put all kinds of
    responsibilities upon the
    preacher
Amen an' he got to bear it
He don't have time, to have
    sympathy for hisself
He don't want nobody to have
    no pity on him
100 The minister should never get
    it in his mind that he's
    being mistreated
Uhh-huh unnecessary loads are
    required of him
He must not have sympathy—
    umm-hmm—with himself

Uhh-huh sympathize with
others
The minister have no time to
feel sorry, for himself
105 The ox—Amen—is used as a
burden bearer
Umm-hmm being strong,
bearing, a heavy burden,
was often laid upon, this
old faithful ox
He grunt, sometime he groan
Amen sometimes falls to his
knees
But he kept on pullin'
110 I wonder you know what I'm
talkin' about?
How the church lay a heavy
burden, upon the pastor
Unnecessary burdens, such—
umm-hmm—as puts us in
the home
Amen—disputes between
husband and wife
All these things—they laid it on
the pastor
115 God from Zion
Sometime, just [least?] a little
for nothin'
Look for the pastor, you think
his car burnin' gas?
Ride from house to house
See about these things—burden,
burden bearer
120 What I'm tryin' to say is it's all
right, t' bear a burden
But Jesus said the other day
Bear ye, one another's burden
Didn't he say so?
Bear ye one another's burden

125 That am, the motto of the
church
Bear ye one another's burden
I think I'm right about it
And when the burden get too
hard
Take 'em on the sheet
130 Lay 'em down there to sleep
Tell Jesus about it
There He is, there He is
Tell Jesus about it
Oh bear my burdens
135 Too hard for me to bear
Jesus'll take your burdens, all
to himself
I think I know what I'm talkin'
about
But y' lay 'em on the preacher
An' look for the preacher
140 Amen!
Is the bearer of all your
burdens
He just can't do it
I know I'm right about it
I say he just can't do it
145 Let's go on a little further
God from Zion
God's plowboy
Must feed
We're goin' on to the feedin'
150 I say God's plowboy
Must feed
His master's sheep
The Lord said to Peter
Feed, my lambs
155 And then He said unto him
Feed, my sheep
The Lord

Didn't have no flock
Didn't have no herd
160 He was talkin' about
God from Zion
He was talkin' about the lambs
Of newborn babes
In Christ Jesus
165 Such as had not yet, fully
developed
He said to Peter twice feed my
sheep
Said to him the last time
Feed my lamb
Ain't God all right?
170 Feed my lamb
Take heed
Therefore
Unto yourself
And to all the flock
175 Which the Holy Ghost have
made thee
Overseer
To feed
The church of God
Huh let's think about it
180 God from Zion
God left the church
In the hands of the preacher
He feed
The church
185 Paul was speakin' here to the
pastors
Who were
Feeders of the flock of God
Each 'n' every pastor
Must not only feed
190 But properly feed

This what I'm tryin' to say to
you
Some feed
The wrong kind of food
Some say
195 They don't have no sugar-tin
Some say
They don't have no sweet milk
I'm tryin' to say to you this
evenin'
Every pastor
200 Must have a home
A sugar-tin
Along with him
Got somebody in the church
Been there twenty years
205 And still needs a sugar-tin
God from Zion
Got somebody here
Umm-hmm
That need a sugar-tin
210 Every now and then
God from Zion
Let's see am I right about it
God
Went up on the mountain
215 The other day
To pray
And while He was up there
prayin'
Some of the
Laborers
220 Said I'll be
I'll go out and get some stuff
And feed the people
Because they're hungry
Went out to pick vegetables
225 And got the wrong kind
Brought 'em on back

Put 'em in a pot
Begin to boil green
Had death in the pot
230 Ain't I right about it?
They tell me
That the pastor
Amen—must know
How to feed
235 And what thing to feed of
I'm going on to close now
God's
Plowboy
Has a right to plow
240 In hope
He that plows
Should plow in hope
It's only right
And fair
245 That the pastor should hope
To share in
The eternal
Things
Of all his members
250 God from Zion
Who
Ahh—goes
Warfare
Any time
255 Of his own
Charges
Who plants the vineyards
And eateth not
Of the food thereof
260 Who feedeth
A flock
And don't drink the milk
Thereof
In this verse

265 We find Paul
Expressin'
To the Corinthian church
The diplomat forms
Of righteousness
270 And able
Also
As he supported
As he
Of labor
275 Also
As he planted
He ate
Of his fruit Amen
As a shepherd
280 He drink
Of the milk
And let us consider
Separate
Each one of these things
285 No soldier
Go to the war
I don't care who he is
No soldier
Go over yonder
290 In that war
Unless his government/pay him
    so much a month
Give his family so much a
    month
No soldier
Volunteer
295 And went to war
Unless his government pays him
God from Zion
I'm tryin' to say here
That no soldier
300 Go here

In the army of God
Unless he looks for a reward
Ain't I right about it?
An' the reward
305 Shall be in the mornin'
In the mornin'
I said in the mornin'
When it's all over
Ohh, in the mornin' [long
    pause]
310 I read that—expect a man to
    prepare, the ground, get
    out there and cut down
    those trees
Break up the stumps, pull up
    the roots, and then hitch
    his tractor—pay a high
    price for his tractor
Go out there and tell 'em ain't
    got none
Get 'em ready to 'pare seed
An' then not do that any more
315 When he did it he believed it
In the fall there, he gonna
    reap—Amen—the work
    done
Jesus said you reap what you
    sow
When man does that he's gonna
    reap what he sows
God from Zion
320 He's gonna reap
A red horse
An' when a preacher preach
    the gospel
He's lookin' in the mornin'
For God to tell him

325 Well done
Ohh well done
Good and faithful servant
You been faithful
You preach sometime in church
330 When there wasn't but a few
    there
Preach sometime
When there wasn't but a half a
    dozen there
You preach sometime
When there's nothin' but
    Sunday school students
    there
335 But you preach right on
Well done
Good and faithful servant
You been faithful over a few
    things
I'm gonna make you rule the
    whole day
340 C'mon, sit down, give y' the
    line of Jordan
I believe y' know what I'm
    talkin' about
After a while
It'll all be over [sings a few
    notes]
I said after a while
345 It'll all be over
We're goin' home
To get my crown
I love that song
I love to sing that song
350 When I've done, the best I can
I wear the crown
Pause to think about it

Missus Lacy used to sing the
    song to me
When I's in the pulpit
    preachin'
355 Sometimes she set me down

Singin' that song
When I've done
The best I can
Give me the crown [sings]

GOD'S PLOWBOY
Version 2

The Reverend Rubin Lacy delivered this sermon May 19, 1968, in Tulare, California. The importance of this sermon (when compared to its earlier version) to understanding structural changes in time has been discussed in chapter 7. I recorded this purely by chance: Lacy had already delivered his sermon in the morning in his own church in Corcoran, and had no plans to do any further work for the day since his winter heart attacks were very much on his mind. However, when we arrived in Tulare (the New Mount Olive Baptist Church, the Reverend W. H. Henry, pastor) the guest preacher was not well and asked Lacy to fill in for him. With about fifteen minutes' notice Lacy preached the following sermon, which was well received. The preacher established good rapport with the congregation early: he had been chatting amiably with them for several minutes before the sermon began so that once he started they responded readily. A faint chant begins around line 85 and is more metrical at line 120. Throughout Lacy held himself in check rather than risk taxing his heart. The performance turned out to be unique because he used materials from several sources, most of which I had been recording the year before; in this sermon he brings them together.

I better get it right   Me talkin' a little here about
                                          this pastor

God almighty, umm
Obey them that have the rule
over you
5 And submit yourselves
For they watch for your souls
As they that must give an
account
That they may do it with joy
And not with grief
10 For that is unprofitable
Not for me
But it's unprofitable for you
If I have to do it in grief
That's the text
15 You'll find it in Hebrew
thirteen to seventeen
That's the text—the pastor of
the church
Is more—have more
responsibility than the King
of England
Because the King of England
Has got to go to church
20 If he see God's face in peace
Hmm?
He got to shake the preacher's
hand
And tell 'im I know God
An' I'm willin' to trust God
25 If he sees God's face in peace
Yet he's a ruler
Over many people
But the preacher's over him
President Johnson
30 Can stay in the Senate all week
With the Senate and Congress
And the House of
Representatives
But on a Sunday mornin'

He gotta go to church
35 An' hear what the preacher
says
Umm-hmm
Why?
Because Johnson
Can't watch his soul
40 But the preacher
Watches over your soul
Umm-hmm
When he's not there
He may be at home in the bed
45 An' you may be walkin' up an'
down the streets
In your town
Sometime Mac is up yonder in
Fresno
An' his people is havin' a big
time
Mac is on bended knee
50 He may be in the bed
But he's on bended knee
Talkin' to God
About your soul
Umm-hmm
55 Sunday mornin'
When Mac comes down here
Down here to his church
First Baptist Church
He's ready to go
60 God has given 'im a message
An' I say he oughta use it
He oughtn'ta let a . . . preacher
He oughtn't let nobody preach
If God gave it to you
65 You oughta deliver it to your
folks
Umm-hmm
I know I'm right about it

You say you been here
    eighteen years
Umm-hmm
⁷⁰ Good preachin' didn't keep y'
    here
Don't let nobody fool y'
Something else kept y' here
I know I'm right about it
God is on y' side
⁷⁵ I know I'm right about it
God give y' a helpmate
That would stand by y'
Through dangerous seas
. . . when you're hungry
⁸⁰ She just be hungry with y'
When y' got a . . .
She's all right
I know I'm right about it
Umm-hmm
⁸⁵ Talkin' about the man
That watches for your soul
The pastor
Is an overseer
Of souls
⁹⁰ He watches, as one, that must
    give accounts
God, has entrusted souls, in his
    care
This tremendous responsibility
Of the pastor
Makes his work and duty
⁹⁵ The most important
Man in the world
Yeah—we will consider the
    pastor
Under three headings
Let's see first
¹⁰⁰ He as a watchman
Second as a preacher

Third as a pattern
Wanta say I may not go far on
    it
Wanta say this evenin' he's a
    watchman
¹⁰⁵ One writer said he's a overseer
I know you know what it is
Some of you come off a
    plantation
Way down in Mississippi
In Arkansas
¹¹⁰ Out in Texas
They had overseers
What did the overseer do
The overseer
Told y' what to do
¹¹⁵ You didn't tell the overseer
But he told you
What to do
On the plantation
Ah—this writer said
¹²⁰ Paul said
Pastors are overseers
God from Zion
Tell the church what to do
Tell the deacon what to do
¹²⁵ And then everything's all right
Well it's changed around
They got to tell you
Jus' won't work
Not to save your life
¹³⁰ Just don't work
The church is goin' backwards
Every day of his life
God from Zion
Yes he's a feeder
¹³⁵ I said he's a feeder
Pastor must know how to feed
Just any old thing

Throw in the trough
Just won't do
140 Must know how to feed
Don't y' remember
When Moses went off that time
Up on the mountain
Left the boys down there
145 Somebody cried out I'm hungry
Went out there in the woods
Pulled up the wrong thing
Went on back there
Put it in the pot
150 Began to boil
Before Moses got back
Some of 'em was eatin' that
    stuff
Everybody begin to die
I want you to know Moses
155 Umm-hmm
Somebody said death
Was in the pot
Pastor must know
What kind of food
160 Is to give his children
He got all kinds of children
Some of 'em's sickly
Some of 'em's healthy
And they all don't eat the same
    thing
165 Sometime
A healthy child
A good healthy member
Can die
On the wrong kind of food
170 Sometime
A weak member
Can die
Tryin' to give him healthy food
Hark Hallelujah

175 Pastor
Must be able
To feed his weak members
When they's gettin' weak
Sometime
180 They got to lose time
Go around to his home
Pat him on the shoulder
Let somebody know
That you care about him
185 Ain't God all right
Somebody
Every now and then
Somebody
Want you to care
190 I wonder
Do y' know what I'm talkin'
    about
God from Zion
Yes he's a watchman
That stands
195 On the wall
Ezekiel said
Stand on the wall
Rap the gavel
Men don't believe you
200 Then their blood
Is not required at your hand
I'm wonderin' do y' hear me
    today
Somebody here
Soft-peddlin' the gospel
205 Tryin' to sooth somebody
Twistin' the Word of God
I'm here to tell y' today
Preach the Word
Preach the Word
210 Don't care who don't like it
I don't care who it hit

Ohh preach the Word
I don't care who don't like it
I don't care who get offended
about it
215 Preach the Word
Umm-hmm
That's another thing the pastor
must do
Oughta be glad to preach
Some of us say well
220 I know y' get tired sometime
But we oughta be glad to
preach
Because God said preach
Umm-hmm
Preach
225 Umm-hmm
Because the gospel
Is the saving salt
That saves the soul
Umm-hmm
230 Preach
Because the gospel
Is the power of God
Unto those of salvation
To everyone that believe
235 Ohh preach the Word
Preach the Word
I said preach the Word
I'm glad God told me
A long time ago
240 To preach my Word
Ohh go eat
Therefore
In other words
Ohh men don't like you
245 I'm on y' side
Preach the Word
That's what He want you to do

Preach the Word
Yes he's a watchman
250 I'm closin' here
I say I'm closin'
Paul here says
I don't mean no harm but tell
me what Paul says
Paul here says
255 The pastor must watch the
enemy
Well—who is the enemy
For I know this Paul says
That after my departuring
Shall grievous wolves enter in
260 Among you
Not sparing the flock
Umm-huh
These grievous wolves
I hate to say it
265 But sometimes
These grievous wolves
Sometimes is preachers
Umm-hmm
And they, will get good
members
270 I don't mean bad members
Out of the church
An' go off an' organize another
church
An' then take another one
there with 'em
After they get off—I know what
I'm talkin' about
275 I seen it done a few years ago
I know what I'm talkin' about
The preacher run off first
And then left the folks there
Without any preacher
280 After he's pulled out

And organized another church
Oh yes—said these grievous
    wolves
Do this to be bragged on
They want to be bragged on
285 Let me use the word pre-enium
It means to be bragged on
Lifted up high
When y' don't deserve it
But I say this
290 Jesus said
If any man exalts his self
He shall be . . .
God from Zion
If any man want to be exalted
295 Let him humble himself
Like Joseph did
When he was down in Egypt
Joseph
Stuck to God
300 He heard through God
Don't care what happen
When the woman caught
    Joseph
Pulled his coat off
Goin' 'round without his coat

305 Suffered to go to jail
Ain't I right about it
He suffered to go to jail
Wonder how many Josephs
Will we find now
310 Joseph suffered to go to jail
Stayed in jail
But listen friend
God was in jail too
Jailer
315 Was a mean man
But the jailer liked Joseph
Give him the key
Told him you take my place
Ain't I right about it
320 I want to say to you
    brothering—Brother
Henry and Sister Henry
Stay on
You pray on
An' you preach on
325 Don't fool yourself good
    preachin' ain't keepin' y'
here—they don't know
what that is in California

THE CHRIST OF THE BIBLE

Recited by the Reverend D. J. McDowell, July 30, 1967, in Delano, California, this sermon was received with great enthusiasm. The occasion was the anniversary service for the Reverend Mr. Moore (see lines 1 and 230) and was well attended by the local clergy. Mr. McDowell begins to chant sporadically at line 55, consistently at line 99. He is clearly singing the lines after 146, and this is sustained until line 306 when he very abruptly returns to conversational prose. The emotional build-up had been so great that the long denouement was needed. This sermon is noteworthy for its images (lines 24 and 34) and for its use of memorized themes. The major portion of the sermon was noted on a five-by-five-inch card that was kept on the pulpit and referred to from time to time. Memorized themes in this piece that have been used elsewhere are in lines 78–96, 235–45, 260–61, and 281–91.

Reverend Moore, Brown, Pastor
   Lacy, Sister Moore,
   Officers, our fellow citizens
   of the kingdom of God, and
   to our Center friends, if
   there be any with us
This is another opportunity for
   us to worship together
I would encourage each of you
   who are here today—let us
   take advantage of it
I'm honored to have this
   privilege of closing out this
   appreciation service
5 Wanta invite your attention to
   the sixteenth chapter of
   our

Lord's gospel by Matthew
And the sixteenth verse
And Simon Peter answered and
   said, Thou art the Christ,
   the Son of the living God
Then John, chapter six verse
   sixty-seven through sixty-
   nine
10 Then said Jesus unto the
   twelve, Will ye also go
   away?
Then Simon Peter answered
   Him Lord, to whom shall
   we go? Thou hast the
   words of eternal life and
   we believe, and are sure
   that Thou art the Christ,
   the Son of the living God,
   the Holy One of God
Wanta talk to you this evening
   from this thought, the
   Christ of the Bible
The Christ of the Bible
I believe you will agree with
   me, this evening, that if
   America ever needed
   Christ in our life, in our
   homes, on our jobs, in our
   city government, state, and
   internationally, we need
   Him today
15 Turmoils, all around us
Frustration and confusion on
   every side
Only the Christ of the Bible
   can solve our problems
We want to talk about Him this
   evening, if you please

Men everywhere seek for some
   form of religion
20 Every man recognizes that
   there is a God who made
   and controls this wonderful
   world in which we live
Even the atheist deep down
   within knows there is a
   God somewhere
Ahh, and everyone in some way
   wishes to have a
   connection between
   himself and the Christ of
   the Bible
The Bible is a book of
   revelations based upon the
   Christ of the Bible
He is a center-piece on every
   table
25 We may reach Him only by
   faith, by faith
First—the first, foremost and
   final task of the church is
   to teach the word of God
And all other activities either
   contribute to or grow out
   of an understanding and an
   acceptance of the authority
   of the word of God
When you see a man breaking
   the law of the land, it only
   means that he doesn't
   recognize the law of God
When you see a man breaking
   the law of God, it only
   means that he's a
   lawbreaker in the land
30 We need God in our life—the
   Christ of the Bible

Jesus—ahh—has come to the
crossroad in His earthly
ministry
So He drew Himself away from
the scenes of His early
labor
On the borderline of Palestine
and a Roman colony
At the foot of Mount Hermon,
where the Jordan springs
from the mountainside
emptied themselves into
the sea, as He would in a
few short months empty
Himself in death for the sin
of the world
35 C'mon, Holy Ghost
The Christ of the Bible
It was here in this—ahh—
secluded place where Jesus
called upon His
Disciples to give a definite
statement of their faith in
Him
Whom say ye that I am?
40 Simon Peter answered and said,
Thou are the Christ, the
Son of the living God
Talkin' about the Christ of the
Bible
Ahh, my friends, we must be
able to answer this
question today
Right now in our hearts, for the
whole weight and worth of
our salvation hinges upon
the answer to this question
To know the Christ of the Bible
is to know the gospel

45 Whom say ye that I am?
What do you say about Him
this evenin'?
We have found Him whom
Moses in the Law and the
prophets did write
Jesus of Nazareth, the son of
Joseph; the Christ of the
Bible cannot be described
in words
Language loses its signifisense
[sic], tryin' to pay proper
homage to the Christ of the
Bible
50 Nathaniel ask him's there any
good thing come out of
Nazareth
Phillip said unto him, come and
see—John one forty-five
and forty-six
Talkin' about the Christ of the
Bible
You see words, are only
symbols of an artist, that
are used in creating images
in the human mind
But mere words fall short—
Amen—and become
insufficient and images
dissolve and vanish because
the Christ of the Bible is
not an aggregation of
words but the perfect
embodiment of the living
God Himself—Isaiah
chapter six verse three,
Colossians, chapter two and
verse nine

⁵⁵ Isaiah, Isaiah declared the other
day that he saw Him, high
and lifted up
Sitting on the throne
He said His strain filled the
temple
Amen! and He asked me a
question
And I had the knowledge that
I'm unworthy
⁶⁰ I am not fit to serve on your
program
I—I dwell among men of
unclean lips
Even my lips, myself they are
unclean
For that reason I can't go
He said—He said, I kept on
watching
⁶⁵ And in a moment and twinkling
of an eye
He ordered one of His
seraphim angels
And he took a pair o' tongs
And took a live coal
For the [order] of God
⁷⁰ And Isaiah said He came even
to me
Touched my lips
Purged my sins
Amen! And dissipated my
iniquities
He asked me again who will go
for us
⁷⁵ I said here I am Lord, send me
Talkin' about the Christ of the
Bible
The only description that be
given to Him that describes

Him as the Christ of the
Bible comes from the
names and titles given in
the Holy Word of God
All the world cannot contain
Him
All oceans cannot bear Him
⁸⁰ All questions cannot confound
Him
All judges cannot condemn
Him
An' all courts cannot try Him
And all rules cannot discipline
Him
All orders cannot compel Him
⁸⁵ And all graves cannot hold Him
down
I'm glad about it this evening
There was no grave that could
hold Him down
Help me Lord Jesus, tell Your
story
In education, He is the period
at the end of every
sentence
⁹⁰ The logic, in every phrase and
the glowing beauty and
meaning in every syllable
Nominations would not elevate
Him
Nations could not entangle Him
Campaigns did not elect Him
Parties could not influence Him
⁹⁵ Epidemics did not surprise Him
Death had no power on Him
This is the Christ of the Bible
Help me Lord Jesus, I feel
something coming now

There is no secret, which He
does not know the smallest
detail
[100] There is no problem, that He
does not have the solution
for
You have a problem in your
life, you oughta tell Jesus
about it
The Christ of the Bible
Ahh, no poet can describe His
character, nor the meaning
of His being
No—no, no one could describe
Him, no one could pin the
character of my Lord and
Savior Jesus Christ
[105] In Genesis, He is the seed of
the woman
Oh yes He is
In Exodus He is the burning
bush, that stopped old man
Moses
Am I right about it?
In Leviticus He is the image of
holiness, standing in the
center of the sanctuary
[110] Help me Jesus
In Numbers He is the star, that
came out of Jacob
The brazen serpent
The smitten rock
And the city of refuge
[115] I'm talkin' about the Christ of
the Bible
In Deuteronomy He is the
interpretation of the Law
I'm talkin' about the Christ of
the Bible

Ahh, in Joshua, He is my
battleaxe, in time of war
Not only that but in Judges, He
is, the separator
[120] In Ruth, He is the true-bred, in
Bethlehem
In First Samuel, He is the true
potentate, for all mankind
In Second Samuel, He is
anointed shepherd
And knows each of His sheep
by name
I wonder are you prayin' with
me?
[125] Goin' on now, in First Kings,
He is Solomon's counsellor
In Second Kings, He is the
troubler of all men He
have
And the destruction of Sister
Jezebel
In First Chronicle He gives
Israel, an everlastin' name
In Second Chronicle, He is, the
complete structure, of
[130] Solomon's temple, and a
buildin' made, without
hands
In, in in Ezra, He is
Zerubbabel's leadership
In Nehemiah, He—He is Israel's
pure religion
I'm wondering, is He your pure
religion this evening?
In Esther, He is the
consolation, of the Jews
[135] And in Job, He is my heart's
pouring in yonder valley

In Psalms, of David, He's the
    mighty shepherd
Am I right about it?
In Proverbs, He is the wisdom,
    that passes all
    understanding
In Ecclesiastes, He is the
    gaining, of more wisdom
140 Songs of Solomon, He is the
    bridegroom, looking
    forward to a bright
    morning
I feel something coming now
In Isaiah He is the warrior,
    wrapped in a dyed garment
Walkin' in the strength of His
    own power
In Jeremiah, He is, the
    message, to the weeping
    prophet
145 In Ezekiel, He is the wheel, in
    the middle of the wheel
Help me Lord Jesus tell Your
    story
Not only that but in Daniel,
    He's the stone
Cut out of the mountain,
    moving down through the
    world
Tearin' down the kingdoms of
    the world
150 Am I right about it?
In Hosea, He is, a mighty
    searchlight
Am I right about it?
In Joel, He's a plague of locusts
I'm talkin' about the Christ, in
    my Bible

155 Not only that but in Amos, He's
    the plowman, overtakin'
    His reaper
I know that's right
Will you pray with me?
In Obadiah, He is Israel's,
    mighty deliverer
I don't know about you but He
    delivered me one day
160 Ever since that day, I been
    risin' an' fallin' in His name
C'mon church, and help me tell
    God's story
In Jonah, He is the speed-cop,
    overtakin' the mighty
    violator
Have you violated? if you've
    violated He'll overtake you
    by an' by after a while
In Micah, He's the hope of the
    church
165 In Nahum, He's a whirlwind, in
    a cloud of dust
In Habakkuk, He is the triumph
    of all missions
I know that's right
In Zephaniah, He is the
    foundation
In old man David's house
170 Not only that in Malachi
He is the refiner's fire
He'll purify you whole
He'll purify your soul
If you want purifyin'
175 I know that's right
In Matthew, He is the lion, and
    the tribe of Judah
Pray with me church

In Mark, He is, the high-cost
   servant
I know that right
180 In Luke, He's the great
   physician
In John, He transcends time
   both ways
He's grace and truth
Help me Lord Jesus, tell Your
   story
In Acts, He's the spirit and
   scope
185 Of all evangelism
Help me Lord Jesus, tell Your
   story
In Romans, He is the one, who
   ascended way up to heaven
I know that's right
In Ephesians, He is, my
   spiritual weapon
190 Am I right about it?
In Philippians, He is my
   abdicator
In Colossians, He's my all and
   all
What about yours?
In First Thessalonians, He's the
   head of the church
195 I know that's right
In Second Thessalonians, He is
   the returning Lord
Are you lookin' for him? Are
   you lookin' for Him Saint
   Paul?
He's in His dressing room right
   now, coming back out to
   His church
In First Timothy, He is, the
   finish of all my pain

200 He's my courage, He's my
   hope, He's my all and all
Are you prayin' with me now?
In Second Timothy, He's the
   joy of my salvation
Am I right about it?
I feel all right right now
205 Something moving in my heart
In Titus, He is my sound
   doctrine
My signpost, my guideline
Am I right about it?
In—in Jude, yes He is
210 He's my doxology, and my
   benediction
In Revelation, I'm Alpha and
   Omega
I know that's right
I started this business, I'm goin'
   to see it to the end
Am I right about it?
215 I don't worry, about man
   destroyin' God's world
God started this world
And God will end this world
Man might destroy himself
But he cannot destroy God's
   creation
220 Am I right about it?
If you don't hear me no more
   Saint Paul
Keep your hand in God's hand
Keep your eyes, on the starpost
   in glory
Step by step
225 You'll have to make this
   journey
I know that's right
But step by step

I'm gonna make an end,
    someday
Am I right about it?
230 Brother Moore if I don't speak,
    in your church no more
Keep your hand in God's hand
And your eyes, on the starposts
    in glory
Lord said He would fight your
    battles
If you'd only be still
235 You may not be a florist
Am I right about it?
But you must tell them, that
    He's the Rose of Sharon
I know that's right
You may not be a geologist
240 But you must tell them, that
    He's the Rock of Ages
I know that's right
You may not be a physician
But you must tell them, that
    He's the great physician
You may not be a baker,
245 But you must tell them, that
    He's the bread of life
Am I right about it?
You must tell them
That He's a friend
That stick close t' his brother
250 He said I'll not cast y' out
In the sixth hour, and in the
    seventh hour
I didn't know I was turnin' you
    out
If y' keep your hand in God's
    hand
Let me stay in you
255 And high in you

I'll lead y' t' high heights
And deeper depths in my fire
Am I right about it?
And not only that
260 You may not be a builder
But you must tell them, that
    He's the chief cornerstone
Am I right about it?
I believe
Right now Saint Paul
265 He's in His dressing room right
    now
Putting on His judgment
    garments
Gettin' ready to come back t'
    this church
We will be waiting
Are you waiting?
270 Are you waiting?
Are you waiting Saint Paul?
Keep your hands in the Lord's
    hands
Keep your eyes, on the starpost
    in glory
Walk, and never get tired
275 Run, and think 'bout the saints
Cause He's the strength
Of my salvation
Promise, said the Lord
In my life
280 And my salvation
Whom do I have to fear?
He's the strength of my life
Whom do I have to be afraid
    of?
He's my all
285 He's my all
He's my bread
When I'm hungry

He's my water
When I get thirsty
290 He's my shelter
When they throw me outdoors
I know that's right
When I don't have a leaning
    post
I can lean on Him
295 Am I right about it?
He won't turn me out
For the psalmist said forty-six
God is our refuge
And strength
300 A well-proved helpmate in
    trouble
I'm in trouble this evenin'
Yes I am
I said I'm in trouble this
    evenin'
I need someone to go all night
    long
305 If you never hear me no more
Keep your hand, in God's hand
He'll make a way for you
The Christ of the Bible
No grave, could hold Him
    down
310 This is the Christ of the Bible
Overtaking the reaper,
    overtaking the violator
Amen!
Don't worry Saint Paul about
    folk misusing you
No no don't worry about folk
    misusing you
315 The Christ of the Bible sooner
    or later, is gonna overtake
    them
He's my speed-cop

See He's my speed-cop
Amen!
He's the chief speed-cop
320 He may misuse me and think
    he's getting away with it
But at the moment—at the
    moment—when he least
    expect—you know this is
    true—
Amen those of us who have
    gotten citations
You're in a hurry, left late
Amen and you're overspeedin'
325 Oh yes I've gotten them
Amen
And the moment that you least
    expect, the Highway Patrol
You look up in your rearview
    mirror and you see a red
    light
Blinkin' in your face
330 He's overtakin' you
So it is with the Christ of the
    Bible
You may mistreat me
You may talk about me
But just keep on livin'
335 The speed-cop gonna take care
    of it
When you don't know anything
    but red lights, gonna be
    blinkin' in your face
And it's no use to say you
    didn't do it
Amen
Because He has your record
340 He have our everything
Amen you can't deny it
And it signed in your name

And you can't deny it
I like that
345 Amen everybody's gonna have
to read their own title
prayer
And you can't deny your own
signature
Oh yes.I've wanted to deny
mine
I've signed mine, Amen and
found out that it was very
difficult for me to pay that
bill

And Amen, I wondered, well
now wait a minute here did
I sign that—yes I signed—
there's the signature right
here
350 Yes that's my signature I won't
deny it
So, if we violate He's gonna
catch up with us after a
while
The Christ of the Bible

PREACH THE WORD

This sermon was recited by the Reverend Elihue H. Brown, July 16, 1967, in Bakersfield, California. It was delivered in honor of a Reverend Mr. Thompson of Bakersfield's St. Immanuel Church; the occasion was his twentieth ministerial anniversary, which must have made him one of the first black ministers who had settled in Bakersfield and was still alive in the community. The many references to the preacher in the desert are a tribute to Thompson's early years. As with all of Brown's sermons, the chanting begins early, here on line 30. Brown stays fairly close to his basic comparison throughout, that of Thompson to Ezekiel, though he makes a number of digressions that are triggered by thoughts in the "main stream." Thompson is a prophet; Brown is reminded of the prophet Daniel (line 54) and then of Ezekiel (line 89). Then he thinks of the Word of God and this reminds him of John (line 124) and then of his own life (line 142), back to the Word and then to Jesus (line 172). The remainder of the sermon employs all the themes and associations that Brown has used earlier. For example, the lines "Tell them/I know my redeemer live/ Because He lives in me" (172–74) are repeated in lines 209–11. Although the Reverend Rubin Lacy preached (ostensibly) on the same subject there is little overlapping.

Son of man I have made thee a
    watchman in the house of
    Israel

Therefore hear the words at my
    mouth and give them
    warnings from me

You'll find these words and
noted expressions comin'
out of the book of Ezekiel
chapter three verse
seventeen
Son of man I have made thee a
watchman
⁵ Unto the house of Israel
Therefore hear the word of my
mouth
And give them warning from
me
Thank you
To Pastor Thompson, and all of
my brother ministers,
visitors, and members of
the Saint Immanuel Baptist
Church
¹⁰ All our other visitors, we are
very gratified that God has
made it possible for us to
be present here this
evenin'
That we can say we thank God
for He has brought us
another milestone in life
There have been many voices
hushed up since one year
ago
But I can remember when we
were here
On this same occasion
¹⁵ I can remember some of the
words came from some of
the members that they had
been along with Pastor
Thompson a long time
But one and all we want to
thank God for a man who

was able to stand on the
wall twenty years
And bring men warnings from
God
You know no man could do
what Pastor Thompson
done out in the midst of a
desert
Unless that God would direct
him
²⁰ Just can't do things of yourself
It takes the Lord to help you
So as God warned and give
these ever-kind words to
the listenin' ear of one of
the major prophets
So as He warned Brother
Thompson as he traveled
twenty years' journey
I want you to know God is still
asking Thompson to bring
them warnings from me
²⁵ There is no way that a man
could walk out in the midst
of a desert and call enough
men and Christians
together
And say let's build God a house
Unless'n God is with him
In warnin' men every now and
then, you can't warn 'em
off your opinion, but you
have to warn them what
God relate to you
Then you confer to them what
God has told you to say
³⁰ I believe this evenin' that we
stay with God's word,
everything will be all right

He said son of man I have made
thee
A watchman over the house of
Israel
I want you to listen to my voice
And I want you to warn Israel
and at my commandment
35 So it was with Brother
Thompson and still is
I want you to warn Saint
Immanuel
With my voice
What I'm talkin' about Brother
Thompson preached soul
That men can hear God in your
voice
40 Want to walk soul
That men can see God in your
walk
Then you can climb to the bars
of Jesus
While the celestial light shines
And men may see your good
works
45 I want you to know that God
this evenin'
He was warnin' Ezekiel
One of the major prophets
Who had been through the sun
Who had been through the rain
50 Men who had gone down in
captivity
And stayed down there under
old Nebuchadnezzar's rule
Stayed down there in Babylonia
They were able to stand up and
speak up for God
I tell you Ezekiel and Daniel

55 Or some of the major prophets
can tell you that God will
carry you through your
troubles
If you wanted to talk about
prayer this evenin'
You'd talk to Daniel and Daniel
would tell you
Just stand in the window
And face Jerusalem
60 And prayer will be all right
I know as for myself
In nineteen years
Thompson had to face
Jerusalem
Started out here brethrens
65 In the desert
Didn't have no place to
worship
Started out in old tent
But he kept on preachin'
Until the Lord build a house
70 Now now now
Devil done told somebody
Thompson is gettin' old
He's worryin' all the people
Need a younger man
75 Man that walked along here
With this responsibility
On his shoulders
Sometime he cry all night long
Tell the Lord
80 Take care of Saint Immanuel
Have a little difficulty at Saint
Immanuel
I know You can take care Lord
I'm not able to Lord
To take care o' little difficulty

85 Ohh I know if You hold my
     hand
   He'll make everything all right
   I want Brother Thompson
   To be obedient
   Like Ezekiel
90 Ezekiel said
   The Lord carried me out one
     day
   Carried me out in the valley
   Set me down in the midst of
     dry bones
   Set right there brethren
95 Ohh after a while
   The Lord said to Ezekiel
   Son of man
   Can these bones live
   Ezekiel said in these words
100 Oh Lord Thou knowest
   One thing about it Brother
     Thompson
   If we wait on the Lord
   Let the Lord know what we
     want Him to do
   Everything will turn out all
     right
105 Ezekiel sittin' out there
   In a valley of many dry bones
   Voice of the Lord said
   Can these dry bones live
   He said Lord God Thou
     knowest
110 Say I want you to prophesy to
     them now
   What You want me to say to
     them Lord
   Tell them ohh ye dry bones
   Hear ye the Word of the Lord

   One thing I want you to know
     this evening
115 If you preach the Word Brother
     Thompson
   Everything will be all right
   Somebody may go home
   Just keep on preachin'
   I know he will this evenin'
120 These words, in solid rock
   These words will stand the
     terrible fire
   These words will be here when
     everything is gone
   Because God, is aware
   I believe you'll read in the
     book of John
125 That in the beginnin'
   Was the Word
   And the Word was with God
   And the Word sure was God
   Don't y' know God is all right
     this evenin'
130 Ohh Lord
   To God some change in him
   Stay with His Word
   If His Word was able enough to
     come to this world and
     develop itself in Him
   And dwell among us thirty-
     three long years
135 Don't you know the Word is all
     right to trust y' in
   I know the Word this evenin'
   It'll lift you up
   When it seems like all your
     friends are gone
   It'll give you strength
140 When you get weak
   I know the Word this evenin'

Will bring you a long ways
The Word churnin' me up
It started my heart to fear
¹⁴⁵ The hour I first believe
Long time ago
In the state of old Arkansas
Thompson I know it saw it then
Every now and then
¹⁵⁰ I stay by the Word
Ohh the Word
Ohh the old preacher's sermon
   begin
Come on to me all you who are
   able
And heavy laden
¹⁵⁵ And I will give you rest
Take my yoke upon you
And learn of me
My yoke is easy
And burden light
¹⁶⁰ Kept on settin' there
One evenin'
Somethin' got all in my head
Started my mouth to talkin'
Started my feet to walkin'
¹⁶⁵ I don't mind runnin' for Him
   this mornin'
Because the Word is in my
   heart
Don't mind cryin' for the name
Because every tear I shed/ is
   shed for a good cause
   brethren
I'm gonna read the . . . Some
   day
¹⁷⁰ Stay with the Word
What I'm sayin' Immanuel
   every time Brother
   Thompson

Tell them
I know my redeemer live
Because He lives in me
¹⁷⁵ Tell 'em that Job said
Ohh the appointed time
I'll wait on the change comin'
So many time men try to move
   before the change comin'
But stay right here
¹⁸⁰ Stay here
And bring them warnings from
   me
Warn them out of God's Word
Tell men when they're right
Doesn't matter how much
   money he pay in church
¹⁸⁵ But tell him when he's wrong
Am I right
So right
To stand on His Word
It's all right
¹⁹⁰ To cry upon the man
I know it's all right
Carry your trouble to the Lord
Ohh have you ever carried
   your burden to the Lord
And leave 'em right there
¹⁹⁵ I declare you're about to this
   evenin'
Never lost a patient
And friend this evenin'
He's a friend
Above all others
²⁰⁰ Don't you know His Word this
   evenin'
To go on out with Ezekiel with
   the dry bones
And start a-rattlin' and shakin'

Don't you know He's gonna let
    this old body . . .
If they're started them old
    bones a-shakin' out there in
    that valley
205 Well, I know it will make me
    move
It getting my feet
I don't mind walkin'
Ohh, get on in the voice
Tell men
210 I know my redeemer lives
Because He lives in me
In the later years
In my flesh
I shall see God
215 Somebody
Somebody this evenin'
May be sayin' in your heart
There is no God
Search the Scripture over
220 I heard the book of Psalms say
That fool
Said in thy heart
There is no God
I know this evenin' there is a
    God
225 God's somewhere
Every now and then brethrens
He's been close to me
Tell me
When I get weak
230 Hold on a little while longer
Sometime
Sometimes
I hold against His courage
But there's a little old fistful
235 To keep on moving
Ohh after a while

He's sure to be all right
I gotta keep on
Carryin' my heavy load
240 'Cause some of these days
I'm gonna lay down my heavy
    load
But I got somewhere . . .
I made a long time ready to go
Ohh the Word this evenin'
245 Warn 'em Brother Thompson
If they don't hear you
You gonna lose your reward
But if you fail to tell Saint
    Immanuel
And they die in the change
250 God will require of your hand
Ohh tell men
I know, for myself
That I been changed
You know what we don't have
    now
255 We don't have enough changed
    men in the world
We have men too scared
To let the world know they
    been changed
Oh I don't mind tellin' the
    world
I know I been changed
260 I know for myself
Ever since that Monday evenin'
I'm goin' home
To live with God
When I lay my burden down
265 I'm going to get my calendar
I'm not sufferin' here in this old
    world brethrens
For somebody to say I'm a
    sufferer

But I'm sufferin' because of the
    grace of God
In my heart
270 Warn them on Brother
    Thompson
Twenty years of service
Bringin' warnin's to one hard-
    head group of folks
God will give you a reward
Who had his wife to stand by
    him
275 Until sickness came along and
    say you take a rest for a
    while
The same is goin' to happen to
    all of us some of these days
I want to say to the members of
    the Saint Immanuel Church
Let us stay by our pastor
He is my pastor like he is yours
280 We want to stay here by him
    and throw around him—our
    arms of protection
Give him his flowers while he
    live
That he can enjoy the heat of
    the sun
Give me my flowers while I live
Doesn't matter how many we
    would bring down through
    the hour
285 After God has called him home
But bring—give him the flowers
    now while he can enjoy
    them
We pray His blessing that he
    will serve many many more
    years

I want you to know Brother
    Thompson it's just hot in
    here
God will give you victory
290 If you'll just hold to His hand
Stood on the wall and watch
It doesn't mean watchin' what
    folks do
But watching Thompson
And you can see what others do
295 Am I right brother preachers
If you stand on a corner tryin'
    to watch all of these folks
    they'll cut a corner around
    that-a-way
But if you just watch yourself
Tell the Lord every every now
    and then give me strength
I am weak but Thou art strong
300 God bless you
I wants to see Jesus
Do you
I have a father gone
I have a brother gone and sister
305 But out of all of that I want to
    see Jesus
Do you want to see Jesus
Do you know you're on the
    right road only way that
    you can see Jesus
You must be on the right road
By and by
310 I will see Jesus
By and by
I will see Jesus [singing]

DRY BONES IN THE VALLEY

Recited by the Reverend Rubin Lacy, July 16, 1967, in Bakersfield, California, this sermon was, despite its poor beginning,
moderately successful. Lacy was slow in getting started because
he spent a lot of his time on politics, local and international. In
none of the other sermons recorded was so much time spent on
such matters. Lines 42–46 refer to the Arab-Israeli "Six-Day
War," then just a month old; lines 85 ff. have to do with a telecast
Lacy had just seen, though he would not identify the speaker.
From this "false prophet" Lacy turns to the duty of the true
preacher and finally gets around to the main point of the sermon.
Most of the opening remarks (the first 120 lines) appear to have
been lost on the congregation; most of them had not seen the
TV program Lacy was criticizing. Sporadic chanting begins at
line 157, with a set piece about John's life as a preacher. Although
off the subject (dry bones), Lacy undoubtedly used it for two
reasons: he was talking about preachers already and this theme
was psychologically related; and since it was a memorized (or
nearly memorized) theme, he could use it to his best advantage
to establish a rhythmical pattern in his audience. A consistent
chant begins at line 203. From John's life as a preacher Lacy
moves to Moses in the desert and then to the wilderness experience of Ezekiel. Momentum had begun to build up (by line
268) when he decided to use material from the gospel song,
"Dem Bones." Near the end he comes to the main story (lines

287 ff.), occasionally breaking into song (lines 337 ff. and 363–78).

We're gonna talk today from
    Ezekiel thirty-seven, and
    fourth chap—verse
Ezekiel thirty-seven and fourth
    verse
Son of man, can these dry
    bones live?
Son of man, can these dry
    bones live?
⁵ Ezekiel said to God, Oh Lord,
    Thou knowest
Ezekiel way back there
    reminded me of Peter
God asked Peter feed my sheep
Asked him again to feed my
    sheep
He said Peter do you love me?
¹⁰ He said Lord Thou knowest
You know You know I love
    You—gotta feed my lambs
So Ezekiel here tells God Lord
    Thou knowest
And the Lord said in the fourth
    verse then you prophesy
Go out there and prophesy
¹⁵ Prophesy to the dry bones
That they might—tell 'em to
    get up and walk, to live
    again
We find here that old—that
    Ezekiel was obedient
Obedience is better than
    sacrifice
It wasn't Ezekiel's business to
    see how God would make
    those bones live

²⁰ Wasn't his business
You know, we as a whole, if we
    are told to do something,
    that we don't see any sense
    in doing that we don't
    think it oughta be did
We talk back
But this prophet didn't argue
    with God, neither did
Abraham—Abram argue with
    God
²⁵ God said to Abram take that
    boy and take him on out
    yonder
Just go on goin' 'til y' get to
    Mount Moriah
And when y' get there I'll show
    y' which one of the peaks
    to get up on
There's a heap o' peaks out
    there
When y' get there I'll show y'
    the one to go up on
³⁰ Take him on out there and kill
    'im
Offer 'im up as a sacrifice
You know Abraham thought
    about that God had said
    that out o' that boy would
    come the seed of all
    nations
Of the tribes to be brr-blest
You know that he thought of
    that
³⁵ But he didn't argue with God

He did not argue with God
Ahh, he just don't be
So, we know Ishmael was here
Son that's begotten by the
    concubine we know he was
    here
40 And he's here today
Amen I say he's here today
Ishmael is troubling Jerusalem
    today
Ishmaelites—they're called
    Arabs
But they're troublin' Jerusalem
    today
45 Israel, is God's chosen people
They're here there standing up
    for their rights
They've fallen many times,
    every time they fall, God
    reaches
His outstretched hand and
    picks them up
You know, if God is for y' He's
    more than the world
    against y'
50 Yes, we, love to argue too
    much, with leadership
Because we can't see it, hmm?
But I think if we do more
    obeying than we do
    arguing we'd get along
    better
God has chosen people, to tell
    you what to do
Hmm?
55 Paul said, Timothy, to be
    mindful over the flock

which the Holy Ghost have
    made thee overseer
Word overseer here doesn't
    mean a slave
Hmm?
But the overseer is to tell you
    what to do, not to tell him
Amen
60 Speakin' of the boss of the
    church—if the church have
    any boss on earth it's the
    preacher
I know some folks don't like to
    hear it but it's true
Because the church is left in
    the hands of the preacher
    whether he like it or not
Hmm?
Said the hands of the preacher
65 Jesus said to Peter the other
    day I give unto thee the
    keys of the kingdom of
    heaven
All that walks around here
    loose, will loose in heaven
All that you bind here on earth,
    I'll bind in heaven
Hmm?
The keys not the key, but the
    key that means the
    skeleton keys or the pass
    keys or whatever y' wanta
    call it—not like the other
    keys
70 Thought He'd ask Ezekiel here
    a question, can these dry
    bones live?

It spell-bound Ezekiel 'cause he
    didn't know
But I love him because he
    submitted himself to God:
    You know, You know, tell
    me what to do
God said go out there and
    speak, God wants men
    today that'll speak for Him
Hmm?
75 We got people here now—
    ahh—speakin' for the folk,
    not God
I want this on the record—I
    want this on the record
I say we got men, here, that
    speakin' for men and not
    God and sayin' they're
    preachers—ministers of the
    gospel
Hmm?
No ministers, of God, is gonna
    let no dollar buy him
80 Hmm?
Simon Peter and John hail a
    man, here come a rich
    man, and offered to pay
    'em
If you just gimme a token so I
    can do that—Amen!—I do—
    I'd make you rich
Peter turned around and told
    him this don't come from
    money
I know it's all right, this don't
    come from money
85 Tryin' to say to you this
    evenin', we have here in
    Bakersfield

We have preachers in
    Bakersfield that's preachin'
    for the folk and not for
    God
Ahh, I know what I'm talkin'
    about because God is not a
    segregated God
I say God is not a segregated
    God
Hmm?
90 I know a man here in this town
    Pastor seventeen or
    eighteen hundred people
Hmm?
Got on the public TV the other
    day
And publicly announced that
    was canvassin' for white
    supremacy
Amen—Wallace, George
    Wallace of Alabama
95 That man—if he's pastorin' two
    thousand people every one
    of those people is with him
'Cause if they wasn't they'd
    leave the church
I know I'm right about it
God is displeased at that
That isn't doin' anything—that's
    not doing the town any
    good
100 That's stirrin' up more trouble
More confusion, more hate into
    our town
And it's comin' from the church
The Missionary Baptist church
    of Bakersfield
Seventeen or eighteen hundred
    members

[105] If he didn't hide it I didn't have
no right to hide it
I wouldn't speak about it if he
hadn't got on TV with it
But I have to answer—some
way or another to answer
him
I want to tell you he's not the
preacher of God
But he's a preacher for the
white supremacy folk, not
God he's not a preacher
but a business of the
people in Bakersfield
[110] I know that
God is no respecter of
persons—you had that in
your lessons this mornin'
They was tryin' to segregate
way back then Peter was
the hardest-hearted one
there was in the bunch, but
God had convinced him on
the housetops that He
wasn't no respecter of
persons
Hmm?
Ahh—but I want you—to
remember that if God's for
you, He's more than the
world against you
[115] Ezekiel here—ahh—believed in
God
When he was a young man he
didn't do like some of us
now
All stiff-necked
Hmm?
And didn't wanna deal, with
nothin' but the big

members of the church
[120] But he went out and sat down
in sackcloth and ashes with
the people
Yes he did, I say he sit down
there with the people
God wants the shepherd to be
with the sheep
How can you feed—Amen—
your sheep when you're in
New Orleans and your
sheep's in Bakersfield
You can't do it to save your life
[125] A shepherd is a feeder
And to feed you gotta be there
I know what I'm talkin' about/
an' you gotta know how to
feed
Everybody that said they can
feed can't feed
I can't come here and feed this
man's sheep like he did
[130] Why? because these are his
sheep
Amen, I can come along here
and boost him
Maybe give them a boost
But the regular feeder—have t'
be the shepherd
He never said shepherds—no
He didn't—over no flock
[135] But He said the shepherd of
the flock
Not shepherds over the flock
Therefore one shepherd at a
time
If one—one—shepherd is
removed, God always have

been able to place another
one there
Ahh, so Ezekiel I said, was a
shepherd
140 He's almost a gospel preacher
One that God told him to stand
on the wall
And rap the gavel
And if men don't believe him,
then—ahh—their souls is
required at their own
hands
But if you stand to rap the
gavel, then if they die in
sin
145 You are responsible for it
Ahh—so many of us—ahh—
ministers of the gospel
Is responsible today because
we're scared to tell the
truth
Afraid we'll lose a dollar
Afraid we'll lose a church
150 I say unto you this evenin', if
God calls me to preach,
and not able to give me no
preachin' to do, it's all
right with me
If He wanted me to sit down,
He say Lacy you've done
enough
That's all right
I can sit down, but I'm not
dischargin' myself
Because I think God oughta do
the dischargin'
155 Ahh—I'm not like some people,
sayin' that a preacher
oughta retire

There's no retirement to no
preacher
Amen—he keeps on—keepin'
on—let's see about—am I
right about it
John was young man
When he started out
160 About twenty-some odd years
old
Like him now, make a
conclusion to the book of
Revelation
Way up yonder, in his nineties
I said in his nineties
Fixin' to go home
165 But yet he never had sat down
And—uhh—discharge his debt
He might have got to the place,
brother pastors
Where he didn't shout as much
as he used t'
And do much evangelistic work
as he used t'
170 But at this particular time
He was sitting down in the city
of Ephesia
Pastoring a church
That Timothy—Bishop
Timothy—
Ahh—had founded a long time
ago
175 Tryin' to say to you we can't
give up, as ministers of the
gospel
Yes sir!
Take this young prophet, out
yonder in the valley, where

many of 'em had disobeyed
God
Y' know, t' hear the light, stay
in the wilderness, forty
long years, all of that was
because of disobedience
They could have been to the
land of Canaan in two or
three days
180 Ahh—but they stay there on
account of they was
disobedient t' God
Uhh-huhh, and, God, set there
an' wandered right there in
the wilderness
But He was good to them
He didn't let them starve to
death
For food and neither water
185 He smote a rock out yonder
Water came up out of the foot
of the mountain
They drink—Amen—the good
cool pure water
An' then it rained down bread
I'm told it was angel's food
190 Food that the angels ate
And they were disobedient
about that
He told them to gather just
what you could eat on one
day
Don't put up nothin' for
tomorrow
Ahh—God has always been
particular about men
stackin' up a whole lot
195 Because you're here today, and
tomorrow you may be gone

I see then they disobeyed God
And began to stack back-stuffs
They just wasn't obeyin', not to
save their lives
And God said the other day,
I'm gonna kill all of y'
200 Every one, that help out the
land of Egypt
With Moses fulfilled with
Joshua
Ahh—I'm gonna say if You do
that, the people'll go out
with the news
That You wasn't able to get 'em
To the land of Canaan
205 God said I don't care what the
folks say
They've been so disobedient
God from Zion
They've hurt me time and again
That He ain't gonna put up
with them no longer
210 God began to kill 'em
Out there in the wilderness
Died out there
Old Moses
Go get your serpent
215 Is rarin' up out there
Go tryin' an' get 'em
See what it all been
Go and got a golden serpent
Rarin' up there out in the
wilderness
220 All of you
Wanta stop dyin'
And wanta get well
Just look up and live
Went out there

²²⁵ Stood under the serpent
So mean
So contribuous [*sic*]
Stood there with the head
    down
Just wouldn't look up
²³⁰ Stood there rather die
That don't be the Word of God
Ain't God all right?
See here
Some years after
²³⁵ Ezekiel come on the scene
That great prophet of God
Told him Ezekiel
Go out yonder
Go an' pastor that land
²⁴⁰ Save everybody
Way they die out there
By the millions
Out yonder in the valley
Prophesy
²⁴⁵ To the dry bones
The Word
The valley is white
Bleached with dry bones
Go out yon
²⁵⁰ And prophesy to 'em
Tell 'em
To wake up
And hear the Word of God
Ain't God all right?
²⁵⁵ God from Zion
Ezekiel went out there
Begin to prophesy
Dry bones
Ezekiel said
²⁶⁰ I heard
A mighty rattlin'

The rattlin' of bones
Shakin' through the valley
Hark hallelujah
²⁶⁵ Rattlin' of a livin' God
Said the bones
Began to get together
Toe bone
Connected to the foot bone
²⁷⁰ Foot bone
Connected to the ankle bone
Ankle bone
Connected to the leg bone
Leg bone
²⁷⁵ Connected to the knee bone
Knee bone
Connected to the hip—thigh
    bone
Thigh bone
Connected to the hip bone
²⁸⁰ Hip bone
Connected to the back bone
Back bone
Connected to the head bone
—To the neck bone
²⁸⁵ The neck bone
Connected to the back bone
And I heard
Him prophesy again
The Word of God
²⁹⁰ Come to the dry bones
Rise and live
God from Zion
Said to Ezekiel
Prophesy again
²⁹⁵ Prophesy
Said again
Came over the bone
Layin' there

With skin on the bones
300 Said prophesy
Some manage t' get up
Prophesied again
Wind was still
No wind blowin'
305 Said to prophesy
Four winds to blowin'
God blowed His hardest
On the winds
Winds blow
310 Breath came into the bones
These bones
Got up shouting
Praisin' God
Ain't God all right?
315 Ohh He'll give you another
    chance
I love the Lord
'Cause He'll give you
Another chance
Ain't God all right?
320 Heard Jesus
Say the other day
To those Pharisees
God from Zion
It'll be more trouble
325 For you
In the resurrection mornin'
Than it was
With those people
In Sodom and Gomorrah
330 Ain't God all right?
Ohh He's a warrior
Fightin' your battles
Ohhh, take my hand
Take my hand
335 If you'll hold my hand

I'm going on anyhow
Lord, hold my hand
Ohh, hold my hand
I don't want to hold His hand
340 'Cause I might turn it loose
There's old folks used to sing
You better mind how you walk
    on across
Your foot might slip, and your
    soul be lost
I don't want, to hold His hand
345 I might be weak and turn it
    lose
But I want Jesus, to hold my
    hand
When y' leave here Brother
    McRoy
We hit the daily highway
Y' tell God to hold me
350 Guide me
Ohh, lead me
Lead me
I know him—what you're doin'
I'm on the highway
355 I may get a guide to show me
Don't let the race-rod [sic]
    come loose
Umm-hmm
Ohh all alone
Sleep with Him
360 I say, to tell Him to sleep with
    y'
And wake y' in the mornin'
And everything will be all right
Give me wings
Just give me wings
365 Oh wings of faith
To fly away

To be at—my soul is . . .
Give me wings
Give servant wings
370 And I'll fly
To be . . .
Just give me wings

Servant wings
Ohh wings of faith
375 To fly away to be . . .
My soul is where I'm at . . .
Ohh give me wings [dissolves in
    humming]

I CAN DO ALL THINGS

This sermon was recited by Assistant Pastor William Robinson, August 13, 1967, in Santa Barbara, California. The failure of this sermon (as an oral performance) can be attributed to Mr. Robinson's lack of experience. At the time of recording he had not mastered the technique of organizing his words into metrical units. As a result he had to think about each line: he was not able to achieve any metrical consistency until near the end (line 181); pauses between lines were excessive, and he was unable to give any sense of metrical continuity. Between lines the regular pastor, C. Earl Williamson, shouted encouragement: "Pray with him church," "Yes, yes," and "You tell it, preacher." At first the congregation was sympathetic but after several minutes they became restless so that by the time Robinson was able to begin a chant he had lost them completely. The length of the lines and the flexibility of the syntax mark them as more akin to written prose than to oral delivery, especially oral presentation in this tradition. There is little of the parallelism characteristic of oral delivery; in lines 26 and 27 the repetition of "through Christ" came about because Robinson couldn't think of what to say next. It was, in other words, an unintentional stall formula. The first traces of oral style—and the first sign of metrical consistency—come at line 93 but could not be sustained. Robinson begins to sing at line 174; the lines remain just as irregular, but at that point we begin to have much more repetition and parallel syntax and resistance against introducing new ideas. Lines 186–

88 nearly repeat phrases that have been used earlier; to the end
of the performance the language is noticeably repetitive: the last
lines at least Robinson has mastered.

Pastor Williamson, Officers, first
    lady, members and visitin'
    friends
Truly I am grateful to the Lord
For blessing me and keeping
    me
And I am grateful to you for
    this opportunity
5 It is always good to be able to
    say something for the Lord
I want to call your attention at
    this time to the epistle of
    Paul to the Philippians
That is the epistle of Paul or
    the letter of Paul to the
    'lippians
In chapter four of that letter
    and the thirteenth verse
    you will find these words
I can do all things through
    Christ that strengthens me
10 I can do all things through
    Christ that strengthens me
To put our hearts in one tune
    will you repeat after me
    these words
I can do all things
    [response]
Through Christ
    [response]
That strengthens me
    [response]
15 So said Paul, apostle Paul
I would like to use, these
    words, for my main
    thought

For the main thought of my
    message, this morning
Could say for the theme, but I
    say main thought of my
    message
Reason I say this is because, if
    you don't get anything
    else, from the message this
    morning you can carry
    these words away from the
    sanctuary with you
20 You can carry this thought with
    you
These are the words of apostle
    Paul
And I am moved or I am
    touched with this saying
Now the main—the key word in
    our thought this morning
I think—I think would be that I
    can do
25 I can do—I think this would be
    the key word
But I would like for you to
    think—think mainly on
    these words through
    Christ, through Christ
Through Christ
This is the lesson that Paul had
    to learn
It's the lesson
30 I will go as far to say that this is
    the lesson that some of us
    will have to learn
That it is through Christ

Not through President Johnson
Not through Rap Brown,
    Stokely Carmichael
Not even through Pastor
    Williamson
35 Oh no
But through Christ
I can do through Christ
But without Christ then I don't
    think that we can do
    anything
We can't do anything, anything
    without Christ
40 I said Paul had to learn this
    lesson
Now I think first of all we
    should, take a look at the
    life of Paul
The man that spoke these
    words
See, in the epistle and at this
    present time we think of
    him as apostle Paul
But it wasn't so from the
    beginning
45 No
There was some time before he
    was known as Paul
Umm-hmm
Well first of all he was born—
    born in Tarsus, Tarsus
A few years after the
    resurrection of Christ
50 And was named Saul
Lord help us today
Was named Saul
He was born of Jewish parent
Who held the rights and
    privileges of Roman—
    Roman citizenship

55 He was instructed in the Jewish
    law to the extent that at
    the age of thirteen he
    would call—he was called a
    son of the law
A son of the law, meanin' that
    he knew the law so well
That he was honored to be a
    son of the law
But I would like for you to
    think that—think on the
    idea of Paul bein' a Jew
And his parent bein' also
    Hebrews that held the
    rights and privileges of
    Roman citizenship
60 Because it is—it means
    something
It means something, it means
    something
You see that first of all there
    were many Jews that did
    not believe in Christ
Did not believe in Christ
Now they believed in God
65 But there were many that
    never—and some even
    today—that don't believe in
    Christ
Some of them are still lookin'—
    lookin' for the risen Christ
And do you know that there
    are many of us today that
    don't believe in Christ
And some of us don't even
    believe in God
After we are able to look on
    the altar of nature and see

the sun and all of His
handiworks
⁷⁰ Read His divine Word but some
of us still don't believe in
God
We say we believe in God
But Pastor W'mson has said
that he's gonna talk about
it and I want to hear it—All
Shook Up
And you know when you fail to
believe in God—when you
be fail—when you fail to
believe in Christ then you
are goin' to be shook up
Oh yes goin' to be shook up
⁷⁵ I said that Paul was a Jew
And it seemed as though that
he was destined
To be a great man to be a great
man—it was discovered in
the early stages of his life
Because we find that he was
brilliant
There was a time when our
poor parents thought of
their children to the extent
that they could look at
them and predict what they
would be when they grew
up
⁸⁰ They would say if you had—if
you had—a large head he's
going to be a preacher
I know when I was a child—
very small—my mother
used to say one day you
are going to be a preacher

I had no thoughts but today
here I am
I am—and I am what I am but I
want you to know I am a
servant of the living God
That is—I feel that is what's
important
⁸⁵ Not to the point of being a
preacher but being a
servant of the true and
living God
Paul said I can do all things,
through Christ
But we also find here that
maybe someone we should
talk about this to our [?]
that you may have a better
understandin'
All things, not all things you
know, there must be some
limitation to this
Anything
⁹⁰ Through Christ—no no not
anything–not all things
Now reverend what do you
mean—you just made this
statement all things
But Paul goes to say here in
this eighth verse
Finally brethren, whatsoever
thing is true
Whatsoever thing are honest
⁹⁵ Whatsoever things are just
Whatsoever things are pure
Whatsoever things are lovely
Whatsoever things are good
Report
¹⁰⁰ You know he named those
things

Whatsoever things are right
Things that are good
Things that are pure
Those things we can do through
Christ
105 No He can't—I don't think—
don't get the idea that you
can jump the jack through
Christ—it's through the
devil
But through Christ
What did Paul start out to do
And I think we should call him
Saul at this time
That we may better identify
him
110 What did Saul start out to do
Right off hand we could say
that he started out to
destroy the Church
He started out to get rid of the
man—the idea of this
Christ
But do you know one thing
God stopped him
115 This Christ stopped him
He could have stopped
altogether but He just
delayed him
Gave him to know that I am the
Christ
Jesus after His baptism you
know became the Christ
At Nazareth—Jesus—but don't
get confused about Jesus
Christ 'cause the Father an'
Son an' Holy Ghost they're
all in One

120 Jesus hears—I'm talkin' about
Christ
We find that Paul, as I said,
went to the synagogue
school
And he achieved so much in
the synagogue school
The teachin' of the rabbis
That he was honored as the son
of the law
125 And upon his graduation from
synagogue school
We find that he went to
Jerusalem to further his
schooling
And there he was taught under
Gamaliel
People like to say that he was
taught at the feet of
Gamaliel
Gamaliel was a great teacher of
the law
130 And he—he was the leadin'
figure in the Sanhedrin
council—whenever they
needed counsel they would
turn to him
He was one that knew the law
So Paul received further
learning in the council
He was taught more about the
law
This is the Sanhedrin council
135 The same council that passed
the judgment upon this
Christ
They knew about it
Paul received training there—
learned more about the law

Increased knowledge and
wisdom
But it is said that while he
there attendin' law school
in Jerusalem he came in
contact with the new
Christian movement
[140] And it is said that it aroused his
hostility
And after the death of Stephen
which he had a share
He was around some place
It is said that he was employed
by the Sanhedrin council
To further destroy—to further
destroy this Christian
movement—Lord help me a
little while
[145] And to make the arrest of all of
Stephen's followers
And it was while he was
exercising this commission
it happened
Because if you recall on the
road to Damascus
As he drew near to the city
And it was along about noon
day
[150] Paul said that somethin'
happened—this same Christ
appeared unto him—came
before him this same
Christ—and He appeared,
and He appeared in the
form of a light, a light that
was so bright
Until it was even brighter than
the sun

Was so bright until it blinded—
and Lord help when I say
it—Paul because it was Saul
Blinded Saul—the light was so
bright—Lord help us—until
it blinded Saul's eyes and
he fell on the ground
While he's on the ground Paul
said he saw someone in
that light
[155] Someone that he had never
seen before
Not only did he see someone
but Paul said he heard a
voice
A voice said to Saul—Lord help
us this morning—
Saul—Saul—Saul why persecute
thou me
Saul why—why—why are you
tryin' to fight against me
[160] Tell me that Saul said who was
Thou Lord
Who are Thou Lord
He said that I am Jesus
Meanin' the Christ
The One that you are tryin' to
destroy
[165] An' my mind go back to God's
word—to Jesus' word when
He said upon this rock I
build my church
And the gates of hell shall not
prevail against it
Upon this rock I build my
church
You see Paul didn't know that
which he was tryin' to
destroy

Founded by that same Christ
170 Paul—Paul didn't know that he
    was playin' with Someone
    that was much bigger
But you know today—today we
    have those that are still
    tryin' to destroy that which
    is right that which is holy
    and that which is just
You still have those who are
    tryin' to destroy the church
    of a true and a living God
Last Sunday I had the privilege
    of hearing a young man
    stand behind the rostrum—
    the pulpit here and say that
    who would believe in this
    Christ idea
He said that I don't think there
    anything to this idea of
    Christ
175 And he tried to make a joke
    about it 'cause he said if
    you had a wife an' you
    would come home and she
    told you she was with child
She told you that she received
    it by the Holy Spirit what
    would you think of it
I'm tryin'—what I'm tryin' to
    say to you today that there
    are those that not only are
    so far out that they no
    longer believe in the Christ
    idea
That they are tryin' to teach
    others
Umm they're tryin' to teach
    others that there is no such
    thing as Christ

180 They are—they are proclaiming
    and saying that God is dead
Trying—and you know what
    they are trying to do—they
    are trying to destroy the
    church
But my Bible tell me
Umm-hmm my Bible tell me
That the gates of hell shall not
    prevail
185 And I want to say—say—to you
    that is a mighty dangerous
    thing
Umm to go around tryin' to
    destroy that which is right
Tryin' to destroy that which is
    holy
Tryin' to destroy that which is
    just
Umm and as I close this
    mornin'
190 Paul had to learn this lesson—
    had to learn his lesson
And we find him saying here—
    saying here today
That I can do all things through
    Christ
Umm at one time in my life
I thought that I could do all
    things through the law
195 At one time in my life I
    thought that I could do all
    things through—under my
    own power
I thought I could do all things
    under my own strength
Oh Lord but ah—but ah today—
    today I'm sayin' that I can
    do all things through Christ

Umm because I realize today
    that my strength lies in
    Christ Jesus
My strength lies in Christ Jesus
200 Everything that I attempt to do
    I shall put Christ before me
And everything that I do I
    should want to know is this
    the will of Christ
If it isn't the will of Christ—
    umm—I should feel like
    that I'm going to fail
The same Christ—the same
    Christ
The same Christ Pastor
    Williamson
205 The same Christ He is available
    today
The same Christ the same
    Christ lives today
He is here today in the form of
    the Holy Spirit

You may not be able to see the
    same Christ
Umm but if you will just open
    up the door of your heart
210 Behold I said at the door and
    knock He said
And if you'll open up I'll come
    in and sup with y'
The same Christ is available
    today
Have you met Him
Do you know Him
215 Open up your heart today
And receive Him
Because if we are to succeed it
    must be through Christ
And if we fail it is because we
    fail to recognize that Christ
He lives today—open up your
    heart and receive Him

THIS SAME JESUS

The Reverend Jerry Lockett was a young man (middle forties) when he preached this sermon in Charlottesville, Virginia, on March 17, 1968. Being young, he had great energy and stamina, but being a relatively inexperienced preacher, his global conception of the performance was fragmented—and consequently his chanting was irregular throughout. His shouting was more powerful than most of his fellow preachers, and he could sustain emotional peaks longer than they, but these shows of strength were not always aesthetically pleasing. He began reciting metrically fairly early in the sermon, around lines 26–28; and he wound down, returning to the immediate world of the Charlottesville church in front of him, at line 349. The structure of his composition is the preacher's well-proven text-context-application.

"This Same Jesus" is a sermon topic that is also in the repertoire of Reverend Elihue Brown, and a comparison of the two performances, particularly the similarity of lexicon, metaphor, exampla from Scripture and tradition, and idea, shows the influence of the oral tradition from which both men borrowed. Lockett's performance was heavily formulaic: "this same Jesus" occurs fifteen times here, and "same Jesus" is uttered thrice more. Quite a few lines (formulas?) are repeated verbatim: 48–49, 86–87, 136–38, 196–97, 213–17, 226–27. Certain other repetitions (such as on the miracles that recount the healing of the blind, lame, and dumb: 4, 8–11, 159–63) are induced by the subject

of the evening's sermon. Lockett was particularly fond of anaphoric sequences: 9–11; 92–3; 112, 114, 118; 146–47; 237–39;
263–65, 270; 274–77; 293–94; 327–29; 330–33; and 335–38.
Lockett advances action with the conventional "after a while"
(182, 220, 234, 281); exclaims "Oh Lord" (59–60, 143–44, 184–
85); and "Lord have mercy" (52–53, 255). A stall formula similar
to that used by the Reverend C. L. Franklin—"Oh church, I
wonder this evening do you know what I'm talking about?"—is
expressed in line 102. Lockett digresses several times: on faith
(24–33) and on conversion (164–70, repeated in lines 175–81);
on the birth of Jesus (36–42, 51–54); about the folly of arguing
with God (43–50); the "conceiving" of the Holy Ghost (58–66,
75); the childhood of Jesus (90–109); his ascension (189 ff.); and
portions of his earthly life (209–71). Lines 127–29 also rhyme,
an unusual but by no mean rare phenomenon in oral sermons.

Dear Christian friends, we want
   you to notice from the
   twelfth chapter and the
   twenty-second verse of the
   book of Saint Matthew
The twelfth chapter and the
   twenty-second verse
Of the gospel of Saint Matthew
Then was brought unto Him
   one possessed with a devil,
   blind and dumb, and He
   healed him insomuch that
   the blind and dumb both
   spake, and saw
5 We might use for a subject this
   evenin', this same Jesus
This same Jesus
No other Jesus but this same
   Jesus
That give sight to the blind
Cause the dumb to talk
10 Cause the lame to walk
Caused the deaf to hear

This same Jesus
No other one, at that time, had
   the power and the
   authority, to do such things
   but Jesus
But Jesus told His disciples,
   before He left
15 The work that I have done, are
   greater works, than ye shall
   do
He left it on record, for
   mankind to walk, so
   respectful, in the presence
   of God, that he'll be able
   to touch the blind
They will see
He'll be able to lay hands upon
   the sick
And they would be healed
20 Providing if the sick ones and
   the blind ones, the deaf
   and the dumb would have
   faith enough in God

You know so many times
people—I've seen it so
ofttimes, people go and
pray with people
And they come away—feel
rejoicing and they got
salvation
Because I've done what God
told me to do
But the individual that is sick
haven't felt nothing
25 Because he didn't have faith
enough in God
But we have faith enough in
God, to believe that God
will do the work
He told you and I to pray for
him
Anoint him with oil
Lay hands on him
30 But God will do the work
We can't do the work
But God will do the healing
If we only got faith in Him
I say this same Jesus
35 That's who we're talking about
this evening
If we let our minds run back
Just a little further
We would see this same Jesus
that we're talking about
When Mary was traveling up
and down the dusty road
40 The mother of Jesus
Was traveling up and down the
dusty roads
When an angel came to Mary
and told her that you shall
bring forth a son into the

world and His name shall
be called Jesus
You know it ain't good to argue
with God's people
It's not good
45 When Mary received those
words she said not so
Talkin' to the angel now
It's not so
Don't argue with God
Don't argue with God—if God
send you a message you
receive that
50 You accept and say thank you
Jesus
She said not so—how can I
bring forth a child in the
world when I know not a
man
Lord have mercy
Good Lord have mercy
I cannot bring forth a child
55 Tell me the angel went on back
home
And carried the message to the
Father
Send the angel on back
And Mary the thing will—
concealed by the Holy
Ghost
Oh Lord
60 Oh Lord
Church—and everyone been's
concealed by the Holy
Ghost
Like a tree that's been planted
by the rivers of a water
You shall not be moved

That's the reason why—so many
men and women is fallin'
by the wayside
65 Because they haven't never
done been concealed
Or contained—or be concealed
And His name shall be called
Jesus
We see Mary—when she got in
a hurry one day
Runnin' over the hills and
valleys
70 Going on over, to her cousin's
house
Going over to cousin Elizabeth
Told Elizabeth
What the angel had told her
Tell the . . . , over there
75 Elizabeth had been concealed,
with a child called John
Oh yes
Spirit . . . with the spirit
Travel with John, leaped with
joy
Even before he was born
80 Because Mary had carried a
good news
Yes my Lord I'm talkin' about
Jesus
I'm talkin' about the lamb of
God
Then we see the same child
After He's born, we seen Him
there
85 When He's about twelve years
old
I'm talkin' about Jesus
I'm talkin' about Jesus
Talkin' about the One

Who brought us a mighty long
ways
90 We seen a child way up in
Jerusalem
Seen Him up there settin' down
amongst the doctors
Settin' up there among the
lawyers
Settin' up there among highly
educated people . . .
pretty good answer
95 Oh my God
Save the man now
I know you got your education
Got it from a man
But I got mine from my Father
100 Which art in heaven
We seen the child comin' on
back home now
Oh church, I wonder this
evening do you know what
I'm talking about
When I say Jesus
I say Jesus
105 The lamb of God
We see in Him one day
When He stepped on the . . .
And He said . . .
I go about my Father's business
110 We see Him when He stepped
on out now
I gotta do the work of the One
that sent me
Tell me that Jesus
For three long years and six
months
Tell me Jesus
115 Went all through the land and
country

Goin' about there giving sight
  to the blind
Yes He was
Tell me that woman
Oh Lord
120 . . . the blood
Had been suffering for twelve
  long years
Had spent all of her means
Didn't have no more money
I can't go to doctor no more
125 But I heard say Lord
I heard that Jesus
Was gonna pass by this way
I wonder one day
Till you and I get on the way
130 Get on the way that Jesus
  passin' by
Thank God—oh church
He give 'em a kiss of His love
Touch us from the crown of our
  heads
On to the sole of our feet
135 We begin to say thank you
  Jesus
Thank you Jesus
Thank you Jesus
Thank you Jesus
That same Jesus
140 When the final hour had come
Walking on about—doing great
  work for His Father
Saved this woman one day
Preacher say ohh Lord
Oh Lord
145 I can guess . . . that kiss the
  men of His garments
I believe . . .
I believe I will be whole

. . . .
  I see a crowd somewhere
150 Got on to the hem of His
  garments
To the great faith that she had
Great God I heard Jesus say
  now
Upon your faith woman
You will be whole now
155 Oh yes
This same Jesus
Told the woman one day
Same Jesus
That give sight to the blind one
  day
160 Same Jesus
Spoke to the dumb one day
Caused them to speak
Deaf to hear one day
That same Jesus
165 Met us one day
When we were on our road
Bent on hell and destruction
Travelin' down the road
Turns around one day
170 Give us a kiss of His love
But now
Oh now
Ways
Oh ways
175 Goin' down the road
I wanta turn y' around
Now when y' run from me now
Great God almighty in Zion
When the love of God come
  upon us
180 Then we turn all the way
  around
And began to run for Jesus

By and by—after a while
When the time has fully come
Oh Lord
185 Oh Lord
I say when the time
I see y' do nothin'
Until the time comes . . .
The time had fully come
190 Of Jesus
To make a departure
Out of this world
And go back home
Take a seat
195 On the right hand of the Father
Oh church
Oh church
I see the Savior now
When the hour fully have come
200 Yes it have
See the enemy at . . .
When he come upon
This same Jesus
I see Him
205 When He went on around
To the table
And He sat down there
And He set up an example for
     you and I
When He sat down there an'
     taught
210 His disciples
How I want you to do
I want you to eat of this bread
In remembrance of me
The bread is my broken body
215 And out of this cup
I want you to drink it
In remembrance of me
This is my spilled blood

That I spilled on account of you
220 And after a while an' by an' by
I seen Him when He went on
     out
Into the garden of Gethsemane
Got down on His bended knee
Begin to call on the Father
225 Which art in heaven
Oh Father
Oh Father
If it's Your will
Remove this cup from me
230 If not Your will
He said then I'll drink it up
. . . Your will
Yes He did
Then after a while an' by an'
     by
235 We seen this same Jesus
All the way the path to Calvary
Goin' on up with the heavy
     load on His shoulder
Goin' on up to Calvary now
I'm goin' up there now
240 Because I've finished my . . .
Right now up yonder now
The judgment's gonna be . . .
Going on up now
Oh yes—seen Him when He
     went on out
245 I seen the Jews
When they hung Him on the
     cross
Had Him pierced
Pierced Him in the side
I seen that clean blood and
     water
250 I heard 'em say now it's all
     finished

Yes it is just as sure as
    Golgotha
This same Jesus
On the third day in the mornin'
We seen this same Jesus
255 Oh Lord have mercy
I tell you my Father
Which art in heaven
Gonna leave Him now
    . . . hurry
260 Goin' down to Golgotha this
    morning
I seen Him there
Oh yes He is
Rolled the stone away this
    mornin'
Rolled the stone
265 Rolled the stone away.
Just about time now
That my Son's due to get up
That . . .
From heaven came on down
270 Rolled that stone away
And Jesus rose that morning
Do y' know church that He
    rose that morning
Did He rise deep in your soul
Oh, can you feel
275 Can y' feel
Can y' feel the fire
Can y' feel the fire burnin' now
I seen Jesus when He got up
Tarried here on earth
280 Forty long days and nights
After a while an' by an' by
When the time had fully come
I heard Him say now
I gotta go over there and meet
    [the boys]?

285 I'm leavin' now
For my Father
Which are in heaven
Is gonna send me trumpetin'
    back
And the trumpet will be the
    Holy Ghost
290 And the trumpeter[?]
And comin' by itself
But He's gonna bring the father
    along with Him
That same thing, church, that
    burned on the table of our
    hearts
The same thing that the Father
    sent back
295 When He sent down the Holy
    Ghost
And I seen these people
When they went on out of the
    Mount of Olives with Him
Goin' far as I can go with y'
    now
Tell me that a cloud rode down
    from heaven
300 Tell me Jesus said stepped
    aboard that mornin'
Yes He did
Tell me Jesus stepped aboard
Rode on back home
Goin' on back now
305 Take a seat on the right hand of
    my Father
Goin' on back home to
    meditate on
I'm goin' on back home now to
    plead for you and I
Yes my Lord
It was so many times

310 I said so many times
Justice would have cut us down
But mercy was standin' at my
feet
They's prayin' a little while
longer
I seen Jesus when He went on
by . . .
315 Tell me that a stranger
Appeared there just at that
time
He said men and brethren
Why ye stand here gazing
Looking up at the heaven
320 He said have you seen a ghost
Same Jesus coming back again
He's coming back children
Just as sure as you're born
He's coming back
325 And He says you'll be hearing
Revelation
When I come back I'm coming
back with my church
He didn't say what His church
is
He didn't say nothin' 'bout
denominations
He didn't say nothin' 'bout
creed or color
330 He said I'm comin' back with
my church
I'm comin' back with my
church
I'm comin' with my church
Comin' back with the clean [?]
Yeah, Father those will go into
God's kingdom
335 Nothin' but the clean [?]
Nothin' but the pure in heart

Nothin' but the pure in heart
Nothin' but the bestest[?] one is
going into God's kingdom
That's why we're working and
striving so hard
340 Try to go into God's kingdom
We'll try to clean up down
here
Yes we is
If we got on a dirty robe, and
we know we got it on
We got to put it off
345 That God's cleanness
Not on the outside, but
cleanness on the inside
Cleanness so that we can love
one another
As He have told us to do
We got the same Jesus' love
within us
350 Then we don't . . .
No . . . with us
No . . . with us
No we can't do it
He said if your load is too
heavy come to me
355 Lay down, and I'm a burden
bearer
I can help you bear your
burden
The only way we can do that—
we got to know this same
Jesus
For ourselves
And the only way we can know
Him is 'cause we got to do
like He told old man
Nicodemus to do
360 Man you must be born again

You don't think that you're
gonna know Jesus, unless y'
been born
By the Spirit of God
I've been by the waters
Yes y' gotta be born, y' gotta
be born, y' gotta be born y'
know what . . .
365 . . . tell the people, the reason
why that y' find so many
people turnin' back to the
world
Is because they didn't get all of
it
They carin' for the little grave
and they baptism[?]
Bring on back eternal youth
just like a bunch of wild
rabbits
And still they bring them back
and let 'em . . . on the altar
370 Till God give 'em something,
then they'll stay still
They'll be then so that they'll
be unshaven [?]
Otherwise—they's like a path in
the winter weather

Wind blow from the east you'll
see the chaff blowin' west
Oh my God almighty
375 Until we become to know with
Jesus we are subject to
being tossed and driven
Under any wind and doctrine—
may God ever bless you,
may heaven ever smile
upon you
Somewhere and someday in
that city's that not made by
hand
But eternal in the heaven that
we may all go in and come
out no more
Then every day will be Sunday
and sabbaths won't never
have no end
380 And there'll be nothing but joy
and peace and happiness
there forever, and forever
more
May God bless you

I AM THE WAY

This sermon, thoroughly traditional in lexicon, use of formula, dependence on folk traditions, and message content, was preached by the Reverend W. T. Ratliff in Durham, North Carolina, on March 10, 1968. He was a mature man then, probably in his mid- to late sixties. The format is that of text (in this case John 14:8)-context-application, a very popular scriptural passage and sermon topic. Although Ratliff's ordinary discourse and ecstatic singing were not as stylistically disparate as were those of most of his colleagues, a noticeable chant begins around line 44; his performative intensity winds down around line 266, and ends in a brief coda beginning with line 268. Throughout, his sermon was stately and dignified. It was a Sunday morning, his congregation responsive; they were about seventy in number.

Several oral sermon techniques may be observed here. Certain repetitions—from scriptural passages to be sure, but recurrent enough to be considered memorized formulas—occur: 33, 38; 7, 42, 281; 79, 94–5; etc. Allusions to "God's hand," widely heard among black folk preachers, occur in lines 141, 170, 178, and 183–84. "I'm so glad," also from a popular spiritual, occurs in 204. "I am the way," naturally enough given the subject of the sermon, is used many times throughout this performance. The Lord is "old man God," line 248, St. Stephen is "old Brother Stephen," line 292. Lines 124 and 138 introduce repetitious sequences. Long, discursive sentences are segmented in performance to provide metrically consistent formulas: 6–7, 199–

200, 217 ff. Certain key words are used as matrices upon which entire utterances are based, and also provide transitions between lines. "Ways" functions like this in lines 12, 13, 15–16, 18–26, 36–37, 39, 268–70, 279–280, 282, 314, and 316. "Peace" is similarly used in lines 242–44, 251, and 254. And Ratliff's favorite exclamations, "Glory to God" and "Thank God," occur throughout.

The main stream of the argument is interrupted—it is hardly a digression—for a folk rephrasing of the twenty-third Psalm in lines 217–22. A more characteristically oral anecdote depicts a conversation between Mary and Jesus, lines 99–119. Her address to him is terminated with Ratliff's exclamation, "Thanks be to God" (103). Jesus' brief response is also concluded with Ratliff's "Thank God" (106). The next two couplets largely repeat each other: "I know I'll see Him again/In the resurrection and the life/You shall see him/Because I know I will." The Lord's response is also repetitive: "But Jesus said/Unto her/I is the resurrection/And the life/And since I's bein' the resurrection and the life/Though he may be dead but yet he shall live again."

We're gonna talk to you out of
   two passages of Scripture,
   this mornin'
Out of the fourteenth chapter
   of John's gospel
And the sixth verse
Will be the words of the text
5 Jesus said unto him
I am the way, the truth, and
   the light
No man comes to the Father,
   except by me
And out of the eleventh
   chapter
Of John's gospel
10 And the twenty-fifth verse and
   Jesus said unto her I am,
   the resurrection and life

He that believe in me though
   he were dead, yet shall he
   live
We're gonna use for a subject
   this mornin' God, and His
   ways
God and His ways
Physically, let us think
   physically this morning on
   our—on our thinking
15 We think about an individual—
   we think about his ways
And his ways doesn't mean, too
   much
In the sight of God
God's ways is beyond man
I believe the—I believe your
   Bible said—God said in His

word that, your ways are
not my ways—neither are
your thoughts my thoughts
20 As high as the heaven is above
the earth is my ways, and
your ways
That's the diff'—that makes the
difference between the
ways of a man and the
ways of God
We, want to say this morning
that—if we want our ways
to mean, anything to us, we
must, blend our ways in
the ways of God
Because our ways is so weak
they fail on every hand
In all our ways it's nothing—
man is like a bubble on the
water
25 Like a trash[?] on the mighty
seas—it flies away
Like a flower—it soon—and
grass which it soon cut
down and withers away
But God's Word will stand
forever
These words were spoken by
our Lord and our master to
the church—at the entrance
of that church
The church was growing in its
infancy
30 When the disciples came to
Jesus
And the master said to them let
not your heart be troubled
Ye believe in God believe also
in me

In my Father's house there are
many mansions—if it wasn't
so I wouldn't've told y'
He said I'll go prepare a place
for y' that where I am
there ye shall be also
35 And if I go away—if I go and
prepare that place there—
you—the way you know
But the church, the unstable
church, said to Him, what
in a challengin' way,
master, we know not the
way
How do we know the Father
when we don't know the
way
He said that in my Father's
house there are many
mansions—if it wasn't so I
wouldn't have told y'
Said I'm goin' to prepare a
place for y'—Thomas said
to Him master how do we
know the way
40 Said we don't even know the
Father
But—in the language of the text
Jesus said unto him, I am
the way the truth and the
light
No man come to the Father but
by me
If y' expect to get to God y' got
to deny—you must deny
your ways
Take up His cross and follow
Him

⁴⁵ You must blend your ways into
    the ways of God, and walk
    therein
Not only that
But
Mary
And Martha
⁵⁰ One day
Jesus you know passed by their
    home so often time
And while passin' by He would
    stop in
And they became to love
The master
⁵⁵ The Lord Jesus
And one day
Their brother taken sick
And while he was sick Jesus
    was on His way
To another city
⁶⁰ And while He was on His way
He got a message that, he
    whom Thou loveth is sick
And, the disciple said master,
    he said, master
What y' gonna do about it
Lazarus is sick
⁶⁵ You know the men—the Jews of
    late sought to stone Thee
There in that city
And You're goin' there again
But Jesus
Remained on there
⁷⁰ And after a while for three days
    Jesus tarried there in the
    city
And as God He said—turned
    there to the little church

That He was training for this,
    war-torn world
That He was training for those
    that had, come up the
    rough side of the
    mountain—glory to God
Those that had . . . their burden
    in the heat of the day
⁷⁵ Jesus the master was walkin'
    with them by day—and by
    night they were walkin'
    and living by sight
Thank God the church today
Is living by faith
Thank God I heard Him say it
Lazarus is asleep
⁸⁰ Jesus knows all things
He's always sleeping not [?]
I'm afraid that I might go wake
    Him out of His sleep
They said listen master
You don't need to go there
⁸⁵ No no y' don't need to go there
    because they gonna stone
    y' to death, when y' get
    there but Jesus said are not
    there twelve hours in the
    day
He that walketh in the day
    stumbleth not, because he
    can see
But y' walk in the night you'll
    stumble
You can't see your way
Thank God—then I heard Jesus
⁹⁰ The voice said master
If y' go I'm goin' with y'
Then I'm goin' with y'
But Jesus said

Lazarus is
95 Asleep
He said well Lord if he's asleep
    he does all right now
But Jesus said he's dead
I'm goin' that I might wake him
    out of his sleep
Mary met Him on His way
100 Said master
If you'd 've been here my
    brother
Wouldn't 've died
Thanks be to God
And He said
105 You shall see him again
Thank God
I know I'll see him again
In the resurrection and the life
You shall see him
110 Because I know I will
But Jesus said
Unto her
I is the resurrection
And the life
115 And since I's bein' the
    resurrection and the life
Though he may be dead but
    yet he shall live again
I'm sayin' to y' this mornin'
Jesus said I'm the way
The truth and the light
120 Your ways
Glory
Your ways is not right
God's ways is all right
I'm sayin' to y'
125 This mornin'
Jesus said
Thank God almighty

Revelation twenty-two
Sixteen
130 And seventeen
He said
I'm Alpha and Omega—the
    beginning and the end
The voice in the void
I was here when there was
    nothing
135 I was here before the world . . .
And I'm still here
Thank God
This mornin' I'm sayin' to you
In my closin' remarks that
140 If y' hold on
To God's hand
God will make a way
Out of no way
I'm saying to you
145 Jesus is sayin'—Jesus is sayin' to
    y' this morning—
    beckenin'—to y'
To look to the hills
Over yonder
Whence cometh all our help
    and aid
I am the way
150 I am the way, the truth and the
    light
What is God's way
The ways of God—what is they
He said I am the way
His ways are holy ways
155 Let us go back and see what
The prophet said about it
He said
It was the only way
To work your way to glory

¹⁶⁰ None of these beasts could
    walk on there—thank God
That's the ways of God
When you see
A child of God
Just livin' right
¹⁶⁵ Glory to God
He's all right [?]
Yes He is
Thank God—y' may say all
    things about Him
But thanks be to God
¹⁷⁰ He's got his hands in God's
    hand
He can take
He can bear it
Thank God let's see now
Brother preacher
¹⁷⁵ Can he bear it
For all times
Yes sir
If y' got your hand in God's
    hand
You can bear hard names
¹⁸⁰ Whole world may turn their
    back on y'
But Jesus said
In His Word
If y' hold onto my hand
I can keep y' in the palm of my
    hand
¹⁸⁵ And all the devils in hell can't
    pluck y' out
If you live right
God will make a way out o'
    your way
Oh yes
Sometimes our ways get dark
¹⁹⁰ Glory to God—those times

Stormy sea
Thank God
You can't see your way
But Jesus
¹⁹⁵ If y' just wanta throw out your
    anchor
Let it deep enough in Jesus
He'll hold y' until the stormy
    ride is over
I'm the way
If you'll just follow me I'll lead
    y'
²⁰⁰ In the paths of righteousness
Though the one as Job says
    may destroy your body
But if you're in God—God'll
    make a way
Yes He will
I'm so glad this mornin'
²⁰⁵ Long time ago
Thank God almighty Jesus
I let Him into my heart
Jesus said if you'll
Be whole
²¹⁰ Thank God of Revelation
I stand at the door and knock
If any man will open up the . . .
I'll come in and serve with y'
And you with me
²¹⁵ I said I was at the table with y'
And I'll talk with y' wherever
    y' go
I'll lead y'
In the paths of righteousness
For His name's sake
²²⁰ Yea though I walk through the
    valley of the shadow of
    death, I'll fear no evil

For Thou art with me, Thy rod
and Thy staff
God and His ways
God's ways is right
Beyond all reasonable doubt
225 You can trust God
Because His ways is right
I'm sayin'
My Christian friend
If you—thank God
230 If you can't see your way
Find God
God
This morning
We-we-we-we're searching
235 The world
And the people
Are searching for peace
And happiness
Thank God the cabinet of the
United States
240 Glory to God
Lookin' for happiness and
peace
Around the peace table
They're trying to find peace
No peace can be found
245 But except in the church
I would that the United States
cabinet
Was here I want to say to y' if
you go back
To old man God
Go back
250 And find God
You'll find peace
Yes you will
Because

In God there's peace and
happiness
255 Glory to God
And the lamb forever more
If you want happiness
Find God
God will make it happen for y'
260 Yes He will
Thank God
He said I
Am He that were dead
And alive forever more
265 Thank God
This mornin' if you'll just find
God
Everything will be all right
We're closing, by saying, God,
and His ways
God's ways is righteous
270 It's a happy way, it's a peaceful
way, it's a joyful way
Turn to the choir this mornin'
That sing, the praises of God
And if you want, to sing the
praises of God that men
might see Christ in your
life, get close to God
Near the light, that God, would
approve of
275 Live so God, can . . . with His
children
And you His Father
And then we can lead the
world to Christ
Without that, we cannot lead
the world to Christ
Get in the ways of God, and
God will make a way

280 He said I am the way, the truth
and the light
No man comes to the Father
but by me
God's way is right and ever will
be right, and if you get into
the ways of God, then, you
can say, like the prophet of
old
Like the apostle of old
Like the one that said
285 I know
The apostle Paul
Without a doubt
I know
That He is
290 The Christ—the Son of the
living God
And my friends, this morning if
we recall one of the old
patriarchs, one that
suffered and died, for
Christ's sake
Old Brother Stephen
As he stood
Out yonder in the . . .
295 To mend this wrong
To live a sinful life
It's wrong
To commit adultery
They begin stonin' Stephen and
yet Stephen didn't even,
try to defend himself
300 He stuck to God, and His
righteousness
Said for God I'm livin', for God
I'm dyin'
And as they stoned Brother
Stephen and as he was lyin'

under the shower of stones
he looked through the
shower of stones—saw the
heavens open
Said Father forgive them—they
don't know what they're
doin'
And you get in the ways of God
305 When they being stonin' you,
you can say Father forgive
them they don't know what
they done
Glory to God—so many—so
many nights a child of God
can bow around His couch
There were hours of the night
when the world had rocked
herself to sleep
Thank God—and then the touch
of God's hand touches the
child of God and wakes
him from his sleep
Hand on his soul—y' been born
again—y' can hear him cry
out thank you Jesus for the
blessing You've bestowed
upon me
310 Glory to God—so many—I
waked up—the Spirit of
God had wakened me so
many nights
Thank God—and I lay there
crying
Thank God—just get happy
Glory to God
I'm the way the truth and the
light—get to think about
God's ways

[315] How He has kept us from
    dangers unseen
I'm the way—the ways of God

Choir's gonna sing—doors of
    the church is open

Index

Note on the Author

Bruce Rosenberg's Ph.D. is in medieval English literature, taken at Ohio State University under the direction of Francis Lee Utley. Under Utley's mentorship and intellectual guidance, Rosenberg became interested in folklore, especially the way in which it interacts with the products of literature. In the last two decades he has published five books and more than sixty articles, most of which deal with this interdisciplinary interaction. *The Art of the American Folk Preacher,* the prototype of the present volume, won the Modern Language Association's James Russell Lowell prize for 1970, as well as a University of Chicago Folklore Prize.

Folk Preacher was written while Rosenberg was teaching at the University of California, Santa Barbara: he has maintained an interest in the subject of folk preaching at his current position in the American Civilization Program at Brown University. Initially supported by a fellowship from the National Endowment for the Humanities, Rosenberg has since been the recipient of a Guggenheim Fellowship, a Fulbright, and a Mellon Professorship (at the University of Pittsburgh), and has received grants from the Newberry Library and the Huntington Library.